2-

The
Social Impact
of
New Religious
Movements

D0887491

Bryan Wilson
Editor

Distributed by
The Rose of Sharon Press, Inc.
New York

Conference series no. 9
First edition
© 1981
by
The Unification Theological Seminary
Barrytown, New York 12507

Distributed by
The Rose of Sharon Press, Inc.
G.P.O. Box 2432
New York, New York 10116

Printed in the United States of America
Library of Congress Cataloging number 81-51152
ISBN 0-932894-09-7

CONTENTS

CONTENTS

FOREWORD

Just what should be taken to count as "new religious movements" is, fortunately, a question which, in introducing these
essays, an editor need feel no obligation to answer. That large
numbers of movements have arisen in recent years justifies the
designation "new", although it is also evident, from the tacit
distinction implied in most commentaries, that there must be a
sense in which "new movements" are so called in contradistinc-
tion to "old sects". Without here pre-empting or prejudicing the
discussion which follows in some of the papers in this volume,
particularly in that of Wallis and, to a lesser extent, in those of Stark,
Bainbridge and Jackson, and Wilson, one might observe that what
appears to come to mind when people refer to the new religions
are several features that are taken to be characteristic. These
elements may be listed as: exotic provenance; new cultural life-
style; a level of engagement markedly different from that of traditional church Christianity; charismatic leadership; a following predominantly young and drawn in disproportionate measure from
the better-educated and middle class sections of society; social
conspicuity; international operation; and emergence within the last
decade and a half.

Not all of the new movements participate in all of these
features, and there are also obvious differences among them,
most evidently in the extent of their claim to possess a monopoly of

truth in doctrine and of validity in ritual or therapeutic practice. The case studies provided by three of the papers in this collection illustrate the diversity on these points, from the relatively exclusivistic Children of God to the very open position of Transcendental Meditation. There is also a sharp distinction between movements the primary concern of which is to canvass a system of physical or mental therapy and those which offer a much more encompassing scheme of salvation. This difference is often one which entails others—for example, the extent to which the individual or the collectivity (and perhaps beyond that the wider society) is the focus of concern. Not only do new religions differ so markedly from each other, however; each one of them is much less monolithic than the press and the public are disposed to believe. Organizations undergo processes of change, and some of the papers in this volume are devoted to the analysis of just such developments. As became evident in the discussion at the conference at which these papers were first delivered, there are variations in the way in which a given movement operates in different social and temporal contexts: as between one country and another, or one period and another, there may be a considerable difference in ethos, tactics, strategy, and practical arrangements. Intense as commitment usually is, there are also variations in the obligations and expectations of different categories of members. All of these considerations need to be borne in mind in any discussion of movements which, for convenience, the general public, and indeed, the sociologists of religion, are inclined to lump together under one nomenclative umbrella.

We may take it that the members of the new movements do not so readily perceive themselves as belonging to one among a number of groups that are to be regarded as "all of a kind", much less that they should be seen as in any way "interchangeable". It is sociologists, seeking an explanation of the more or less simultaneous emergence and expansion of new movements in the Western world in broad, facilitating social circumstances, who are likely to see new religions as comparable entities.

The processes of technical, organizational, and economic

change, and their consequences for social structures, relation-ships, values, and life-style, may be taken as the context within which the new religions have come into being, at least as socially significant movements. The invocation of the factors involved in social and cultural change is, however, not enough to explain the emergence of any one particular movement; to account for its origins; to indicate the causes of its growth; and least of all to convince its followers that these are the terms in which the move-ment should be understood. Indeed, in the case of "old sects", any such endeavour to explain what the members themselves would regard as a distinctive act of God, occurring at a specially chosen time in history, would, in itself be a suggestion impudent if not blasphemous. It is, therefore, all the more remarkable that among the leadership of new religious movements there are those who are prepared not merely to tolerate such explanations, but also, for discussion of these issues, to meet sociologists on their—the sociologists'—own ground.

The sponsorship of the conference at which eight of the nine papers in this volume were delivered, and the imprint under which they are now published, are those of the Unification Church. Obviously, no one in the Unification movement would, or could, accept sociological explanation as ever affording a final under-standing of the factors that have brought that movement into being: and, indeed, it must be said that sociological analysis is still a long way from providing adequate explanation of any—let alone of all—of the new religious movements. Yet to engage in debate, and, further, to facilitate such debate, about the social causes, contexts, and consequences of their own movement is, on the face of it, a surprising gesture on the part of the Moonies. It is even more surprising that they should sponsor a discussion in which sociolo-gists easily, if not lightly, compare one new religion with another, in a way which cannot but appear misguided to the deeply-committed religious conscience—and the followers of new religions are almost invariably deeply committed. Even within the well-established denominations, where allegiance is usually less intense, the authori-ties have, at least until very recently, looked askance at sociological commentary on religions, regarding any extra-theological explanation of religious matters as almost an affront to their dignity. With the ushering in of ecumenism, the established denominations (excepting perhaps the Roman Catholics and some Baptists) have come to accept that they must be considered as on no more than equal terms with other churches, but this new, and still equivocal, spirit of tolerance has by no means eliminated the hostility towards non-religious explanations of religion among churchmen of the traditional denominations. One might expect new movements, beginning with the fervour of newly propounded truths, and embracing a membership almost all of whom are first-generation converts, to stand more resolutely for their own world-view, and to take a less mellow attitude towards external, and to them extraneous, appraisals. Yet, here we have an evidence of exactly the opposite. In this case at least, (and there is evidence of similar openness in some of the new religions in Japan, Soka Gakkai, Rissho Kosei Kai, Tenrikyo, and Konkokyo, among others) we find religionists who readily accept the need for scholarly sociological enquiry, and whose leaders are even eager to hear what sociologists have to say.

The difference in attitude between the new religions, on the one hand, and, on the other, the established denominations and old sects, may in part represent the less exclusivistic orientation of religions arising in eastern societies and cultures. But it may also reflect, and this is perhaps more pertinent, a shift in the self-interpretation of the leaders and followers of new religions in an age in which social phenomena of all kinds are interpreted less and less in moral or theological terms, and increasingly by reference to empirical evidence about society itself. This is not to suggest that sociology as a discipline has successfully established itself on the basis of a large body of cumulative and reliable findings, cogent analysis, and convincing theories. Not even the most chauvinistic professional, in what is an aggressively chauvinistic discipline, could assert that. It is only to recognize that, with all its abundant shortcomings, sociology is now accepted as the source of the language, the assumptions, and the apparatus for socially acceptable types of explanations of all those phenomena that depend on social interaction. Such explanations are not entirely accommodated to the religious perspective *per se,* which always proceeds on the assumption of another, other-worldly, reality—whether spirits, a god, a law, a transterrestrial sphere, or a metaphysical system of causes and effects—outside of nature and, even if marginally within the range of human influence, none the less, beyond the bounds of social creativity. Yet, the idea that religion is a social product, and that conceptions of salvation and of what must be done to attain it are socially determined has become a kind of modern common sense, which appears to be far less uncongenial to the votaries of the new religions than to traditionalists.

It would be perhaps too much to say that, in attracting sociological enquiry, and more especially by their ready accept- ance of it, the new movements have become not simply the objects of sociological study, but also almost the clients of sociol- ogists. Their leaders have among them those who are ready to consult outside experts in order to acquire a sociological under- standing of their own operation, their relative success, effectiveness, influence, and oganizational resilience and competence. Stated thus, the matter is over-stated, but the trend is there, as is evident from the publication of a volume such as this, and from the fact that it issues from a conference promoted by the educational authori- ties of the Unification Church and participated in by a number of their own members who were engaged in graduate studies in various American universities. The reader of these papers should, therefore, remind himself as he reads the unrestrained comments of the authors, whether in the discussion by Mrs. Barker of just to whom Moonie ideas appeal, or the manifestly agnostic exposition of the theory of compensators by Professor Stark, that these papers were delivered to, and discussed by, a number of young highly-educated members of the Unification Church, and are published by the movement's own publishing house. Simply by remembering these facts, the reader will, I suggest, acquire an apprehension of at least this particular new religious movement somewhat different from any that he is likely to obtain by the sometimes sensationalized accounts that are so much grist to the mill of the mass-circulation media.

In the foregoing, I have quite deliberately used the word "client" to intimate something of the status which the new religions have, in some limited degree, adopted towards sociologists of religion. The word may provoke raised eyebrows. It should, however, be clear that, as clients, the new movements are neither the controlling sponsors nor the financing agents of sociologists, who remain committed to the methodological canons of ethical neutrality and objectivity. Rather, the movements are to be compared to any other organizations which might seek information and even advice. If sociologists have any expertise at all, it should not be surprising that those whose social activities they study should seek to have that expertise made available to them. Hitherto, sociologists of religion have not been very much used to being consulted. The instances have been few, but occasionally and randomly even in the old religious establishments there have been those who, in recent years, have recognized that theology, ecclesiology, and philosophy, even when these subjects are alleged to be based on divine revelation, are insufficiently grounded in empirical reality to provide even traditionally-based institutions with guidance in their operations in an increasingly complex and rapidly changing social context. Some religionists, particularly in the new religions, have recognized that sociologists of religion sometimes know more than they do themselves, particularly in comparative terms, about the relations of religion and the state, or the effectiveness of different missionary methods, or the ways in which processes of schisms are likely to develop. On all these matters, religious movements have, in recent years, consulted sociologists, and, in conflicts pursued at law, sociologists of religion have become expert witnesses, useful to the court precisely because detachment and objectivity is accorded to them more readily than it is to even the most conscientious of religionists.

The new religions have given an impetus to demands such as these on sociological expertise. The conference at which the essays in this volume were delivered was another type of occasion for consultation. Obviously, it cannot be supposed that a collection of papers, covering diverse aspects of the circumstances and consequences of the new religions, is in itself likely to provoke any change of course on the part of any new movement. Even a long-term systematic enquiry into a movement in all its aspects might not occasion such a change. But papers such as these explore facets of the interrelation of new religions and society in ways that might influence the thinking of those who heard them or who now read them, whether they are themselves members of new religions or outsiders. To expose themselves to the possibility of such influence from outside experts is the substance of the daring challenge to its own members which the Unification Church has issued. In doing so, it shows itself to be willing to risk more, and to have more openness of purpose, than some much larger and longer-established denominations.

If the Unification Church has shown itself to be unafraid of the consequences of an encounter with sociologists of religion, have these sociologists anything to fear from attending a conference organized by the Unification Church? There are those who roundly condemn the participation of academics in conferences sponsored by the Moonies, who, through their various affiliated organizations, promote frequent academic meetings, particularly for scientists and social scientists. Chief among these critics has been Professor Irving Louis Horowitz. With a vehemence somewhat unbecoming an academic, he has suggested that such occasions amount to the exploitation of academics by an organization that seeks to use them as a means of legitimating its own concerns.[1] He objects in general to the private donor obtaining the services of the "scientific recipient", and does so, in particular, because he disapproves of many of the activities of the Rev. Moon and of the Unification Church.

The thrust of his attack is double-edged. He objects to sponsors obtaining the services of academics. And he has particularly attacked those academics who attended the International Conference On the Unity of the Sciences (sponsored by the Rev.

Moon) because of what he described as their conservatism and anti-communism in leading "a vanguard thrust into backwardness". The political convictions which so powerfully colour Professor Horowitz's comments have no relevance for the conference on The Social Impact of New Religious Movements. His objection of academic service to those who sponsor conferences fails to recognize that, at least in the free world, ideas are free. Without this conference, sooner or later, the participants would, in all probability, have addressed the issues on which they presented their papers. Moonies might then have heard them or have read them. If the ideas in the papers are of use—to Moonies or others—should the authors do anything other than rejoice? As things are, the Moonies stimulated the expression, exchange, circulation, and publication of these ideas, and if they are of service, they are likely to be so as much to the rest of the academic community, at least to the sociologists of religion, as to anyone else.

The exchange of ideas in a completely free and unconstrained atmosphere, among a small group of specialists who could not otherwise have met, either at that time or in a meeting with such a specific focus of interest, could be nothing but a welcome academic opportunity, which those who participated were happy and right to seize. None of them finds need for excuse for their attendance, but such is the climate of opinion to which Professor Horowitz has contributed, that there is a danger that academics might begin to doubt their freedom to speak, here or there, for fear of intemperate and unwarranted censure. Using an analogy, which is perhaps deliberately intended to be offensive, Horowitz says, "If a conference held on crime as an American way of life were sponsored by the Mafia, one can imagine a perfectly reasonable series of essays by top-flight scholars; but I hardly imagine that the crookedness or crankiness of the sponsors would be entirely irrelevant to the output."[2] The conference from which these essays are drawn was a conference on new religions sponsored by a new religion: I do not believe that what Horowitz might call "the crookedness or crankiness" of the sponsors has any relevance to the output whatsoever. Whether this volume is, as I believe, a clear refutation of the assumptions on which Horowitz makes his case, the reader may judge for himself. Its publication certainly makes it clear that scholars more involved with the new religions in their academic work than he is himself, are not to be stampeded by condemnations—all too McCarthy-like in tone—into abandoning their legitimate concerns.

Those legitimate interests include an interest in the Unification Church, and although by no means all the sociologists who participated in the conference had had any close contact with that particular movement, all came in the hope of learning more about it. Their hopes were not disappointed. Some of us, without belonging to any of the religious organizations involved (and most of us perhaps belonging to none) had, in any case, attended other conferences sponsored by religious bodies—by the Vatican, by the Anglicans, by the Seventh-day Adventists. Nowhere had the atmosphere been less constrained than it was in this conference sponsored by the Unification Church.

The preliminary remarks of the President of the Unification Theological Seminary, Mr. David S.C. Kim, which are published in this volume, are themselves an indication of the extent to which the Unification Church leaders have become aware of the animosity that their activities arouse. Such is the hostility of the climate that has been created, that Mr. Kim acknowledged that, for a sociologist to attend a conference sponsored by the Moonies, might be to entail some hazard to his profession. Those who attended did so in the clear conviction that, in a free society, such a consequence must be risked, and in the knowledge that, by taking that risk, they would indeed reduce the hazard. The participants had been assured that they would be free to say what they liked; that they would control the publication of their own papers; that they would not be subjected to any unwanted propagandist address; and that their attendance would not be exploited for propagandist or ideological purposes. Those assurances were all honoured. The conference was small, encompassing some two dozen participants, and the candour of debate was unimpaired. The general consensus was that the papers should be published, and the

Seminary authorities invited me to act as editor. In the discharge of that task, I was given a completely free hand. I alone selected the papers to be published, and did so solely on the criterion of their academic suitability for publication. None of them has been edited except for stylistic purposes. I alone decided that the volume should not include reports of general discussion, and I did so in part because, as is almost invariably the case with impromptu discussion, the written record of that discussion had an inevitable uneven, and at times fragmentary, quality, and partly for reasons of space. At no time did the sponsors seek to influence my judgment in the slightest.

The papers in this volume fall into four groups. Three of them treat of the general social context in which the new religions have arisen into prominence in western society, focussing on the broad processes of social change. James Hunter uses the theoretical apparatus developed by Arnold Gehlen and other German sociologists, whose work has received too little attention in English-speaking countries, to examine the consequences of technological change on everyday life. The unease, not to say anomie, that has followed has produced a general social climate in which some sections of the population, and particularly the young, have become disposed to seek a new integration of the values that govern their lives. It is the specific disorientation of the young, and the attractiveness to them of a vigorous reassertion of the sacred, which provides the core of Professor Fichter's study. Writing as a Jesuit, he none the less maintains a detachment and objectivity in appraising new movements, and frankly acknowledges the points at which the traditional churches have failed. It is the disruption of traditional religious culture that is the central concern of David Martin's contribution: in an implicitly dichotomous assessment, in which he shows how the churches have abandoned their creeds, rituals, beliefs, and morality, he suggests that this ready relinquishment of their traditional cultural heritage has opened the way for new forms of religion to a public which the older churches no longer influence.

The three movements depicted in the case studies in the

second group of papers differ significantly from one another—in ideology; in the specificity of their soteriological concerns; in organizational structure; and in the demands made on their converts. The issues of analysis also differ among these three papers. Eileen Barker illustrates, from the extensive material that she has gathered from interviews, the social profile of those who join the Unification Church. Roy Wallis concentrates primarily on the changes in the policy and style of the Children of God as that movement has encountered a variety of organizational and leadership problems. He augments his discussion with a suggestive comparison with two older sects. Using a very different style of enquiry, William Sims Bainbridge and Daniel H. Jackson discuss the factors affecting the growth and decline of the Transcendental Meditation movement, and the reaction to them reflected in changes in what the movement claims to offer to its votaries. Their paper is the only one in the collection that was not delivered at the conference. It was made available subsequently, and clearly fitted neatly into the section in which new movements were described in individual detail.

The theory that lies behind Rodney Stark's contribution will be recognized by sociologists as an important development of the widely-known relative deprivation thesis: in a deftly constructed analysis that will assuredly stimulate research and provoke response, it opens new perspectives on the perennial issue of the extent to which new movements are to be regarded as religious. Perhaps the most controversial essay is that of Anson D. Shupe Jr., and David G. Bromley, who take up an aspect of the response to new religions which in itself is too seldom recognized as a distinctive sociological problem in its own right. Today's new religious movements, more than new religions at any other time (as the final essay by Wilson emphasizes) operate in a world in which the media dominate the climate of opinion. Obviously, the cases from which the atrocity stories are culled, and which Shupe and Bromley discuss, are the extreme cases of defection from a religious movement. These widely-publicized cases, with their dramatic conflicts between parents (and deprogrammers) and converts, and subsequently between ex-converts and their former religious associates, should not obscure the fact that, among those who defect, most do so in much less dramatic circumstances, and without vituperative recriminations. Shupe and Bromley make clear the ways in which disenchantment is deliberately induced, and by which reaction to a change of heart is reinforced to become an over-reaction.

The conference at which all but one of these essays was presented was acclaimed by the participants as one of the most successful at which they had ever been present. It was small, intensive, intellectually stimulating, and academically rewarding. It is for others to judge the quality of the papers, here presented for their scrutiny, but the participants themselves, most of whom are well-established contributors to the sociology of religion, would certainly affirm that the conference was an occasion for learning, conducted in accordance with the best academic standards of debate, and entirely conducive to the free, open, and untrammelled development of their academic concerns.

Bryan R. Wilson
All Souls College
Oxford
January 16, 1981

FOOTNOTES

1. Irving Louis Horowitz (ed.), *Science, Sin, and Scholarship:The Politics of Reverend Moon and the Unification Church*, Cambridge, Mass.: The MIT Press, 1978, pp. 260-81.
2. *Ibid.*, p. 275.

WELCOMING ADDRESS

David S.C. Kim

Ladies and Gentlemen, on behalf of the Unification Theological Seminary faculty, staff, students and alumni, I greet you all with heartfelt respect and admiration, and welcome you officially to the city of Berkeley—so widely known in academic circles, where more than three hundred academicians and scholars are working in the field of religion. There are theologians, church historians, Bible scholars, religious psychologists and counselors, as well as social scientists who are engaged in the study of the sociology of religion, of marriage and the family, or one or another related topic. You name it! Berkeley is a highly academic community and a melting pot of many religions. Since in Berkeley there is such a dynamic religious influence, the opening of the First International Conference on The Social Impact of New Religious Movements may certainly have its own powerful effect not only on scholars in Berkeley and other parts of the United States, but also on religious circles throughout the entire world.

A few minutes ago, I expressed my feeling of admiration for you all. I mean that word "admiration" in a double sense: I not only admire your scholarly accomplishments in your respective specialized fields, but I also admire your courage in coming and participating in a conference such as this one, sponsored by the "Moonies." You must have been tossing it around in your head for a long time, trying to decide whether or not to come. But in spite of impossible hazards to your profession, you have all gathered together with us. I admire your courage and your decision to attend.

As you probably know, religious and racial prejudice has led to our being unfairly treated. Since 1954, we have been persecuted and ridiculed in Korea, and as our movement grew, we have met similar treatment in the United States and throughout the world. We have continually faced national and international efforts to destroy the Unification movement. Even those who do no more than simply associate with us are often criticized, and sometimes they are exposed, to tremendous pressure from their supervisors and colleagues alike who have been influenced by our adversaries. They jeopardize their academic and scholarly status by associating with us. This is the reason I admire your courage in coming.

If our movement were shown by skilled social scientists like yourselves to contain a blueprint to make this troubled world better for all of us, if it were shown to be related to God's contemporary dispensation for mankind and the world, and if it were shown to be related to genuine truth, then your association with us would be an enormously blessed one. Not only would you contribute to the academic community and to your specialized field, but you would also contribute significantly to "building the Kingdom of God on earth" in our lifetime. This is precisely the ultimate goal of the Unification movement. To help accomplish this goal, we have for many years sponsored conferences such as this one in order to help bring about an "academic ecumenism" in which different disciplines can find a common goal and can work together as a team to bring eternal peace on earth and make it a better place for us all.

On what basis can I make such a big statement? We would simply like to lay the facts before you. We are totally opening ourselves to you for your inquiry and research into our movement. We have nothing to hide. I urge you to inquire into and to investigate our movement, which is one of the more controversial religious movements in the history of religion. We have survived—and even flourished—through the turmoil of judicial, legislative, and administrative investigations against us launched by the U.S. government. In spite of all this, we have been expanding our work in many different areas and in many new enterprises, be they spiritual, financial, educational or cultural in nature. I can assure you that it is absolutely worthwhile to pay attention to our movement and to make further inquiries into it.

I sincerely hope this conference will stimulate you and other scholars as well, and that our present discussions will lead us to cover broader and deeper topics in the future. On the basis of our accomplishments here, we will develop future conferences of wider scope.

Again, I sincerely thank you for coming and for your participation. I again extend a warm welcome to all of you. May God bless you and your families abundantly during your stay in the Bay Area.

Thank you.

THE NEW RELIGIONS: DEMODERNIZATION AND THE PROTEST AGAINST MODERNITY

James Davison Hunter

The development of the pervasive cultural innovations (particularly religious innovations) of the past decade and a half induced a considerable incredulity in the social sciences. Many social scientists had accepted the idea that modern society was increasingly secular in character, and had come to suppose that the secularity of the social system implied not only the decline of religious or supernaturalist assumptions in the operation of the social order, but also the diminution of supernaturalist dispositions on the part of individuals. Even theological currents had reinforced these modern liberal and positivistic assumptions—as evident in the successive fashionability of increasingly anti-traditional theologies, from demythologization, and secularization theology, to eventually the "death of God" theology. In this context, the resurgence of religion, as manifested in the new religious movements, came first as an unpredictable irritation, and eventually as a significant challenge to the long-established and even hallowed assumptions of the majority of social scientists. Only when some of these movements had become routinized did social scientists seriously begin to explore the organizational structure and the substantive features of the plurality of new religions and, perhaps more important, the reasons for their emergence in the first place.

A variety of plausible explanations and interpretations from diverse theoretical perspectives have been offered to account for

1

the appearance of the new movements. Surprisingly, little if any of the research undertaken in Anglo-Saxon countries into these new religions has either utilized or even invoked the insights of the German humanistic tradition of the social sciences—a tradition distinguished by such classical figures as Max Weber, Ernst Troeltsch, and George Simmel—nor made use of the extensive and pertinent contributions of such writers as Arnold Gehlen, Peter Berger, Brigitte Berger, Anton Zijderveld, Thomas Luckmann, Hansfried Kellner, René König or Helmut Schelsky. In what follows, I seek to provide the groundwork for a perspective on the rise of the new religions which exploits the insights afforded by the German humanistic tradition, and which uses them to increase our understanding of the constitutive character of the new religious movements. I shall try, in addition, to locate this perspective among a few of the more recent interpretations offered, briefly exploring their commonalities and differences.

Modernity and the Crises of Meaning

The perspective which is derived from the German humanistic tradition of sociology maintains a deliberate and unflinching affinity with the concerns and aspirations of classical sociological thought. Most generally, these concerns focus on the problem of individual existence in society, and more specifically, on the problem of individual existence in *modern societies*. At issue are the essence and character of modernity and its impact on the nature and course of individual life. These fundamental questions provided the *daemon* of inspiration behind most of the writings of the patristics of sociological thinking; and in this regard, it can be noted that the "early fathers" interpreted this problem as a religious problem, and adduced solutions which relied upon their development of an understanding of the differing aspects of the religious dimensions of social life. This preamble aside, it is within this stream of the classical tradition that one may find the first clue to understanding the riddle posed by the rise of the new religious consciousness.

Modernity is typified by a number of salient features. Among

the most important are institutional differentiation[1] and bureaucratic augmentation.[2] This process results in a structural bifurca-
tion—a split between public and private spheres of life;[3] intense
cultural pluralism which follows from urbanization and the proliferation
of the media of mass communications;[4] and social mobility and
geographic mobility, among other things. The resulting effect of
the intense convergence of these uniquely modern processes is
what the German social theorist, Arnold Gehlen, has aptly described
as *de-institutionalization*. Requisite to the full appreciation of the
meaning of this concept is its placement within the larger context
of Gehlen's general theory of institutions.[5]

The basis of Gehlen's theory of institutions is in an understanding of the biological constitution of the human animal. The
biological research of such scientists as Adolf Portmann, J. von
Uexkull and F. Butendijk has indicated that in relation to the rest of
the animal world, the human organism is incomplete at birth, in the
sense of what Gehlen calls *instinctual deprivation*. There is no
biologically grounded structure through which humans may channel
their externalizing energies; moreover there is no single ecological
environment to which the human organism must become accustomed. Unlike the rest of the animal world, the human experience
at birth is open and unchanneled. Yet this is a situation which is to
man biologically, and therefore psychologically, intolerable. Institutions, according to Gehlen, are *human artificial constructions* that
provide for men what our biology does not. They function like
instincts in that they pattern individual conduct and social relationship in an habitual and socially predictable manner. Not only do
they establish behavior with a pattern, but institutions also provide
human experience at the cognitive level with an intelligibility and a
sense of continuity. By living within the well-defined parameters of
a matrix of such institutions, humans need not reflect on their
actions—they can take their social world for granted. While institutions exist as a stable background to human experience, there is
also a foreground—the zone of life in which the individual makes
deliberate and purposive choices. The former provides the structural context for the latter. Institutionalization occurs when an

aspect of the foreground of human experience becomes habitualized and routinized so as to become a part of the background. Thus, for example, child-rearing is institutionalized when random behavior of the parent towards the child becomes habituated in a society, and then embedded in a normative (often moral) structure of rules, codes, and procedures. Institutionalization is complete when the rules and procedures guiding child-rearing practices become a feature of the society's taken-for-granted experience. De-institutionalization occurs when an item of culture is transferred from the background to the foreground. Thus, for instance, marriage is de-institutionalized when the normative codes regulating a specific type of social arrangement lose their plausibility, and thus the structure and functioning of the nuptial relationship become open-ended—a matter of choice. According to Gehlen, one of the most important aspects of modernity is that the foreground of choice is growing, and the background of stable institutional patterns is receding. Modernity is characterized by an unprecedented degree of de-institutionalization.

Yet the processes of de-institutionalization are not uniformly distributed in the social world. The public sphere—the sphere of massive bureaucracies organizing such areas of human activity as government and law, business and commerce, labor, health care, communications, the military, and oftentimes, religion—remains highly institutionalized. All these institutions remain quite capable of patterning the thought and the social relationships of individuals within that public sphere, and, when occasion arises, of imposing the force of social control. Because these institutions in the public sphere are extensive and complex, and because, within the public sphere, what is demanded of men is thought, behavior, and relationships that are functionally rational, so these institutions become remote from the individual, and alien from the private sphere of life in general. As Zijderveld has argued, they are very often experienced as infinitely abstract, incomprehensible, and, in the extreme situation, as possessing the quality of unreality.[6] Experience in the public sphere typically disconfirms and contradicts experience in the private sphere.[7] Thus, while the processes of de-institutionalization have not infiltrated the public sphere, its institutions have, nonetheless, "lost their grip" on the individual. They are intrinsically unable to provide the individual with an overall sense of concrete, personal attachment which reinforces personal meanings and purpose. To find these things, the individual must turn elsewhere. That elsewhere is the private sphere—the sphere of personal and family life and other primary relationships. Yet, it is in the private sphere that the processes of de-institutionalization have gone furthest. The areas of child-rearing; courtship; marriage; sexuality; vocation; religious belief and practice; consuming patterns; leisure; and the basic norms which guide social behavior and social exchange—are, in advanced industrial countries, all radically de-institutionalized.

Thus, the dilemma of modernity, in which all individuals are variously caught, is an oppressively formidable public sphere, which is structurally incapable of providing individuals with concrete and meaningful social confirmation of their sense of reality (including their understanding of social processes, subjective meaning and personal identity), and an enfeebled private sphere, which is distressingly under-institutionalized, and which is structurally unable to provide reliable social parameters for the more mundane activity of everyday life and a plausible, well-integrated system of meaning which gives location and purpose to the individual's total life experience.

The condition of modernity, then, necessarily posits a crisis of meaning for individuals. The situation translates into human consciousness as a psychological anomie, with the individual experiencing a *spiritual homelessness* (Camus) or *weightlessness*,[8] metaphorically floating without dependable, faithworthy (taken-for-granted) institutional anchors. Simultaneously, these factors converge to fashion an historically unique personality structure—the *other-directed individual*,[9] concerned with *impression management*,[10] or *Protean Man*,[11] performing chameleon-type identity shifts through the course of his biography according to the different social groups of which he is a part—in a situation defined appropriately as a *permanent identity crisis*.[12]

Naturally, the crisis of meaning (the experience of homelessness) varies in degree according to the relative proximity to the forces of modernity of both the individual himself and of the social structure to which he belongs. Those furthest away from the processes of modernization (empirically this means those of low level educational achievement; non-urban domicile; non-industrial and non-bureaucratic occupation; lower income levels; ethnic or minority racial origin; female gender, etc.) are less likely to experience these strains in their fullest and most sustained intensity. Those closest to these processes (those characterized by higher educational achievement; urban-suburban domicile; industrial or bureaucratic type of occupation; higher income level; dominant racial origin; male gender, etc.) are more likely to experience this type of cognitive uneasiness. Yet, despite these apparent social advantages, it is from among those in closest proximity to these forces, and therefore from those who experience these social-psychological strains most acutely, that protest is most likely to come.

The Anthropological Protest Against Modernity

The protest is, in essence, not cultural, social or political, but rather anthropological. This is to say that the protest against modernity is rooted in the nature of the species, *homo sapiens*.

It is a commonplace that human beings have a remarkable capacity for adjustment in the face of difficult social and natural environments. Nonetheless, there are definite limitations to this human malleability. The death of the human organism marks the human limit of adjustment to the harshest of natural ecological conditions; insanity marks the limit of adjustment to intemperate socio-cultural conditions. Prior to reaching those limits however, humans almost invariably struggle to resist the environment when the strains endemic to that environment threaten to become too great to bear. Man will in most circumstances pronounce the "No" of protest *when it is perceived* that the "Yes" of accommodation means the end of one's humanity—biological or psychological. Humans have a limited capacity to adjust to the conditions of anomie—a situation which is experienced as lacking any enduring, subjectively meaningful and relevant design. To do so is, as Turnbull's Mountain People exemplify, to risk extinction. Human beings almost inevitably react against these conditions.[13]

Holding these broadest theoretical generalities in reserve, one may say that what we have characterized as modernity structurally engenders precisely those conditions that are anthropologically intolerable. Thus, modernity itself spawns discontents among those who experience and induce protest—a protest that has been called the *demodernizing impulse*.[14]

Although this protest against modernity is fundamentally anthropological, it may and often does take social, cultural, and political expression. Historically, the expression of the demodernizing impulse in all these three forms is not new. The past two centuries of Western history are replete with examples. The mysticism of the Transcendentalist movement which was popularized by Emerson and Thoreau; Eastern mysticism advocated by upper class intellectuals in the Theosophical Society and, later, in the Vedanta Society; the Shaker movement; late nineteenth and early twentieth century Fundamentalism; and even aspects of the larger Romanticist movement in art and literature in the nineteenth century—may all be understood as various cultural expressions of the anthropological protest against modernity. The most recent significant expression of the protest is the counter-cultural movement of the 1960s and early 1970s, which extends, in its successor movements, to the present. Perhaps the most important cultural aspect of this latter phenomenon are the burgeoning myriad of new religions.

Thus, I am now in a position to state propositionally that the source of the new religious consciousness is in the anthropological protest against modernity. More precisely stated, the new religious consciousness is a cultural expression of the anthropological protest against the anomic structures intrinsic to modernity. As a demodernizing movement, the new religions are a sign that in some sectors of modern society, the strains of modernity have reached the limits of human tolerance, and are thus symbolic, at both the collective and the social-psychological levels, of the desire for relief and assuagement.

One point of clarification should be made here. Although new religions are here all classified as demodernizing movements, these movements do differ considerably one from another in the thrust of their challenge to modernity. Some of them embrace ideologies and adopt strategies of organization and activity, and promote life-styles which have the appearance of being not merely consonant with modernity, but even of being an espousal and a celebration of it. Let me exemplify: Scientology and the Unification Church are movements that are both decidedly pro-science and pro-technology, and so, ostensibly pro-modern. Scientology appears to claim, in its very name, as well as in its quasi-scientific therapeutic procedures, the imprimatur of science and technology. Nonetheless, much as it claims to offer its votaries better techniques based on fundamental "scientific" research, for the improvement of their intelligence and their lives, Scientology is itself rejected by modern science. Its claims are unsubstantiated by those outside the movement. In its salesmanship (its attempt to induce those who do become involved to continue in ever more advanced courses); in its development of increasingly metaphysical theories; and also in the segregated and intense total organization of the lives of its inner cadres, Scientology also manifests characteristics that can readily be seen to be at variance with the normal practice and assumptions of modern everyday life. Structurally, if not ideologically, the movement stands counter to much of modern life and social organization. In particular, of course, it claims to neutralize the anomic effects that life in modern society produces, and it offers the prospect of a life without this type of strain and tension, first for individuals and, ultimately, for mankind at large. That utopian ideal is radically anti-modern. The Unification Church also endorses modern science, but the structure of the movement, particularly in its communal organization and in its emphasis on individual care, stands in sharp contrast to the structural arrangements and the value-orientations of modern life.

What is unique about the counter-culture in general and the new religions in particular, in relation to demodernizing movements of the past, is a quantitative shift. Demodernizing movements of the past remained sequestered in fairly small and isolated socio-cultural enclaves. The new religions are representative of a large-scale cultural phenomenon. Never before has a demodernizing movement been so pervasive and so rapidly and so widely disseminated, attesting to the extent to which the discontents of modernity have become diffused. The new religions are unique because of a qualitative shift as well. The protest represented by the rise of the new religions is, as a whole, more extreme than that of most other demodernizing movements of the past, leading to much more radical departures from the assumptions of everyday life. This is brought into relief by the radical disjunction which many of these religions manifest between their own life-style and values and those of the dominant patterns of the modern societies in which they arise.

Principal Features of the New Religions

More than a symbol of the need for relief, the new religions are concrete attempts to resolve the perplexities experienced by modern man. In attempting to provide such a solution the new religions are distinctively characterized in that they in greater or lesser degree reflect the opposition to the strains imposed by the double-bind of modernity, an overly rational, abstract public sphere and a radically de-institutionalized private sphere. To take the latter dimension first: if the dominant social psychological effect of modernity is the experience of "homelessness," then, the most likely solution will be an attempt to restore a sense of "being at home" by reconstructing or reimposing institutionally reliable meanings upon existence. As it is true for demodernizing movements on the whole, so it is with the new religions, namely, that the principal feature of the spirit of protest is an *absolutism* or *totalism*.[15] This manifests itself at the cognitive level as well as the socio-organizational level of human experience.

At the cognitive level, this is expressed in a variety of ways. Within the new religions absolutism is present, almost by definition— the "pure consciousness" advocated by Transcendental Meditation; "eternal bliss" offered by the Hare Krishna movement; "receiving

Knowledge" from the Divine Light Mission; achieving "God Con-sciousness" through the Healthy Happy Holy Organization; and undergoing "Transpersonal Experience" (*e.g.,* being, essence, self-actualization, "oneness," "Cosmic awareness," "transcendence") in the Human Potential Movement, to name a few. All, in one form or another, profess to offer a superlative, providing its possessor with an ultimate system of relevance which transcends the bland ordinariness and meaninglessness of everyday life in the mod-ern world.

At the socio-behavioral level, absolutism is expressed variously as a communitarianism, which may vary from the part-time quasi-communities[16] such as the encounter group and sensitivity training groups of the human potential movement to the communities of the neo-Christian movement and the communal *ashrams* of the neo-Eastern religious movement. As Zablocki points out, communi-tarianism (specifically the communal structure) is basically a modern phenomenon which, however, may be understood as a demodernizing form of social organization.[17] Indeed the protest and reaction to the experience of homelessness produced by modernity is such that the social structure of the new religions in many cases approximates, when it does not replicate, a *total institutionalization*—a microcosmic totalitarianism as a means of tangibly re-establishing a home-world for its members.[18] Synanon, the Unification Church, and the Children of God are especially notable in this regard.

Parenthetically, it may be noted that it is not happenstance that communitarianism, in its various forms, is a predominant mode of social organization in the new religions. It provides perhaps the only type of social structure by which a socially deviant meaning system can be plausibly maintained among its members. It provides a thorough insulation and protection from the cognitive contamination that a sustained encounter with "the world" necessarily brings about. It therefore performs a cognitive survival function. The quasi-communitarianism of the human poten-tial movement functions similarly to ensure that the individual maintains a cognitive allegiance to his/her world-view.

Thus the cognitive and organizational absolutism implicitly offered by the new religions is counter-poised against the institutional ambiguity of the modern social world. It offers to bridge the hiatus between public and private spheres, renewing a symbolic and actual symmetry in individual life experience. In this way, the new religions offer cognitive easement from the tensions that such institutional ambiguity begets. Although it is certainly the principal characteristic of the spirit of protest, absolutism is not the only one. It must be understood in association with another important feature, one born specifically in protest against the abstract character of the public sphere.

As was previously advanced, social experience in the public sphere is typically unsatisfying. Its structures confront man as an abstract and incomprehensible labyrinth; its rationality is detached from subjectively meaningful values and aspirations. These things are, therefore, perceived as "not real," or as unnatural perversions of social existence. All demodernizing movements exhibit, to a greater or lesser degree, a rejection of the "cold, lifeless and artificial forms" of thought, behavior, and relationship, and manifest an affinity for the expressive and particularistic at all three levels. The emotionally spontaneous is understood to be "more natural" than the rationally engineered; the subjective experience of reality is understood to be "more real" than the objective, institutionally defined reality, and therefore, the former is assigned greater positive value than the latter. This is particularly true for the new religions. The ideological elements of expressivism and particularism can be seen in the mysticism of the neo-oriental and neo-Christian groups (from Zen to Charismatic Renewal) as well as in the orgiastic rituals of the human potential groups (e.g., Silva Mind Control, Arica, est, and others.)

Yet, I should note, in this regard, that the orientation toward expressivism does not simply result from a disaffection with the functional rationalism and utilitarianism of the public sphere. There is an important structural process which encourages this response. That process is what Gehlen refers to as *subjectivization.*

According to Gehlen, subjectivization is a corollary process to de-institutionalization. When, over the course of time, stable institutional routines and habits are rendered implausible or inconceivable—no longer taken for granted—behavior, morality, and the like are transplanted to the realm of choice. Individuals then must necessarily turn inward to the subjective, and must seriously and continuously reflect, ponder, and probe their new-found choices. This is not to suggest that each individual constructs *ex nihilo* his own life patterns. Options already exist because of the pluralization of cultures. Although innovation is inevitable, it is essentially this plurality of cultural options upon which the individual must reflect and from among which he must choose. Personal independence (*e.g.*, doing one's own thing in life), then, is not simply a social fashion, but rather a structural necessity. Yet, this process presupposes that the individual may engage in a process of turning to his own subjective apprehensions in determining his choices. Helmut Schelsky called this phenomenon the "permanent-reflectiveness" intrinsic to modernity.

One consequence of subjectivization is a shift in self-perception. In more archaic societies, identities were assigned at birth and were socially reinforced throughout the course of the individual's biography. With the de-institutionalization of identity, the question of personal identity shifted to the foreground of choice. Choosing "who one is" again presupposes the process of subjectivization. Hence the "self" becomes a territory without boundaries, ready to be explored, probed, excavated, and charted. The lack of institutional supports for identity make the territory liable to change. Thus, there are always new depths of the self beckoning to be explored.[19]

Subjectivization, the structural process necessitating a "turn within" to reflect on life patterns and identity (and not so much a failure of the moral character of the individual), fosters a *subjectivism* within the culture—an orientation marked not so much by vanity and egoism as it is by an incessant preoccupation with the complexities of one's individual subjectivity, pleasing or displeasing as that may be. Subjectivism may vary in degree from society to society. In the extreme, subjectivism may translate into a narcissism.[20] The latter is particularly encouraged by the dynamics of modern monopoly capitalism. Regardless of this variability, it is an orientation built into modernity and therefore a salient feature within the culture of all modern societies.

This structurally-rooted subjectivism provides a buttress, if not an added dimension, to the highly subjective expressiveness which ensues from the protest against the abstract rationalism of the public sphere. Most demodernizing movements, then, are accented by strong traces of subjectivism.[21] This is particularly true of the new religions. Within the human potential movement "transpersonal techniques are used to achieve the sense realization of Self beyond the everyday self. Put another way, they facilitate an encounter with one's being."[22] Thus, personal-growth programs overtly foster a subjectivism among those who follow them. By fostering it, they also legitimate such subjectivism. Although usually less overtly, the neo-Eastern and neo-Christian religions perform the same function. In this latter case, the exploration of one's subjectivity is usually couched in terms of aligning one's being with one or a number of cosmic forces or deities—an exercise which may take a considerable time, effort, and, often, expense. In all of this, there are, as Joseph Fichter has noted, strong narcissistic qualities about the movements.[23] They are narcissistic in the sense that the "self" is deliberately assigned an inflated significance, indeed, an historically unprecedented preeminence as against the collective weal.

What is suggested, then, is that there is an underlying infrastructure to all cultural manifestations of the anthropological protest against modernity. It takes shape in opposition to the dilemma of modernity. Its most rudimentary feature is a cognitive and socio-organizational absolutism. This is accented, however, by an orientation toward expressivism and subjectivism which may reach narcissine proportions.

Other Theory on the Topic

It is, of course, clear that the interpretation offered here is not in fundamental conflict with that put forward from other theoretical perspectives. It is not presumed that this perspective offers an entirely unique approach to the phenomenon. Yet, it can be argued that it does have its own distinctiveness and, at least, that it throws new light on the subject, providing a basis on which an integration of previous theory on the subject may be accomplished.

A number of attempts to account for the rise of the new religions have been advanced and have been catalogued under several broadly defined rubrics.[24] One perspective contends that the cause of the re-charismatization within the culture is found in the response to *normative breakdown and value dissensus*. One important proponent of this view is Charles Glock, who argues that it is the proliferation of scientific rationalism in the culture which "undermines the underlying assumptions of the old imageries, the cultural values and social arrangements informed by them and the inherent ability of these world-views to give meaning and purpose" while offering "no clear alternative formula either for organizing society or for living one's life."[25] Along similar lines, Robert Bellah contends that "the deepest cause...was...the inability of utilitarian individualism" and technical reason, dominant within the culture, "to provide a meaningful pattern of personal and social existence, especially when its alliance with biblical religion began to sag because biblical religion itself had been gutted in the process."[26]

From a related perspective it is argued that the effect of structural differentiation on individual existence (e.g., the fragmentation of identity into functionally specific roles) encourages the formation of groups which offer a holistic conception of both reality and the self.[27] Very closely connected with this perspective is the view which emphasizes the quest for a sense of community among individuals who are dissatisfied with their life experience in an atomized and structurally disjointed "mass society."[28] The result of such a quest is the development of functional alternatives to extended families and traditional communities— communes and quasi-communes—which are capable of solving the problems of disjuncture by reintegrating the individual's life experience into a coherent totality, thus protecting their members from the world, or providing them with adjustment for a renewed participation in the world.[29]

Without belaboring a body of literature familiar to all students of modern religion, it is clear that there is a great deal of overlap between these explanations and the perspective put forth here. Yet, most of the interpretations that are offered focus upon one or another isolated aspect of a larger problem. The problems of scientific rationalism, the instrumentalism of utilitarianism and technical reason, structural differentiation, and the atomization of mass society are all different though related features of modernity. The *composite effect* of these is captured in what has here been labeled the dilemma of modernity, in a word, an abstract and overly-rational public sphere, and a de-institutionalized private sphere. The elaboration of the perspective offered here, especially of the concepts of de-institutionalization and subjectivization, brings into relief structural dimensions hitherto unaccounted for in the literature which seeks to account for the rise and character of the new religions.

Perhaps the most important contribution of the perspective offered here is the deliberate connection of the perplexities intrinsic to modernity with a philosophical anthropology. The varying perspectives gain added coherence when viewed in relation to a philosophical conception of man. The answer to the question "why have the new religions emerged?" may, then, be more adequately understood.

Normative breakdown, value dissensus, and the resulting moral ambiguity are causal factors in the upsurge of the new religions because there is an anthropological requirement of stable and reliable parameters for individual existence. This latter is something which modernity fails adequately to provide, but something which the new religions promise to supply. There is a quest for community, not simply for unnamed "needs," but because of the anthropologically grounded fact of human sociality— something obstructed by modernity: something promised by the new religions. Finally, a fragmented personal identity and a fragmented general conception of reality is a causal factor because of the anthropologically-rooted demand for a world that has a more or less total and integrated intelligibility, a world that makes sense— which is again something intrinsically denied by modernity, but something which is offered by the new religions. All of the perspectives of causality that we have reviewed declare, or imply, that the new religions offer to meet a human need not presently met. But rarely, if ever, do they state what that need is and why it exists. I suggest that these differing perspectives might be interpreted in light of these philosophical considerations, specifically as rooted in the anthropological protest against modernity.

As such, this perspective offers a broader interpretive framework for understanding the new religions. The new religions are to be understood as a demodernizing movement, unique in its own right, to be sure, yet still one among others in the historical legacy of modernity in the West.

Conclusions

The foregoing are broad brush strokes. They lack shade and nuance, detail, and qualification. Clearly a major theoretical synthesis is necessary to refine, and improve upon, the propositions here outlined. Notwithstanding theoretical imprecision, the foregoing has offered a purview of a theoretical tradition, the contributions of which have been largely ignored in research on the new religions, but the insights of which invite serious consideration. Its propositions are not abstract and/or merely the results of "grand theory," but are capable of being subjected to the rigor of empirical analysis. The assimilation of the special insights of this tradition within empirical research on the new religions might prove to be a very fruitful alliance in a further understanding of the rise of the new religions in the modern world.

FOOTNOTES

1. See Talcott Parsons, *The System of Modern Societies,* Englewood Cliffs, N.J.: Prentice Hall, 1971, Anton Zijderveld, *The Abstract Society,* Garden City, N.Y.: Doubleday, 1970, and Thomas Luckmann, *The Invisible Religion,* New York: Macmillan, 1967.
2. See Peter Blau, *Bureaucracy in Modern Society,* New York: Random House, 1956, Jacques Ellul, *The Technological Society,* New York: Vintage, 1960.
3. See Peter Berger, Brigitte Berger, and Hansfried Kellner, *The Homeless Mind,* . New York: Vintage, 1974, T. Luckmann, *op. cit.,* Richard Sennett, *The Fall of Public Man,* New York: Vintage, 1978, Jürgen Habermas, "The Public Sphere," *The New German Critique,* 3, 1974.
4. Peter Berger, *The Heretical Imperative,* Garden City, N.Y.: Doubleday, 1979; P. Berger *et al., op. cit.;* Robert Nisbet, *The Quest for Community,* New York: Oxford University Press, 1953.
5. See Arnold Gehlen, *Urmensch und Spätkultur,* Bonn: Athanaeum, 1956; see also P. Berger and H. Kellner, "Arnold Gehlen and the Theory of Institutions," *Social Research,* 32, 1, 1965.
6. See A. Zijderfeld, *op. cit.*
7. P. Berger *et al., op. cit.*
8. Lionel Trilling, *Sincerity and Authenticity,* Cambridge, Mass.: Harvard University Press, 1972.
9. See David Riesman, *The Lonely Crowd,* New Haven: Yale University Press, 1966.
10. See Erving Goffman, *The Presentation of the Self in Everyday Life,* Garden City, N.Y.: Doubleday, 1959.
11. Robert Jay Lifton, "Protean Man," *Partisan Review,* 25, 1, 1968.
12. P. Berger, "Modern Identity: Crisis and Continuity" in Wilton Dillon (ed.), *The Cultural Drama,* Washington: Smithsonian, 1974; Orrin Klapp, *Collective Search for Identity,* New York: Holt, Rinehart and Winston, 1969.
13. Let me be direct about what is implied in this point. Namely, that at the core of these propositions is a certain philosophical anthropology—one that underlies the entire German humanistic tradition in sociology. The central presupposition of this philosophical anthropology is that man has a craving for meaning that has the force of an innate drive. Berger's elaboration of this in *The Sacred Canopy* is helpful. Men are congenitally compelled to impose a meaningful order upon reality. This order, however, presupposes the social enterprise of ordering world-construction. To be separated from society exposes the individual to a multiplicity of dangers with which he is unable to cope by himself, in the extreme case to the danger of imminent extinction. Separation from society also inflicts unbearable psychological tensions upon the individual, tensions that are grounded in the root anthropological fact of sociality. The ultimate danger of such separation, however, is the danger of meaninglessness. This danger is the nightmare *par excellence,* in which the individual is submerged in a world of disorder,

senselessness and madness (Berger, 1969:22). While all philosophical anthropologies reside in the domain of unverifiable conjecture, the validity and utility of this particular philosophical anthropology is supported by the afore-mentioned research on the biological constitution of man. Without the instinct to order human activity and thought, the human organism is rendered helpless. Instinctual deprivation *requires* humans to make up for this inadequacy through the construction of institutions which function like instincts. The biological, and therefore psychological, survival of the human organism depends upon this.

14. P. Berger, B. Berger and H. Kellner, *op. cit.*

15. See A. Zijderved, *op. cit.*, p. 120.

16. See J. Marx and D. Ellison, "Sensitivity Training and Communes: Contemporary Quests for Community," *Pacific Sociological Review,* 18, 4, 1975.

17. See Benjamin Zablocki, *Alienation and Charisma,* Riverside, N.J.: The Free Press, 1980.

18. The total institution is an ideal-type, not to be found in social reality. Even in the most totalitarian societies or micro-societies there can be found non-institutional or anti-institutional behavior and thought. Social organizations are *more* or *less* institutionalized or *more* or *less* totalitarian than others. The new religions, in most cases, tend to be among the *more* institutionalized examples. Thus, for example, in the Unification Church, although members do have the choice whether to marry a particular individual (after three years of membership), the selection has already been made for them. They have only to answer 'yes or no' not 'which one?' Yet should they agee with the Rev. Moon's selection, they do not have a choice as to when they get married, how they get married, or whether to live in proximity to one another before or after marriage. These aspects of the church's organization are totalitarian. The list of examples to be found in the Unification Church or in many of the other new religions of totalitarian control could easily be extended.

19. See Ralph Turner, "The Real Self: From Institution to Impulse," *American Journal of Sociology,* 85, 6, 1976.

20. See Christopher Lasch, *The Culture of Narcissism,* New York: W.W. Norton & Co., 1979, Tom Wolfe, "The Me Generation," *New York Magazine,* August, 1976, and R. Sennett, *op. cit.*

21. There is one qualification to this. Subjectivization occurs in situations where there is a high degree of institutional ambiguity. Thus the strong institutional control which some new religions impose upon their membership militates against this subjectivism.

22. D. Stone, "The Human Potential Movement" in Charles Y. Glock and Robert N. Bellah (eds.), *The New Religious Consciousness,* Berkeley: University of California Press, 1976.

23. Joseph Fichter, "The Trend to Spiritual Narcissism," *Commonweal,* 105, 6, 1978.

24. T. Robbins, D. Anthony, and J. Richardson, "Theory and Research on Today's 'New Religions,' " *Sociological Analysis,* 39, 2, 1978.

25. C.Y. Glock, "Consciousness among Contemporary Youth: An Interpretation" in C.Y. Glock and R.N. Bellah (eds.), *op. cit.;* see also Allan Eister, "Culture Crises and New Religious Movements: A Paradigmatic Statement of a Theory of Cults" in Irving Zaretsky and Mark Leone (eds.), *Religious Movements in Contemporary America,* Princeton: Princeton University Press, 1974.

26. See R.N. Bellah, "The New Religious Consciousness and the Crisis of Modernity" in C.Y. Glock and R.N. Bellah (eds.), *op. cit.,* p. 339; see also, Steven Tipton, "Getting Saved from the Sixties," unpubd. doctoral dissertation, Harvard University, 1978; Christopher Evans, *Cults of Unreason,* New York: Spectrum, 1973; A. Mauss and D. Petersen, "Les 'Jesus Freaks' et Retour à la Respectabilité, ou la Prédiction des Fils Prodiques," *Social Compass,* 21, 3, 1974.

27. Cecil Bradfield, "Neo-Pentecostalism: A Preliminary Inquiry," paper presented to the Eastern Sociological Society, 1975; see also, John Marx and Buckart Holzner, "Ideological Primary Groups in Contemporary Cultural Movements," *Sociological Focus,* 8, 4, 1975.

28. See J. Richardson, M. Stewart, and R.B. Simmonds, *Organized Miracles: A Sociological Study of the Jesus Movement Organization,* New Brunswick, N.J.: Transaction Books, 1978; see also, Cecil Bradfield, "Our Kind of People: The Consequences of Neo-Pentecostalism for Social Participation," paper presented at the Association for the Sociology of Religion, 1976.

29. See J. Marx and D. Ellison, *op. cit.*

YOUTH IN SEARCH OF THE SACRED

Joseph H. Fichter

Daniel Bell recently remarked that during the first half of this century almost every serious sociological thinker expected religion to disappear from industrial society before the year 2000.[1] C. Daniel Batson more recently remarked that "in spite of the immense importance of religion in the lives of millions of people, psychologists have tended to treat religion as a vestige of prescientific civilization soon to disappear and therefore not worthy of consideration."[2] Bryan Wilson, in a response to Daniel Bell, opined that the founders of sociology all "saw sociology as itself an alternative to theological knowledge." Religion in its ideas, practices and institutions, was an anachronism in the development of modern society.[3]

Social scientists, whether they study religion or any other institution, want to be seen as very rational people who deal only with empirical evidence. They could hardly take seriously the central religious fact of transcendence which escapes the research instruments of social science. "How can they believe such obvious nonsense?" is the cynical reaction to the belief system of so-called "deviant" religious cults. Sociologists "pride themselves on their positivistic common sense," wrote Lofland in the first American study of the Moonies. He observed that the sociologist who tries to explain how cult members maintain their religious faith emphasizes the inadequacy of such "world-views as cognitive systems."[4]

The focus of this paper is on young people who have encountered God and who believe that that encounter is of central importance to themselves and society. Instead of trying to explain away, through common sense, the religious experience of young Moonies, I want to take them seriously when they say, with their theologian, Young Oon Kim, that "any religious search is man's attempt to restore the original relationship of love with God."[5] In other words, these young people are claiming that religion is precisely what it appears to be: a probing relationship in search of truth, transcendence, and the sacred. To commune with the Infinite, to be in the presence of God, to experience the trans-cendent—here we are talking about the essence of religion.

The Crisis of Secularity

It has been part of the positivist conventional wisdom that religion is in crisis and that young people in particular are in rebellion against God. This wisdom is now being questioned, and the forecasts are spoken in a weaker voice. It appears now that secularity, not religion, is in crisis. "The most obvious fact about the contemporary world," writes Peter Berger, "is not so much its secularity, but rather its great hunger for redemption and tran-scendence."[6] In talking about the "new religions," Wuthnow observes that "virtually all accounts of contemporary religious movements have described them as youth phenomena. People over thirty have been said to be scarce either as members or as supporters of these groups."[7]

In broadest terms, we may say that secularity is a negation of the spiritual and an affirmation of the material. Most often it is seen as a replacement for religion, even an opponent of religion. In a book that was out of date even before it was published in English, Acquaviva talked about the "Eclipse of the Sacred." Like so many of the positivists he was sure that we are witnessing the end of the sacred. He wrote that "from the religious point of view, humanity has entered a long night that will become darker and darker with the passing of the generations, and of which no end can yet be seen." He conceded that perhaps some people may feel a need for religious faith and practice, but humanity is completely enmeshed in "uncertainty, doubt, and existential insecurity."[8]

Taking their usual broad overview of culture and society, social scientists apply Toennies' thesis to a kind of cosmic drift from small, simple, moral, and God-fearing communities to large, complex, individualistic, and sensate societies.[9] The neat, all-embracing formula for this drift combines three simultaneous long-term trends: industrialization, urbanization, and secularization. The quick hypothesis accepted by sociology students is that people who live in cities, in a technological culture, logically lose interest in religion. The acceptance of cultural determinism suggests an almost inevitable trend in the succession of Sorokin's cultural stages from idealistic to ideational to sensate.[10]

Distinctions abound between spiritual and material, natural and supernatural, reason and religion, and there is a recognizable shift from one to the other. Durkheim insisted that every society makes a distinction between that which is profane and that which is sacred.[11] If this is said in measurable terms, these phenomena are proportionately different according to the type of religion existing in the society. The sacred is more pronounced in an immanentist religion as among most primitive people and in the religions of Hinduism, Buddhism, and Taoism. The profane is likely to be more emphasized in a transcendental religion, as in Judaism, Islam, and Christianity.

Secularization then is a process, a shift, from the sacred and the religious to the profane and the material. A double transformation of thinking occurs in this process: one is a desacralization of attitudes toward persons and things, the other a rationalization of thought which is logical, scientific, objective, and free of emotion. What this means is that the religious world-view, whether immanent or transcendental, is no longer the basic frame of reference. This is the triumph of the secular which has been taken as an article of faith, a practically unshakable dogma of sociological theory.

One can understand why secularism is so attractive to the typical American sociologist, why it fits in so neatly with contemporary ideological baggage. Secularism is rooted in humanitarianism and democracy. It tends to reflect the rational and scientific forces that are said to be responsible for the enormous progress achieved in the Western world. This philosophical ideal is often called secular humanism, and it is synonymous with morality independent of any value that "transcends the natural, historical and social order of man."[12] It is interesting to note Tillich's remark that the great problem facing Christianity is not the opposition of non-Christian religions, but the pervasive strength of secular humanism.[13]

An argument can be made, however, that, at least among sociologists, the transcendentalism of religion has been replaced by the immanentism of secularism. To the extent that this has occurred in the American population, therein lies the crisis of secularism. A peculiarly appropriate label for this phenomenon is "utopian materialism." It has to be called *materialism* because "it reduces man to his most instinctive and spontaneous aspirations, apart from any ethical experience." It has to be called *utopian* because out of these aspirations there should emerge "a degree of consciousness and human fulfillment that can come only from man's ethical development."[14]

This concept of utopian materialism is probably known by another name to students of economic theory who hold the notion that the satisfaction of private interests eventually redounds to the benefit of the total society. This is not the same as the celebration of the "me decade," of a narcissism that is automatically and logically antisocial. The paradox in the concept of utopian materialism is that the fever to consume, the gratification of desires, and the satisfaction of possessive instincts, are thought to be for the commonweal. Out of these will emerge "the nobler attributes of mankind—liberty, peace, love, fullness, justice—and thus bring about a genuine utopia of happiness."[15]

Secular Enslavement

Utopian materialism is a trap; humanistic secularism leads to its own brand of conformism. This is not how Harvey Cox interpreted the ideology of secularism in his popular celebration of the secular city. He saw it as "a new closed world-view which functions very much like a new religion." Although he conceded that it can become a menace to openness and freedom, he said that the *process* of secularization is "almost certainly irreversible, in which society and culture are delivered from the tutelage to religious control and closed metaphysical world-views. We have argued that it is basically a liberating development."[16] I want to argue the exact opposite: that large numbers of people have been programmed into a routine of consumerism, materialism, secularism.

Desacralization and rationalization were meant to liberate us from fantasy, emotionalism and sentimentality, but much of the contemporary literature of protest complains that we have been therewith enslaved.[17] Rationality has been rightly credited with enormous progress in Western economics, education and government, but at the price of human freedom. The consequence is that human beings are everywhere regulated and controlled, and confined to tasks and goals that have no deep meaning or value for them. The fact that the socio-cultural system has been "rationalized," that is, planned in a logical and technical fashion, does not mean that the people who are routinized into the system are acting and thinking in a logical or reasonable manner.

It may appear over-dramatic, even sensational, to talk in terms of cultural enslavement, imprisonment, dehumanization, but there is a point at which normal behavioral conformity becomes a kind of abnormal behavioral lockstep. Any introductory textbook in sociology points out that customs and mores have to be institutionalized for the maintenance of an orderly social life. Human beings are socialized, not only as children learning the ways of the culture, but all through adulthood with conformity and adaptation to the requirements of the society. Human behavior is modified and institutionalized as an alternative to chaotic social relations and eccentric personal conduct.[18]

This universal fact of socialization must not be interpreted at any simplistic level of psychological compulsion or cultural determinism. Quite aside from religious affiliation, the fact is that our behavior is patterned to the expectations of the various social groups to which we belong: we are indeed programmed to think and act in ways that are acceptable and approved in the larger society. Ruth Benedict said this clearly when she pointed out that we are the "creatures of culture," while at the same time recognizing that we are also the "creators of our culture."[19]

The impress of our culture is strong upon us, so that we feel odd in acting otherwise. The process of patterning and programming is obviously selective by one's experiences in social relations, which "allow entry of only certain aspects of reality. This is what is meant by one's consciousness: the categories by which one perceives the world." Richard DeMaria notes that the secularized person does not get an entry on religion: "An excessively individualistic, ego-centered consciousness, one which has been shaped largely in terms of individual survival in a hostile world, cuts one off from that special perception which is known by many names, but which seems common to so many reports of religious experience."[20]

It appears that there are always some people who reflect on the tyranny of the sensate culture, question it, investigate it, and then raise their awareness of alternatives. We hear constantly of the need for consciousness-raising, to become aware that there are alternatives to the system in which we have been socialized.[21] Perhaps it is safe to say that people sense that "something is missing" that could make for a more satisfactory life. This seems to be what the Blacks are seeking when they complain that there is no "soul" in contemporary Caucasian society. Women raise their consciousness to a greater awareness of injustice and inequality. In a religious context, the theology of liberation speaks for the Third World, especially Latin America. One of the most important functions of theology, writes Gustavo Gutierrez, is "critical reflection, the fruit of a confrontation between the Word accepted in faith and historical praxis."[22] Pentecostals and evangelicals generally speak of breaking the bonds of worldliness.

Despite these stirrings of discontent with the world as it is, one may suggest that there are many people who are both unreflective and undisturbed, or at least their annoyances are more specific and personal. They may be only vaguely uneasy that the daily routine can best be endured with long stretches before the television or other frivolous ways of passing the tedium. If they feel a sense of entrapment, they may be quite content to leave things as they are. To be liberated from the grip of this utopian materialism allows us to seek the more worthwhile pursuits of human living; it helps to elevate us above and beyond the debilitating patterns of self-satisfaction.

Deprogramming Youth

It is not at all popular to suggest, as I do, that the whole process of socialization that we all experienced as young Americans was also a process of brainwashing, mind control, behavior modification. In other words, we were all programmed into our culture to accept the American way of life as the most natural and logical in the world.

The concept of brainwashing as a deliberate technique of indoctrination seems to have been originally applied to the Chinese communists who practiced thought control of the citizens.[23] This method seems to have a peculiarly Asiatic connotation, as when American prisoners of war were subjected to such treatment by the Viet Cong. The effect was that the individual abandoned his former loyalties, subscribed to a new and different ideology, and readily confessed the errors of his previous commitment. Originating in a non-Caucasian culture, it was seen as reprehensible and sinister, and "brainwashing" is the term then used to describe any psychological influence of which we disapprove. It becomes a logical charge to make against the Korean, the Rev. Sun Myung Moon.

While the term is now employed fairly loosely it appears to remain uni-directional in the sense that the people who do the brainwashing are left-wingers, socialists desiring to introduce some foreign un-American ideology. It is not popularly applicable to people who have adopted the right-wing ideology of Milton Friedman, William Buckley and similar conservatives. It is an interesting fact also that the switch from a religious to a secular ideology is not thought of as brainwashing, even though the individual was deprogrammed out of a church and reprogrammed into the secular culture. To the typical secular social scientist this would be the logical and reasonable step for the individual to take.

While religionists, pastors and parents, bemoaned the defection of youthful believers from the church, the typical social scientist saw this as a demonstration of the expected evolution of secularization. The trend to secularism is an inherent trait of developing civilization. It is charted into the long-term program. There were other youth "problems," like drugs and delinquency, but the repudiation of religious values was not one of them. It seemed logical that American youth be rebellious about the rigid rules of the church, and that they seek to escape the religious traditions of their parents and family.

It appears that church leaders for the most part—especially in the mainline churches—miscalculated or misinterpreted the discontent of youth. Their response was an attempt to accommodate the church to the apparent desires of the people. If young people in particular were going secular, perhaps it was time then for the churches to move in a more liberal and secular direction. They began to liberalize the doctrines of both theology and morality. Even the Catholic Church, a traditional bulwark against the secularizing tendencies of our time, seemed to come to terms with modernity. The hope was that the fractious young Catholics could be retained, or regained, by the relaxations introduced in the Second Vatican Council. But it was too late. Robert Bellah opines that "the Catholic Church finally decided to recognize the value of the modern world just when American young people were beginning to find it valueless."[24]

In the light of recent pronouncements coming from the Vatican one might guess that Pope John Paul had heard Bellah's comment. As the Church moved to modernize itself, many of the old-timers were saying that it is now much easier, more pleasant and relaxed, to practice Catholicism. Conservatives had watched the Catholic Crisis as seen by Thomas O'Dea,[25] and the Gathering Storm predicted by Jeffrey Hadden.[26] What was thought to be an attractive readjustment for young people seems to have turned in upon itself. The generation that wanted to escape the harsh demands of religious mandates is replaced by a generation that now complains: "everything is mixed up. You can't get a straight answer from the priests. You don't know what to believe anymore."

These observations lead us to a double generalization: young people are turning away not only from the religious orthodoxy but also from the secular orthodoxy. What is taken for granted as the proper acceptable urban modern culture has become unsatisfactory for youth. The objective system of traditional religious doctrine and practice has also become unpalatable for young people. This is a double kind of deprogramming that leaves the pious elders confused. They are glad to see their children turning away from secularism, but they are unhappy to see them turning to a religious cult, which they see as quite alien to their own.

The terminology of brainwashing, of programming and deprogramming, may be new but the concept, when applied to religious conversion, is as old as the rivalry between peoples of different religious affiliation. Before the present era of ecumenical goodwill and interfaith understanding, the Jew who became a Christian was obviously coerced to do so. The young Protestant who converted to Catholicism was certainly bewitched by the wiles and deceptions of Rome. The so-called "fallen-away" Catholic who joined a Protestant Church had come under some evil influence that prevented him from thinking clearly. Ecumenism now absolves the switching of members among the large-scale American religions: the charge of brainwashing is brought only when people are "victimized," and "tricked" into joining some new religious cult, especially one with an oriental flavor.

It seems quite legitimate, then, to say that the process of conversion from utopian materialism to transcendental religion is a process of deprogramming. The convert has repudiated the behavior patterns into which he had earlier been programmed, socialized, indoctrinated. The convert has called into serious question the values of his previous way of life, or at least some of them, and has raised his consciousness to prepare for change. "Conversion then," says DeMaria, "can be viewed as a method of re-education whereby one seeks to 'undo' the unbalanced or unhealthy programming with which he or she has grown up."[27]

Factors of Conversion

It is characteristic of the secularist mentality that the religious act, the search for God, the religious conversion, must immediately be suspect. There must be "something wrong" with the individual who says that he or she has freely chosen to join a religious cult. There must have been delusion, seduction, trickery. Talking about young people who join cults, Levine offers the description: "Deliberately and carefully sought out and recruited by cult members, they are, and for some time remain, unaware that they have been selected as prospects by the proselytizers. The latter resort to every ruse imaginable to induce the young person to join the cult."[28]

This type of description of conversion to the Moonie cult is provided generally by three kinds of people. The first type are the people who have abandoned the group, are disgruntled about the experience for whatever reason, and are ready to blame others for their defection. "If the charge of mind control comes from ex-members, we have to ask how much of it is self-justification to explain away their once ardent commitment to a cause they now reject."[29] They are in many ways similar to ex-Catholics who are ready to blame priests and nuns and other teachers for having subjected them to indoctrination in the catechism class of the parochial school.

The second type consists of the parents, many of whom have spent thousands of dollars in trying to retrieve their children from the clutches of the Unification Church. Berkeley Rice reports that "under the leadership of Rabbi Maurice Davis of White Plains, the national organization that has been formed of parents who have lost their children tries to locate them through the network of ex-members. If the parents wish, the organization puts them in touch with professional deprogrammers, like Ted Patrick, who may try to rescue the children for fees that can run to several thousand dollars. The deprogramming can be more brutal than any brainwashing the church may practice."[30]

The third type are the "expert" behavioral scientists who are ready and willing to assert that young people in their right minds simply do not choose to follow a leader like the Rev. Moon. Some tend to be contemptuous of such religious movements. C. Daniel Batson observes that, "for the most part mainstream psychology has treated the Unification Church and other psychoreligious cults with amused neglect."[31] The objective social scientist is not driven by the frustrations of ex-cultists or the disappointments of forsaken parents. He is moved by the high-minded devotion to the search for truth.

In spite of the hysterical charges of trickery and seduction into the religious cult, it is safe to say that the overwhelming majority of young people who become cult members do so freely and deliberately, and for reasons that make sense to them. Anyone who wants to know what the reasons are has to face the fact that the motivation is both complex and multiple. A convert may express a single main reason for joining the religious group, but upon deeper self-analysis will reveal that several motives are present simultaneously. One of the favorite explanations was the so-called "deprivation" theory;[32] another was the assertion that only certain "personality types" are likely to succumb to the attractions of the new religion.[33]

Instead of relying on speculation concerning forms of deprivation or on arbitrary classifications of personality types, let us look at the reasons people give for decisions to affiliate religiously. In the earliest sociological study of the Moonies in America, Lofland described the seven steps, or stages, of the conversion model, from the perception of "considerable tension" to the involvement with "intensive interaction." The crucial stage seems to be that of "religious seekership," in the sense that all of these people "defined themselves as looking for an adequate religious perspective and had taken some action to achieve this end."[34]

We are talking here about a religious act, the effect of which is commitment to a religious group. The search for the sacred is, of course, above all a religious experience. If we speak in terms of needs and motives, we recognize here that the essence of religion is not fellowship, or theological doctrine, or a moral code. It is transcendental experience, a channel of contact with the sacred and the supernatural. The expression of this experience may be formalized in liturgies, spiritual devotion, cultic worship, but it is in essence what Berger calls the "inductive" concept of religion.[35] This is sharply distinguished from the deductive and reductive concepts of religion.

Since motivation is multiple and complex, there are other supportive reasons why young people join a religious cult; and they are the same reasons why they join secular communes, country clubs and other primary groups. Probably the most frequently mentioned factor is simply the search for congenial fellowship.[36] Young people are attracted by the possibility of consorting with amiable people of their "own kind" who show concern for them. This is a response to the "love bombing" that is said to occur for the benefit of recruits to the Unification Church. Like novices in a religious order, they feel that they are being treated with warmth and affection directed at them as special persons.

Another supplementary motive may be termed a search for freedom, the break away from the kinds of confining routines we have already described as the content of utopian materialism. This is something quite different from anarchy, or from the simplistic notion that the young person just wants to "do his own thing." It seems safe to say that the behavioral conformity into which he had been socialized and indoctrinated had become distasteful, meaningless and valueless. Perhaps he is not sure why he rebels at the patterns of a sensate culture, except for the vague feeling that there has to be more to life than this.[37]

Still another subordinate motive appears to be in contrast to the search for freedom, but actually coincides with it. The person turns away from the irrational demands of a sensate conformity and seeks authoritative, dependable and reasonable norms. "They hunger for an authority that will simplify, straighten out, assure— something or somebody that will make their choices fewer and less arduous."[38] In other words, there is a need for an orderly system of norms and regulations on which the individual can depend and to which he can give obedience. In his study of the Moon movement, Sontag reflected that "at least some of our young people today are looking for discipline, structure, strong parental figures, and they are willing to pour their commitment into a life of sacrifice and missionary zeal."[39]

Consequences of Religion

Sociologists should not be faulted if they cannot reach the essential aspects of religion. By definition, and by the nature of their craft, they have to take a secular approach to the kind of data that are empirically verifiable. This is, of course, a limitation on the degree to which they can achieve a genuine understanding of a phenomenon that by its very nature has to include the relationship to the divine, the transcendent, the "beyond." Yinger suggests that many modern intellectuals, including social scientists, have no parallel to this in their own lives. "A supernatural view of the world has become meaningless to them; they are repelled by a boastful and worshipful nationalism; they feel comfortable with a quiet kind of scientific secularism, motivated by idle curiosity with perhaps a nudge from a desire to help solve some human problem."[40]

There are some sociologists who profess a supernatural belief and who practice religion, but like the atheists or complete secularists, who maintain that religion is substantially false, they avoid the super-empirical and simply look at the relation between religion and society. Religion is studied, therefore, as a cultural and social phenomenon with man-made institutions and man-controlled organizations. The empirical and demonstrable data about religion are not derived from the sacred scriptures as the inspired word of God, nor is there any need to talk about divine revelation as the source of research data.

Unable to penetrate the core of religion, the sociologist must content himself with studying the consequences of religion. When we ask why young people join a religious cult we seem to be asking what religion does for them. What good is religion? What benefit do people get from it? Essentially for the individual, religion provides meaning in the search for the sacred; it satisfies the need for transcendent experience. Joining the religious group also responds to the need for companionship, for freedom, for orderliness.

The demonstrable fact is, of course, that religious groups and believing people continue to exist in our reputedly sensate materialistic society. They do hold theological beliefs; they do follow religious patterns of conduct. The functional assumption we make is that since these phenomena survive, since rational human beings embrace them; since they are empirically demonstrable, they must have some utility. People must find religion useful in the sense that it is satisfying some human and social need. This is not a proof for the truth of any religion. The non-functionalist could argue that it might exist even if it were useless.

What we are saying is that the sociologists of religion tend to accept the notion that religion is functional for people in society; and they ask the question: What precisely does religion do for people? What are the consequences of religion? What is its utility? The tendency then is also to bypass the question of the truth or falsity of institutionalized religion. At the same time, the anthropologist, Leonard Glick, proposes that "Religion reflects, sustains, and legitimizes the social order," and he warns that we "should not labor with the misconception that our world is one in which religion is disappearing. For, to the contrary, the evidence is that new religions are arising all the time, that people do not respond to new problems by abandoning religion but by developing a new religion on the ruins of the old."[41]

The generalization that religion is useful, even necessary, for the survival of society rests on the functional theory that religion develops social solidarity among its adherents. Like all such neat theories, this one did not long go unchallenged. The utilitarian theory of integrative religion was questioned, researched, expanded and refined. Robert Merton observed that the "spaceless and timeless generalizations about the 'integrative functions of religion' are largely, although not of course entirely, derived from observations in non-literate societies."[42] Social critics who bemoan the general disintegration of Western civilization seem to feel that there are no remaining cohesive forces available to hold society together. Richard Fenn argues that secularization has undermined traditional bases of social authority and "dissolves traditional cultural wholes."[43]

If the sociologist no longer sees religion as an integrative force for society, the psychologist may argue that religion has certain therapeutic benefits for the individual. This, of course, continues the secular scientist's interest in religion as an instrumentality by and for human beings. It recalls Will Herberg's statement that religion basically requires that human beings pay attention to God. Religion should not be seen primarily as a form of social welfare, as though it were meant to accommodate God to the wants of human beings.[44] It is in this same vein that Robert Friedrichs remarked that people who believe in biblical religion "deem at their core that faith rooted fundamentally in its utility is doctrinal heresy."[45]

The sociological reflection about religion, the functional theory about its cohesive quality, the concept of its social utility, will hardly promote a religious revival. These speculations are probably of little or no interest to the person who is moved by deep religious faith. With some scorn he may ask whether that is the best that can be said about religion: that it is useful for humanity. For the believer the point of importance is that religion has not disappeared: it has not been swallowed up into secularism.[46]

The Religious Function

If we cut through all the secular, sociological, and psychological theories about what religion "does" for people as individuals or in groups, we arrive at the believer's conviction that religious activity is an end in itself. The religious function is precisely what it appears to be: an encounter with truth, transcendence, the sacred. Regardless of what we say about it, whether or not we think it is nonsense, the recruit to the Unification Church believes that he was created to respond to God's love "to be one in heart, will and action with God."[47] When we study the members of religious cults we have to take them seriously when the members say they are in search of the sacred.

The thoroughgoing secularist is embarrassed by the concept of a personal relationship with God, and probably the majority of sociologists would scoff at the idea. They are reluctant to accept the fact that some people do somehow move out of the secular routine of the material world and actually experience the transcendent. This says nothing about theology, the study of which is an intellectual exercise, nor about the acceptance of a code of morality which guides human behavior. Neither theology nor ethics is at the core of religion: the encounter with the Holy.

In Christian history, the ascetics and the mystics who were recognized as saints prepared themselves for union with God through self-denial, fasting, and mortification. Their prayer was essentially a communication with God, perhaps more often in praise and thanksgiving than in supplication. The concept of the "presence of God," and of the "indwelling of the Holy Spirit" is traditional among the members of religious orders, in seminaries, monasteries and convents, and is a common recognition among the large numbers of lay people who go on spiritual retreats.

In other words, the basic religious experience, the personal relationship with God, is not a rare and newly discovered phenomenon by a few eccentrics in religious cults. The experience of being "born again" is almost routine among evangelical Protestants, and is now claimed by many charismatics across ecumenical lines, Catholics as well as mainline Protestants. Many Christians have made a public profession of acceptance of Jesus as personal savior, and in some mystical way feel that they are saved, or at least that they would like to be saved.

The Unification theologian Young Oon Kim refers to the Eucharist as the presence of Christ among Roman Catholics and Eastern Orthodox.[48] She quotes Karl Adam: "The faithful Catholic does not merely hope that Jesus will come to him. He knows that he does... Holy Communion is a living intercourse with Jesus truly present."[49] She quotes also the Russian Orthodox Zernov: "The Eucharist is the meeting place between Jesus Christ and the believer, personal, intimate, unique. It makes the Christian a new creature by elevating him into the Divine Presence."[50]

To say that one has had this religious experience once in a lifetime, or even several times, is not the same as describing the change that remains permanently after the conversion experience. The question, "have you been saved?" may refer to that one-time experience. The question, "are you saved?" seems to imply that the individual is in a permanent state of religiosity, remaining in the grace of God (to use old-fashioned language) until one loses God's friendship through sin.

What the genuine religious convert realizes is that "life is different" as a result of the experience of conversion. This is willingly testified by persons who have had the "baptism in the Spirit" among charismatics and pentecostals. Many recovering alcoholics talk about the "spiritual awakening" that brought them new insights and a different level of behavior. The convert moves into an area that is sacred and supernatural. As Berger says, "the experience of the supernatural opens up the vista of a cohesive and comprehensive world. This other world is perceived as having been there all along, though it was not previously perceived and it forces itself upon consciousness as an undeniable reality, as a force bidding one to enter it."[51]

Parents who insist that their children have been mesmerized by Rev. Moon, or brainwashed by his followers, are willing to spend large sums of money to have their offspring deprogrammed. They obviously do not comprehend what a religious conversion means to the convert. Sontag sees them as young people who "are attracted by the demand for selfless devotion to a cause to usher in the new world of God's kingdom now for all people."[52] Lofland pointed out that "a person who accepts the primary postulates and uses the everyday schema finds that reality is enormously transformed: everything becomes meaningful and understandable, more understandable perhaps than to those who rely on common sense."[53]

The secular skeptic who seeks solid rational proof of religious phenomena is not likely to accept the facts of conversion and the authentic experience of life's transformation. What we are talking about here is obviously a matter of religious faith. Psychologist Batson tends to deal sympathetically with the phenomenon of large numbers of young people who are joining the new religions. He suggests that his fellow psychologists, as secular skeptics, may well begin to examine their own value presuppositions which are threatened by the prevalence of religion.[54]

FOOTNOTES

1. Daniel Bell, "The Return of the Sacred?" *British Journal of Sociology*, 28, 4, 1977, p. 421.
2. C. Daniel Batson, "Moon Madness: Greed or Creed?" pp. 218-225, in Irving Louis Horowitz. (ed.), *Science, Sin and Scholarship*, Cambridge, Mass.: MIT Press, 1978.
3. Bryan Wilson, "The Return of the Sacred," *Journal for the Scientific Study of Religion*, 18, 3, September, 1979, pp. 268-280.
4. John Lofland, *Doomsday Cult*, Englewood Cliffs, N.J.: Prentice-Hall, 1966, p. 193. Perhaps it should be noted that "the positivistic systems, to an important degree in the very process of transcending their scientism, reintroduced, in modified form, both nonempirical cognitive components and nonrational components into the picture." Talcott Parsons, *Action Theory and the Human Condition*, New York: The Free Press, 1978, p. 247.
5. Young Oon Kim, *Unification Theology and Christian Thought*, New York: Golden Gate, 1976, p. 40. She also quotes Blaise Pascal, who points out that the God of the Christians "is a God who fills the soul and the heart which he possesses." p. 37.
6. Peter Berger, *The Heretical Imperative*, Garden City, N.Y.: Doubleday, 1979, p. 184.
7. Robert Wuthnow, "The New Religions in Social Context," pp. 267-293 in Charles Glock and Robert Bellah (eds.), *The New Religious Consciousness*, Berkeley: University of California Press, 1976. It seems odd that the study of thirteen "new religions" took place in Berkeley in the early seventies and paid no attention to the Unification Church which had been studied there by Lofland in the early sixties.
8. S.S. Acquaviva, *The Eclipse of the Sacred in Industrial Society*, New York: Harper & Row, 1979, p. 201. The book was written in Italian about two decades before its English edition appeared.
9. Ferdinand Toennies, *Community and Society*, East Lansing: Michigan State University, 1957.

10. Pitirim Sorokin, *Social and Cultural Dynamics*, Boston: Porter Sargent, 1957, pp. 20-39.
11. Émile Durkheim, *The Elementary Forms of Religious Life*, New York: Macmillan, 1915, p. 37. For a clear exposition, see Robert A. Nisbet, *The Sociology of Émile Durkheim*, New York: Oxford University Press, 1974, ch. 5, "Religion," pp. 156-186.
12. Sidney Hook (*Philosophy and Public Policy*, Carbondale: Southern Illinois University Press, 1979) sees secular humanism in opposition to organized religion.
13. Paul Tillich, *Christianity and the Encounter of the World Religions*, New York: Columbia University Press, 1963.
14. In a document titled "Violence and Society" this utopian materialism is called a "sort of neo-paganism with Christian cravings" and when it fails there result frustration, aggression and violence. See *Promotio Justitiae*, no. 15, December, 1979, pp. 162-171.
15. *Ibid.*, p. 165.
16. Harvey Cox, *The Secular City*, New York: Macmillan, 1965, p. 20.
17. The youthful counter-culture was seen as a "reaction against certain aspects of the rationalistic and utilitarian individualism of the recent phases of development of American society and industrial societies generally." T. Parsons, *op. cit.*, p. 320.
18. Perhaps the most quoted early author on this phenomenon is William Graham Sumner, *Folkways*, Boston: Ginn, 1906. A kind of evolutionary determinism is associated with the "cake of custom."
19. Ruth Benedict, *Patterns of Culture*, London: Routledge, 1935.
20. Richard DeMaria, "A Psycho-Social Analysis of Religious Conversion," pp. 82-130, in M. Darrol Bryant and Herbert W. Richardson, (eds.), *A Time for Consideration: A Scholarly Appraisal of the Unification Church*, New York: Edwin Mellen Press, 1978.
21. Larry Reynolds and James Henslin, (eds.), *American Society: A Critical Analysis*, New York: David McKay,1974.
22. Gustavo Gutierrez, *A Theology of Liberation*, Maryknoll: Orbis Books, 1973, p. 79.
23. See the study by Robert Jay Lifton, *Thought Reform and the Psychology of Totalism: A Study of "Brainwashing" in China*, New York: Norton, 1961, p.3.
24. Robert N. Bellah, "New Religious Consciousness and the Crisis in Modernity," pp. 333-352, in Charles Glock and Robert Bellah, (eds.), *The New Religious Consciousness*, Berkeley: University of California Press, 1976, Peter Berger had said that Catholic opponents of radical aggiornamento had a "good deal of sociological instinct." *The Sacred Canopy*, Garden City,N.Y.: Doubleday, 1969, p. 170.
25. Thomas O'Dea (*The Catholic Crisis*, Boston: Beacon Press, 1968) was sure

that there would remain "the Catholic sense of the importance of the spiritual, of the immediacy of God, and of the reality of the Church mediating man's relation to God." p. xii.

26. Jeffrey Hadden (*The Gathering Storm in the Churches*, Garden City, N.Y.: Doubleday, 1969) warns of the crisis of belief and authority in the Protestant clergy and sees it also "at work within Roman Catholicism." p. 5.

27. R. DeMaria, *op. cit.*, p. 89.

28. Edward M. Levine, "Deprogramming without Tears," *Society*, 17, 3, March/April, 1980, pp. 34-38. "Prospective members are completely unaware that they are being recruited or that they have unwittingly entered the first phase of what is actually a process of indoctrination."

29. Frederick Sontag, "Sun Myung Moon and the Unification Church: Charges and Responses," pp. 20-43, in I. L. Horowitz, *op. cit.*

30. Berkeley Rice, "The Pull of Sun Moon," pp. 226-241, in Horowitz, *op. cit.* p. 239.

31. C. Daniel Batson, "Moon Madness: Greed or Creed?" pp. 218-241, in Horowitz, *op. cit.* p. 222.

32. Five kinds of deprivation are related to membership in religious movements by Charles Glock, "The Role of Deprivation in the Origin and Evolution of Religious Groups," pp. 24-36, in Robert Lee and Martin Marty (eds.), *Religion and Social Conflict,* New York: Oxford University Press, 1964.

33. Even after admitting that both the definition and classification of personality are arbitrary, Kephart decides that people who join modern communes can be classified as: the Parent-Haters, the Deep-Feelers, the Noncompetitors and the Borderliners. William Kephart, *Extraordinary Groups: The Sociology of Unconventional Life-Styles,* New York: St. Martin's Press, 1976, pp. 287-292.

34. John Lofland, *op. cit.*, p. 44. Rosabeth M. Kanter (*Commitment and Community* Cambridge, Mass.: Harvard University Press, 1972) pointed out that the nine successful communities (lasting from 33 to 184 years) she studied "began with some kind of religious base." A whole section of her book, pp. 111-125, treats of "Transcendence."

35. The deductive derives from a set of theological beliefs, while the reductive excludes the transcendent and makes religion a secular phenomenon. The advantage of the inductive option, says Berger, "is its open-mindedness and the freshness that usually comes from a nonauthoritarian approach to questions of truth." Furthermore, "implied in this option is a deliberately empirical attitude, a weighing and assessing frame of mind." Peter Berger, *The Heretical Imperative*, Garden City, N.Y.: Doubleday, 1979, p. 63.

36. This is mentioned first in a series of six "clusters" of reasons by Harvey Cox, *Turning East: Why Americans Look to the Orient for Spirituality*, New York: Simon and Schuster, 1977, p. 95.

37. In a book about the youthful counter-culture, which despite its title has nothing to do with religion, spirituality or God, Frank Musgrove (*Ecstasy and Holiness*,

Bloomington: Indiana University Press, 1974) suggests that the problems of youth are rooted in "differences of values."

38. H. Cox, *op. cit.*, p. 98.
39. F. Sontag, *op. cit.*, p. 209.
40. J. Milton Yinger, *The Scientific Study of Religion,* New York: Macmillan, 1970, p. 11.
41. Leonard Glick, "The Anthropology of Religion: Malinowski and Beyond," pp. 181-242, in Charles Glock and Phillip Hammond (eds.), *Beyond the Classics? Essays in the Scientific Study of Religion,* New York: Harper & Row, 1973.
42. Robert Merton, *Social Theory and Social Structure,* London: Macmillan, 1957, p. 28.
43. Richard Fenn, *Toward A Theory of Secularization,* Storrs: University of Connecticut, 1978, p. 53. In his review of this book, N.J. Demerath thinks "Fenn is disappointed that the Durkheimian vision of an integrated society informed by a comprehensive symbol system is no longer apt, if it ever was." *Journal for the Scientific Study of Religion,* 18, 3, September, 1979, pp. 314-315.
44. Will Herberg, *Protestant-Catholic-Jew: An Essay in American Religious Sociology,* Garden City, N.Y.: Doubleday, 1955.
45. Robert Friedrichs, "An Articulate Witness," *Journal for the Scientific Study of Religion,* 18, 3, September, 1979, pp. 313-314.
46. A Conference sponsored by the Methodists at Notre Dame University was held in November, 1979 on the "Loss and Recovery of the Sacred." It was reminiscent of the exchange between Daniel Bell and Bryan Wilson on "The Return of the Sacred."
47. Frederick Sontag, *Sun Myung Moon and the Unification Church,* Nashville, Tenn.: Abingdon, 1977, p. 102.
48. Y. O. Kim, *op. cit.,* 1976, pp. 296-299.
49. Karl Adam, *The Spirit of Catholicism,* New York: Image Books, 1954, p. 198.
50. N. Zernov, *Orthodox Encounter,* London: Clarke, 1961, p. 74.
51. P. Berger, *op. cit.,* p. 42.
52. F. Sontag, *op. cit.,* p. 209.
53. J. Lofland, *op. cit.,* p. 197.
54. C. Daniel Batson, *op. cit.* p. 224, referring in particular to Donald Campbell, "Reforms as Experiments," *American Psychologist,* December, 1975.

DISORIENTATIONS TO MAINSTREAM RELIGION: THE CONTEXT OF REORIENTATIONS IN NEW RELIGIOUS MOVEMENTS

David Martin

Although it would be difficult to relate the growth of new religions directly to the decline of old ones, and certainly so in the sense of any direct transfer of members from old to new, none the less, viewed within a much wider context, the recent and contemporary processes of declining social influence, doctrinal diversity and doubt, and organizational uncertainty within the mainstream churches have a conspicuous coincidence with the emergence of the new religions in the last two decades. In size, of course, there is, despite the volume of publicity which the new movements have been given, no reasonable comparison to be made. The major churches still command the allegiance of millions in every Western country, while the new religions, at least in the West, even when taken altogether, amount to but a tiny proportion of the religiously committed public. But in quality of commitment, the new religions are impressive, and it is perhaps this intensity and certainty which not only attracts their own new members but which excites public attention. It is, thus, not inappropriate in any discussion of the impact of the new religions to examine the general religious situation, and in particular the radically divergent contemporary trends that are apparent within most of the major denominations, which together represent what I call a process of disorientation.

When we concern ourselves with the situation of mainstream religious bodies we are, of course, confronted by considerable diversity. However, certain broad trends are clear, even though there are powerful contrary pressures and contradictions. These broad trends may be organized around the following themes: bureaucracy and charisma, ecumenicity and fragmentation, liturgical change and politicization. In discussing these themes, I take many of my examples from the British context, not because it is specially important, but because I know it and do not find it exceptional, except perhaps in the remarkable extent of sheer apathy.

About the first theme I have least to say. The process of bureaucratization has continued for a long time, as is shown, for example, in Thompson's study of the Church of England. *Bureaucracy and Church Reform.*[1] However, some of the consequences of that process have become more manifest of recent years, and these are provided with controversial documentation in such a book as James Hitchcock's *Catholicism and Modernity.*[2] These consequences actually overlap the themes of politicization and liturgical change, and for this reason they are not all dealt with under the specific heading of bureaucratization.

Most churches have recently undergone extensive reorganization in which their bureaucracies have been actively involved and appreciably extended. These reorganizations have affected plant, personnel, specialist agencies, government, giving, and charitable and welfare activity. That terms like plant and personnel can be used at all is a sign that the rationalizing techniques, and the vocabulary of managerial science, have not left the churches in splendid isolation. The very existence of Peter Rudge's *Ministry and Management*[3] indicates the advent of the organizational approach.

The most dramatic harbinger of change was perhaps provided by the Paul Report which endeavoured to rationalize the resources of the Anglican Church.[4] The quirky variegated scene, in terms of remuneration, career structure, and geographical distribution was to be tidied up. Clergy were to correspond more to a secular profession, and their deployment was to reflect contemporary social geography. At the same time, they found themselves involved in a more continuous reorganization into team ministries (parallel to group practice in medicine) and into units much larger than the traditional parishes.

At the same time, the very concept of the local parish was challenged and many clergy, particularly the more active and activist, were attracted to specialist ministries and agencies. These agencies might include (for example) industrial mission. The industrial missioner eschewed the traditional evangelical intent, and took on the role of enabler, or ecclesiastical resource-person in the industrial context. Another agency which exhibits a trend away from explicitness and traditional notions is that of Social Responsibility. Thus, the old concept of moral welfare, which had its most characteristic expression in family case-work, was meta-morphosed into social responsibility. This meant that individual charitable endeavour and moral rescue succumbed more and more to a more structural analysis relying to a decreasing extent on individual pious motivation. The level of concern rose above individual initiative and took over some of the conceptual apparatus of sociology. Training supplemented, and even sometimes supplanted, goodwill.

More centrally, a considerable apparatus was developed within the denominations, in the British Council of Churches or National Council of Churches at the societal level, and internationally at the level of the World Council of Churches. This apparatus might be variously concerned with race, education, pollution, or international relations, and comprises mini-ministries attached to mini-parliaments. There is, however, a considerable distance between these supposedly 'representative' agencies and their grassroots, and the cast of mind of many who staff them.[5]

Within such agencies, it is often difficult to discern any recognizable Christian point of view, or even, sometimes, much reference back to religion and the classical bases of Christian norms. Dr. Edward Norman has, of course, recently described what he regards as a discernible assimilation to the views of the secular liberal intelligentsia.[6] Even though his case may be exaggerated, none the less this shift is enough to arouse a determined opposition as, for example, in Mrs. Whitehouse's N.V.A.L.A. (National Viewers and Listeners Association)[7] and the Christian Affirmation Campaign. Doubtless, there are some implicit linkages between those who undertake cultural conservation and explicit conservative politics, but concern extends considerably beyond such linkages. To the expert in the agencies, these spontaneous exposiations of concern are typically confined to moralistic outrage based on the individualistic premise and concentrating on sex, manners, and violence, especially when these invade the home through the media. Mrs. Whitehouse represents a 'moral entrepreneur', opposed to the psychological and moral *laissez-faire*[8] of the experts.

Tendencies in education reflect similar shifts, though not without counter-pressures. Just as a distinctive Christian (or, at any rate, *traditional*) morality has been partly abandoned, so too a distinctive Christian socialization is frowned upon. The term 'pluralism' is so deployed as to suggest that a child should not be exposed in depth to any one, specific, historical tradition. This has the paradoxical effect of strengthening the socialization of religious minorities with an ethnic base, but weakening the socialization of the young in 'mainstream' bodies. The content of religious education has become even more morally abstract, or experimental, while any induction into beliefs or practices is equated with 'indoctrination'. Hence the partial abandonment of the school assembly, on the ground that it involves some corporate involvement in a belief with a particular provenance. Hence, likewise, the erosion of acquaintance with specific scriptures. Texts, beliefs, and moral convictions are abstracted into broad congeries of attitude, up for inspection maybe, but not proposed for inculcation. In short, morality loses specific historic density and is reduced to what are believed to be minimum acceptable functional necessities, or approved 'democratic' wisdom in the style of Harvard's Lawrence Kohlberg.[9]

However, this evacuation of content runs too close to a decline of control and corporate identity in the state school system not to arouse sharp reactions among parents who desire continuity, or self-control, or intellectual discipline. Schools with religious traditions have not entirely abandoned these, and this creates a demand for them from those who resist the *laissez-faire* in the secularized system. Even in the British public (i.e. private) schools, which have had a religious character, the erosion of any discernible Christian profile has engendered a desire to draw some line which defines what a distinctive Christian education might be. The Bloxham Project dealing with Religious Education in 'public' schools includes this amongst its objects.

A parallel initiative exists in higher education. The post-war attempt to provide a secure cultural frame for higher education in Britain, which was associated with such Christians as Sir Walter Moberley and A.D. Lindsay, has too obviously collapsed not to arouse anxiety. Liberal Christians in particular faced a situation in which the Student Christian Movement became so 'open' and (for a period) so politicized that active religiosity was confined to semi-fundamentalist cells.[10] Since the beginning of the 1960s, the mainstream Christian witness of S.C.M. among students became shadowy and disorganized, so much so that there was some minor revival of denominational associations. Liberal Christianity collapsed over its own internal contradictions and appeared parasitic on orthodoxy.

The foregoing paragraphs were included under the very broad head of 'bureaucracy', although not all the various tendencies are closely linked to processes of bureaucratization. Juxtaposed to bureaucracy is charisma, more particularly the Charismatic Movement. In shifting outside the sector of 'enthusiastic' evangelicalism and classical Pentecost, charismatic outbreaks now embrace sizeable constituencies in the Roman, Anglican, and other sometime established churches. On the one hand, charismatics may be seen as a form of grassroots ecumenism, in which the flame of the Spirit overleaps the bodies of doctrinal nicety and organizational difference. On the other hand, charismatics are divided among themselves, and not merely as between old-style Pentecostals and recent devotees of tangible spiritual graces. Enthusiasm separates enthusiasts from others who do not aspire to such graces, and breeds minor divisions amongst different messengers.

The Charismatic Movement is, arguably, both an attempt to overflow the old channels, and a response to the fact that these channels are sorely missed. But it is associated with more general tendencies that run directly counter to the mutations discussed above, i.e., the evacuation of a distinctive Christian presence and stance. Charismatics foregather in intense, dynamic huddles, forming, dividing, and reforming, and set over against 'the world'. For those who enter into such groups 'the world' does *not* set the agenda, and morality is *not* emptied into structural analysis. Personal conversion is a necessary precondition of social change (or social health). Charismatics entertain an element of sectarianism which affects the Christian churches at large.[11]

Just as the new sects represent a fresh and sharp demarcation of boundaries, so there is an alarmed appreciation of the corrosive consequences of weak definitions and low profiles. There are large secular animals abroad who break into the kraal and steal. Lots of congregations have abandoned all sense of the inclusive community, for which a national church may provide a real if weak focus. Such Laodiceanism cannot be afforded, or so it is believed. Those who want Christian baptism for their offspring are to be identifiable communicants, not intermittent attenders of the conventional *rites de passage*. Here, then, we have the direct contrary of smudged definitions.

However, the Charismatic Movement is not in all respects the direct contrary of relaxed profiles and definitions. In two ways it offers its own form of relaxation. One is that tough content tends to succumb to feeling. The specific meanings attached to words are affected by a generalized euphoria, of which speaking with tongues is just one incidental manifestation. Although charismatics are orthodox, they do not aspire to intellectual embodiments of their faith.

The other way in which boundaries are relaxed concerns roles. Roles in the religious context function as markers, just as words do. The construction of a defined pattern of roles is partly undermined by the free flow of the Spirit. This means that Pentecost easily presents the spiritual analogue of the Encounter Group.

It runs alongside and intermingles with the touchy-feely culture, which is designed to invade the defensible space of the individual, to loose him and unbind him. Such loosenings have their dangers, of course, since demons can be unleashed as well as good spirits and high spirits. Hence the revival of possession, the recurrence of exorcism, and, by extension, the cult of spiritual healing. Indeed, the new efflorescence of 'spiritual' phenomena, both good and bad, is something that marks the contemporary scene both within and without the Charismatic Movement.

The fact that the Charismatic Movement represents 'grass-roots ecumenism' has already been referred to. However, the ecumenical movement itself is far from a grassroots phenomenon. Clerical sponsors of ecumenism bend every rhetorical device in the service of unity and excoriate the 'sin of division'. Until recently, the rhetoric of 'the mind of the Spirit for our days' usually cowed opposition, but now the disadvantages of unity are more extensively canvassed and recognized. The ecumenical movement, itself sponsored amongst the church bureaucracies, is now in deep trouble, though the churches still hope to 'covenant' together in the eighties.

The key date for unification set in 1964 was to have been Easter 1980. However, several events interfered with the timetable. The Spirit waits for the churches. One was the fact that the Church of England did not minister the requisite majority for Anglican-Methodist Union. Meanwhile, the Methodist Church haemorrhaged under the strain.[12] Again, the Presbyterian-Congregationalist Union which, because of the historic links between the two churches, was the most plausible installment of unity, was not a conspicuous success. The new United Reformed Church continued the trajectory of decline. The appearance of the ordination of women simultaneously split the Anglicans from the Roman Catholics and from the Free Churches. The *via media* of Anglicanism split into camps and into provinces with opposed policies. The newly traditionalist Pope looked to the Orthodox rather than to the Protestants and Episcopalians. The submerged and fatal rock of papalism reappeared. Perhaps the ecumenical thrust succeeded

sufficiently to point up its own contradictions, notably the preference for ecclesiastical equivalents of the multinational, founded on
marriages of convenience rather than on doctrinal affinity.

Fragmentation is the reverse process to the centralizations
sponsored under bureaucratic aegis, even though elements of
fragmentation have come about in the train of bureaucratic initia-
tives, notably in the field of worship. One aspect of fragmentation is
the division which Towler and Coxon have pointed up between
pietistic Puritans and radicals of all sorts.[13] The divide is particularly sharp within the clergy, where it achieves its more emphatic
expressions, but it exists between clergy and laity as a continuous
latent tension.[14] I have already indicated that the lay constituency
of the churches, somewhat skewed towards the middle class and
suburbia, is more conservative than the clergy, and recognizes
that clerical radicalism is deeply entrenched in the higher specialist agencies. Liberation theology provides the natural focus of
radicalism, even though its dedicated proponents may be quite a
small minority.[15]

A dramatic instance of fragmentation is provided by the
emergence of a self-conscious traditionalism which affects the
Roman Church and the Anglican Church in particular. The disciples of Archbishop Lefevre are only the visible sign of a much
deeper unease extending to doctrine as well as to liturgy. The
break-away movement in the American Episcopalian Church is
largely at the 'Catholic' end of the spectrum and also contains
some political radicals, as is indicated by its main publication. In
the Anglican Church in England, the old party spirit dividing
Evangelicals and 'Catholics' shows signs of reviving, fostered by
the context provided by quasi-parliamentary organs of government, and both are opposed by a third force, 'The New Synod
Group'. The New Synod Group consists of those who organize
against the organized.

Within the broad evangelical movement, the House Churches
have largely severed themselves from (or rather grown up outside)
the official organizational format. These groups meet for mutual
edification and may adopt some semi-communal form, such as

living closely together in adjacent housing.

The last topic concerns liturgical change which is a sensitive indicator of many of the shifts already mentioned: the communal emphasis, politicization, fragmentation, and ecumenism. Liturgical change has attempted to break down the entrenchments of individual piety and to institute a communal emphasis which can foster spontaneous relationships. It typically adopts the circle as its preferred social form in which people and priest encounter each other personally and face-to-face. The congregation is renamed the 'people of God', and the clerical 'president' orchestrates an atmosphere of participation. Sometimes, this expresses itself in the self-service sacrament, where people are simply encouraged to pass a loaf one to another.[16]

In the new liturgies there is an emphasis on positive feelings rather than corruption, on simple, almost childish texts, and on the immanence of the divine. This means that the classic verbal expression of Christianity, which appealed to profound aesthetic impulses is deposed as far as possible. The sacred and the numinous are often dismissed as non-Christian categories.[17] 'Majesty' for example is downgraded as irrelevant, and *bon homous* good fellowship takes its place. It is claimed that the Holy Spirit works through the fellowship, and is inimical to 'high' forms of worship. It is also claimed that emphasis on sin or unworthiness is regressive, which means that doctrines of penitence and redemption, especially the atonement, cease to be regarded as meaningful.

It is paradoxical that the new liturgies are promoted from above in the supposed name of 'the people', and that they carry both the ecumenical thrust and the tendency to fragmentation. The liturgies are produced in various specialist agencies, the International Consultation on English Texts (a non-denominational body), and the International Commission on the English of the Liturgy (which is Roman Catholic), and all their productions bear some family likeness. No doubt this is intended to foster ecumenical contexts, to reduce variety and the sense of distinctiveness. However, since these liturgies often allow a large range of options and are supposed to be adopted by local decision, the result is a lack of common language and common form. In this way, 'Common Prayer' in the old Anglican sense has largely ceased to exist. Moreover, the occasional attender or half-believer now finds himself disenfranchised, unable sometimes even to join the Lord's Prayer.

This disenfranchisement further points up a tendency already noted in relation to baptism, which is the planned withdrawal from the idea of a national church and from Civic Religion.[18] The churches, faced with apathy and secularity, feel that it is no longer possible or indeed proper to hold the sacred canopy over society as a whole. They therefore dismiss not only the local community but also the national society, concentrating instead on inter-church contacts and the building up of dedicated Christian cells. Culture and civilization are abandoned to the world, and the classical expressions are not merely condemned as complex but as positively 'elitist'. In short, the tendencies which have thinned the content of education, de-emphasizing moral discipline, excellence, richness, tradition, and history, have successfully established themselves in the Church. The Church's attempt to disentangle itself from the world follows the trajectory that the world has already set.

It remains only to indicate what should already be obvious with regard to the way this ensemble of shifts and mutations bears on the emergence of new religious movements. First of all, there is a loss of any sense of the transcendent as traditionally understood. God has been incorporated at the interface of human relationships. Profound feelings of awe, majesty, and mystery find little chance to express themselves; and quiet personal meditation is almost disallowed.

Second, 'God' is conceived of as a summary symbol of liberation, and Christian eschatology begins to merge with secular concepts of human progress. He takes his place as a kind of demiurge implicit in the evolutionary process, more particularly in the evolution of society towards utopia. 'Structural reforms' replace charitable endeavours.

Third, these various shifts take place under the aegis of agencies and bureaucracies, the personnel of which resemble their opposite numbers in the secular intelligentsia. They share the same milieux as secular intellectuals and test their views by liberal, especially left-liberal, assumptions. The classic opposition between 'Church' and 'World' disappears in a welter of 'celebration', and is replaced by a tension between unredeemed capitalist society and utopias of various kinds. The pervasive sense of evil is eroded, leaving small interest in redemption. Why confess sins when society is to blame? Why should the divine son shed his blood to cure psychic and social maladjustment? The Church becomes an association which plays down its links with either the community or the state, and instead builds up a separate internal dynamic. It no longer wishes to carry forward the sense of generational continuity or the richness of a cultural inheritance.

Reference has been made in the preceding paragraph to liberalism. It is worth emphasizing that those denominations with the largest liberal component were those which have suffered most. No doubt the Roman Catholic Church has also suffered somewhat from the delayed advent of liberation, but those churches which have for long faced in a liberal direction are conspicuous by their lack of resistance to the secular infection. The Methodist Church and the United Reform Church were less able to reproduce themselves, and presented a demographic profile more skewed to the elderly and the female. By contrast the Baptist and Independent Evangelical Churches were less affected, and likewise the evangelical sector in the Anglican Church grew in numbers, vigour, and self-confidence.

By way of an addendum, I propose to illustrate certain of the mainstream disorientations by indicating issues in the English religious context in which I personally have been involved, and which touch on this matter of cultural inheritance. What is significant here, perhaps, is the active role played by sociological and historical analysis in the process. Bryan Wilson's analysis of ecumenism and Edward Norman's analysis of the relationship between the clergy and the secular intelligentsia constitute active agents in what is happening, and are quoted and combatted. The participation of sociologists in the liturgical debate helped to shape discussion, and perhaps even altered opinion. These debates over ecumenism and over liturgy have been part and parcel of a crisis in the clergy, a lesion between university and church, and a loosening of the tie between church and state, church and culture, church and society.

What needs to be recollected is that English religious consciousness and the religious aspect of the nation have been shaped by two books, the Authorized King James Version of Scripture and the Book of Common Prayer. The former has had the greater influence, since it has included dissent as well as the established Church, but even so, Dissenters, Catholics, and Jews may often have some acquaintance with the Book of Common Prayer. They were, with Shakespeare, Milton, and Wordsworth, the prime constituents of the religious mind, central to an educated sensibility, and, incidentally, the point of reference for popular hymnody. The Authorized Version was, as Thomas Huxley once commented, the religious form of the national epic.

In the course of two decades, both pillars have been weakened, partly by trends in education, but much more massively by the active demotion attempted by the Church itself. This has involved an accelerating spate of new biblical translations which try to shift from the specific poetic and religious registers to a register which is unspecific in character and informational or colloquial in style. The underlying justifications have included the need for easily assimilated material and for clarity of expression, and the claim that the less educated are put off Christianity by obscurity. Falling numbers in the sixties reinforced this line of thought.

In the theological field, there were certain shifts which went against a distinctive, festive, objective, shared, religious language. One was the emphasis on spontaneity, which derived from existentialism, and which decried external form. The classical notion, whereby predetermined shape informed and created a complete world, succumbed to the corrosion of informality and the vagaries of subjectivity. The very notion of a classic form was undermined. And at the same time there was a denigration of specific transitions, as from the secular to holy ground, from the outer court to the inner court. Religious language was seen as associated with that transition, a marker of difference.

Equally important was the sense of unease about the idea of a national church in a plural society. The BBC, for example, disclaimed its national religious mission as originally set forth by its first governor general, Lord Reith, and adapted to plurality. That decisive shift is clearly connected with the way in which the schools thinned the content of Religious Education, and shifted in the direction of generalized moral teaching and the pursuit of psychological maturity. It also links with the way in which the churches, and in particular the Church of England, felt that the weight of sustaining the sacred canopy had become too heavy for the available supports. The Book of Common Prayer became embarrassing because of its long-term association with the idea of lifting up the whole community; not to mention its vigorous insistence on sin and redemption rather than on healthy-mindedness.[19] Thus, we see here a weakening of the markers of the sacred, a thinning of content in the media and schools, and a pluralism which undermined any overall communal framework of religion. At the same time, the clergy have a much diminished income, and they have a lower educational attainment, and they have begun to exhibit a mixture of political radicalism, role uncertainty, and withdrawal symptoms vis-à-vis the society at large. This withdrawal went hand in hand with successful demands for ecclesiastical autonomy, by which the former control of Parliament was largely devolved on to the General Synod. Immediately, the classic texts acquired an association with the *status quo ante,* in that the new clerically and bureaucratically controlled church set about their demolition. There was no apparent widespread call for such a move; it simply mushroomed in clerical consciousness. It is just this clerical confusion which is such a major element in the contemporary disorientation of mainstream religion.

In what way might we briefly suggest that this mainstream disorientation bears on reorientation in the new religious movements? In this context I would like to refer to material on the Unification Church, since it has been carefully investigated both in the U.K. and in the U.S.A. If the Unification Church can in any way be said to stand as representative for new religious movements, the relation of disorientation to reorientation can be tentatively suggested.[20]

In the Unification Church we observe a demographic profile more or less the reverse of that obtaining in the mainstream churches. The new movement is much more male and there is within it a concentration of people who are in their twenties. Almost universally, mainstream religions are relatively weaker in the representation of the twenties age group. However, the new movement resembles the mainstream churches in recruiting more successfully from the higher status groups.[21]

If we observe other characteristics which have been noted, the picture acquires a sharper focus. Members of the new religious movements tend to come from good families where there is some Christian background. Thus they draw on a deposit which is already there. At the same time, however, members of the new movements report a sense of something missing, and a feeling that the conventional bodies do not match up to their *religious* expectations; they offer no confident hope for the world; and they appear suffused with 'hypocrisy'. Such hope as the old churches have is part and parcel of the liberal fragmentation. The theology which they have to offer no longer offers a comprehensive explanation. The neophyte in the new religious movement feels he has lighted on *the* key and that all his experiences make sense.

Once he takes hold of the key he enters into a personal devotional discipline which offers secure markers and boundaries. One such marker is that between good and evil, black and white. It is reported that the convert often has precisely this tendency to see in terms of black and white. Where the Christian Church itself offers such markers the new religious movement makes little headway. A born-again Christian or an adolescent of vigorous evangelical faith is not normally a convert to a new religion. It is where the definition is lacking, the markers removed, and the sense of meaning evacuated that a new religious movement can make some impact. Mainstream disorientation and reorientation in new religious movements constitute a symbiosis.

FOOTNOTES

1. Kenneth A. Thompson, *Bureaucracy and Church Reform*, Oxford: The Clarendon Press, 1970.
2. James Hitchcock, *Catholicism and Modernity*, New York: The Seabury Press, 1979.
3. Peter F. Rudge, *Ministry and Management*, London: Tavistock Publications, 1968.
4. Leslie Paul, *The deployment and payment of the clergy*, London: Church Information Office, 1964.
5. For a fairly conservative account of the W.C.C. *cf.* Ernest W. Lefever, *Amsterdam to Nairobi*, Washington: Ethics and Public Policy Center, 1979. Good background material is provided in Michael Novak (ed.), *Capitalism and Socialism*, Washington: American Enterprise Institute for Public Policy Research, 1979.
6. Edward Norman, *Christianity and the World Order*, Oxford: Oxford University Press, 1979; *idem, Church and Society in England 1770-1970*, Oxford: The Clarendon Press, 1976. A good example of Christian social and ethical comment is provided by John Habgood, *A Working Faith*, London: Darton, Longman and Todd, 1979.
7. *Cf.* a forthcoming work on N.V.A.L.A. by David Morrison and Michael Tracey of the City University, Barbican, London.
8. Roy Wallis, *Salvation and Protest*, London: Frances Pinter, 1979. Also, *cf.* Christie Davies, "Moralists, Causalists, Sex, Law and Morality" in W.H.G. Armytage, R. Chester and J. Peel (eds.), *Changing Patterns of Service Behaviour*, London: Academic Press, 1980.
9. Peter Scharf (ed.), *Readings in Moral Education*, Minneapolis: Winston Press, 1978. For a broad overview *cf. A Groundplan for the Study of Religion*, London: Schools Council, 160 Great Portland Street, 1977.
10. A helpful analysis of this exists in manuscript by Steve Bruce, Queen's University, Belfast.
11. For reading *cf.* for example, Richard Quebedeaux, *The New Charismatics*, Garden City, N.Y.: Doubleday, 1976; Luther P. Gerlack, "Pentecostalism: Revolution or Counter-Revolution" in Irving I. Zaretsky and Mark P. Leone, *Religious Movements in Contemporary America*, Princeton: Princeton University Press, 1974, and Ralph Lane, "The Catholic Charismatic Renewal Movement in the United States", *Social Compass 25, 1*, 1978/1.
12. For an account of schism and ecumenism among Methodists *cf.* Robert

Currie, *Methodism Divided,* London: Faber and Faber, 1968. Perhaps the earliest criticism of ecumenism as clerically-inspired is in Bryan R. Wilson, *Religion in Secular Society,* London: Watts, 1966. Supporting evidence is in Alan Bryman and C. Robin Hinings, "Participation, Reform and Ecumenism" in Michael Hill (ed.), *A Sociological Yearbook of Religion in Britain* No. 7 London: S.C.M. Press, 1974.

13. Robert Towler and A.P. Coxon, *The Fate of the Anglican Clergy,* London: Macmillan, 1979.
14. *Cf.* Anthony Russell, *The Clerical Profession,* London: S.P.C.K., 1980.
15. *Cf.* David A. Martin, "The Cultural Politics of Established Churches" *Japanese Journal of Religious Studies,* 1, 1-2, Vol. 6, Nos. 1-2, March-June, 1979.
16. For a moderate expression of a 'modern' view *cf.* Michael Perry, *The Paradox of Worship,* London: S.P.C.K., 1977.
17. John G. Davies, *Everyday God,* London: S.C.M. Press, 1976.
18. *Cf.* Oliver R. Johnston, *Nationhood: Towards a Christian Perspective,* Latimer Studies, No. 7, Oxford: Latimer House, 1980.
19. For protests and analyses concerning these trends *cf.* Brian Morris (ed.), *Ritual Murder,* Manchester: Carcanet Press, 1980, and David A. Martin (ed.), *Crisis for Cranmer and King James,* Manchester: Carcanet Press, 1979.
20. Perhaps the best short account of new religious movements in general is Bryan R. Wilson "The New Religions", *Japanese Journal of Religious Studies,* 6, 1-2, March-June, 1979.
21. I am relying in these remarks on the analysis provided by Eileen Barker.

WHO'D BE A MOONIE?
A COMPARATIVE STUDY OF THOSE WHO JOIN THE UNIFICATION CHURCH IN BRITAIN

Eileen Barker

The title of this paper allows for a certain ambiguity by permitting a note of incredulity—"how *could* anyone?" (a "why" as well as a "how" question)—to creep into a particular reading of its wording. This is not unintentional for, although my main concern is to present relatively straightforward and unadorned statistical information about the sorts of people who do actually become Moonies, the information has been collected[1] and is presented with the "why" rather than the "who" questions in mind. There is little space to make explicit all the hypotheses with which the research has been concerned (some of which I have discussed elsewhere),[2] but it is hoped that the reader may adduce some of these hypotheses and, perhaps, will be able to develop theories of his or her own through an examination of the data.

Who is a Moonie?

"Moonie" is the name by which members of the Unification Church (UC) have become known in popular parlance. The movement, which was founded in Korea, in 1954, by the Reverend Sun Myung Moon, now has a following of some hundreds of thousands in South Korea and Japan. After struggling without much success to establish a foothold in the West during the sixties, the rate of growth of the UC in Europe and North America increased dramatically in the seventies, giving rise to considerable media coverage.

Members of the UC accept the movement's theology, one version of which has been published under the title *Divine Principle*.[3] It is based on an interpretation of the Bible that Reverend Moon claims was revealed to him by Jesus and by God. It is a messianic, millenarian theology, which exhorts believers to accept responsibility for their role in restoring the Kingdom of Heaven on earth. In Europe and America, members typically live in communal centres, and work long hours in fund-raising in the streets or in trying to get new converts. The church does, however, own several businesses, in which some members work, and others have administrative or teaching roles. The Unification Theological Seminary in New York State has about a hundred full-time students doing a two-year program in religious education. The seminarians, who are among the elite of the movement, must have completed at least one first degree to qualify for entry to the seminary.

The UC is a hierarchically-structured organization which expects full commitment and obedience from its members, who are unlikely to have much time to keep in touch with their family and former friends. After they have been in the movement for some time (usually at least three years), Reverend Moon might suggest marriage partners for his followers, and they (if they accept the choice) may then be Blessed in a mass marriage ceremony with hundreds of other UC couples. This is one of the very few church rituals—and certainly the most important.

Since the end of 1978, there has been a growth in what is known as the Home Church movement. This is part of a plan to extend the UC at a grassroots level. Members spend a proportion of their time going into the community and offering help to people who live in their particular 'parish'. At the same time, there has been the development of Home Church members. These are people who accept, or at least feel a fairly strong sympathy for, the teachings presented in *Divine Principle* but who, for various reasons, do not commit themselves to living in a centre or to working full time for the UC.

Since the mid-seventies, being a Moonie has taken on a new dimension as a result of the growth of organized opposition. Parents and various religious and political bodies have, with the support of a largely 'anti-cultist' media, accused the UC of splitting up families, exploiting the young, financial skulduggery, political intrigue, and (thus providing a justification for the practice of 'deprogramming') of brainwashing and mind control over its members.

The accusations of brainwashing, were they to be unequivocally true, could provide an immediate and easy answer to the question, "Who'd be a Moonie?". The answer would of course be: anyone who fell into the clutches of the Moonie brainwashers. In fact this is not the case. In England, nine out of ten of those who attend a weekend workshop do not become Moonies. In the Bay Area of California, where the social pressure put on the potential recruit is considerably greater, a far larger proportion joins the movement;[4] in Scandinavia, where *Divine Principle* is more likely to be studied in the potential convert's own home away from practically any pressure, the proportion joining is considerably lower— the turnover rate of those who do join is also lower.

It follows from such comparisons of those who, in different areas, *do* become Moonies that while some people might become Moonies under certain circumstances, others are more likely to do so under different circumstances. It is also probable that some people are very likely to become Moonies under a very wide range of circumstances, and others under practically none.

No one becomes a Moonie without the intervention of some sort of action by existing members of the UC, thus, it is necessary to know what the UC is seen to offer, as well as the social context within which the decision to become a Moonie is made.[5] But as neither the UC alternative nor the social context for the decision to join or not to join are sufficient factors to explain why some do and why some do not become members, it is just as necessary to examine both the individual's predispositions and his presuppositions. His predispositions are his values and inclinations as they have been developed up to the time he first makes contact with the UC, and his presuppositions relate to the ways in which he has experienced society and imagines its various manifestations—home, work, college, church, etc.—compared with the alternative offered by the

UC.[6] In other words, in order to find out who becomes a Moonie it is necessary to look for answers to the related questions: "who would *not* be a Moonie?" and "who would be, or not be, a Moonie under what circumstances?". That having been said, however, it is upon the predispositions and presuppositions with which the potential Moonie comes to the Unification Church that this paper mainly concentrates.

Methodology

The central focus of the study that I have carried out over the last four years has been of the Unification Church in Britain, but for comparative purposes, research has also been undertaken into the UC (and some other new religious movements) in America and in Europe (especially Scandinavia). In practical terms the research has been concerned with three main populations (each of which can be further subdivided): UC membership itself; involved outsiders; and control groups.[7]

The UC research involved participant observation, interviews and questionnaires. I stayed at various centres, including the seminary, and visited many others. I also attended several workshops and more advanced courses to observe and compare recruiting and other teaching methods. Just over thirty in-depth interviews, averaging eight to nine taped hours each, were carried out on the basis of a random sample of the British membership. These were supplemented by hundreds of informal interviews. During the latter part of 1978, all members resident in Britain whose English was sufficiently good, all the seminarians in New York State, and a few other Americans were asked to fill in a 41-page questionnaire. There was a gratifyingly high response rate of almost 80%, and this rose to nearly 90% when a single page questionnaire was sent to non-respondents, thus giving a total of 434 cases, just over half of whom were British. Home Church members were treated as a separate group, a few interviews being carried out, and all the application forms analysed. The actively involved outsiders who provided information were mainly parents and the anti-cult organizations. Contact was also made with various other groups such as religious bodies and the media. It is also possible to add to this category interviews with some ex-Moonies, several of whom I had interviewed or known while they were still in the movement.

For the reasons indicated above, it was necessary to select a series of groups with which the membership of the UC could be compared if the boundary between those who would, and those who would not, become a Moonie were to be as clearly defined as possible. The first available group was the population as a whole. Publicly available statistics[8] provided an initial profile of the sorts of people who might be more, rather than less, likely to join the UC. Next a group matched with the UC membership for age, class, educational and, to some extent, religious background, but itself having no connection with the UC, was asked to fill in a 36-page questionnaire similar to that filled in by the Moonies. The information gleaned from this control group of 110 cases indicated that many of the characteristics thought peculiar to the UC membership were in fact shared by the middle class youth of the day, and it was therefore decided that a further control group was needed. This was composed from those who attended Unification Church workshops during the year 1979. Workshops are residential courses during which the potential convert is introduced to the beliefs and practices of the movement, mainly by way of lectures on *Divine Principle*. In Britain, the potential convert is initially invited to attend a two-day workshop (frequently held at a weekend) and then to proceed to a seven-day workshop. After completing this the potential recruit may proceed to a twenty-one-day workshop during which he will hear the lectures in greater length and learn more about the sort of life that he will be likely to lead if he decides to join the church.

I was able to obtain quite a lot of basic information (sex, date of birth, occupation, nationality, religious background and the sex and nationality of the member who first contacted the potential recruit) from the application forms of the thousand or so who had attended a two-day workshop in the London area, and from nearly six hundred people from the southern half of England who attended (and those who had left) a twenty-one-day workshop. In addition, a

6-page questionnaire was sent to the group who had attended the two-day workshop and who had provided legible addresses in Britain. At the time of writing, this had yielded a response of 131 cases which, as far as could be inferred from the information culled from the application forms appear to be significantly representative.

Of the questionnaire respondents, 82% completed the two-day course; 44% started, and 31% completed, the seven-day course. Of the 28% who proceeded to the twenty-one-day workshop, only 14% 'graduated' (the other half leaving before the course was completed). Of the total, 12% became full-time members (but a third of these had left by the time that they filled in the questionnaire), and 9% had become Home Church members (but over half of these had left by the time they filled in the questionnaire). The final figure of 8% full-time members and 4% Home Church members is perhaps slightly higher than the actual percentage of joiners, probably because workshop attenders who had given overseas addresses were not contacted.

Where to find Moonies: A preliminary search.

Members of the UC (and indeed of several of the other new religious movements to be found in the contemporary West) are, typically, young, from 'privileged' rather than 'disadvantaged' backgrounds, and, in Britain and the United States, twice as likely to be male as female. The extent to which age, sex, and class can be seen as strong indicators of where it might be useful to start a search for the potential Moonie can be demonstrated by using these three variables (which are for all practical puposes independent of each other) in considering the current situation in Britain.

In May 1980, the resident British membership of the UC numbered 588, a figure which excludes the 531 'Crusade' members from Japan and the rest of Europe. In other words, roughly one person in every hundred thousand (or 0.001%) of the total British population would be a Moonie. However, (1) whereas, of the general population only about four million are between the ages of twenty-one and twenty-six, this age group comprises half the UC population; (2) half the UC population come from the middle or upper middle classes, which represent only about 13% of the population as a whole; (3) while the general population is (at that age) fairly evenly divided between the sexes, 68% of the Moonies are male. It is thus possible to say that in the category of middle and upper middle class males aged between twenty-one and twenty-six roughly one in every 2500 (or 0.04%) would be a Moonie.

But can that one Moonie be separated from the other 2499 non-Moonies? It might be thought that if one were only to continue adding further factors it would eventually be possible to produce a complete profile of the UC member. However, quite apart from the methodological problem that most of the other relevant variables tend to have positive but quantitatively unknown relationship with each other, it should be remembered that over 80% of the UC membership has already been left out of account—although two thirds are male, one third is not; although half is aged between twenty-one and twenty-six, half is not; although half comes from the "top" 13%, half does not. In other words, to look for a single set of characteristics to delineate the UC membership would not work. Different sorts of people become Moonies for different reasons.

That said, however, the fact that it is possible to increase the statistical density of Moonies forty-fold by merely using age, sex, and class does suggest a fairly potent first clue as to who is likely to be a Moonie. In what follows, various other variables and areas of life will be examined in order to try to elicit some of the rather more complicated factors that could be influential in preparing people for eventual conversion. At the same time, several variables will be noted that do *not* seem to be significant or peculiar to the UC despite the fact that pundits sometimes pronounce them to be crucial.

Health

Health during childhood and adolescence was one of the many subjects on which the data revealed that between the British UC members and the British control group which had been matched for age and class and the group which had attended the London workshops there was less difference than between the British UC and UC members from other countries. This suggests that national differences were frequently more significant than were differences between Moonies and non-Moonies. The remarkable similarity in the internal distribution of British UC, the control group, and the workshop responses also served as something of a reassurance that there was not much more distortion of responses from UC members than from non-members who, it might be assumed, would have little interest in 'skewing' the results in any particular direction. It also served to suggest that when there *was* a noticeable difference between the UC and non-UC responses, this could be of some significance.

As might be expected from their age, the great majority of respondents enjoyed either excellent or good health. This was most true of the American seminarians and least true of the non-British European Moonies. As already indicated, histories of health for the British UC and the control group were almost identical, a slight disparity occurring just before the former joined the UC when they were marginally less healthy than the control group, and then, at the time of filling in the questionnaire, when the UC reported having marginally better health than the control group. It must be stressed, however, that these differences were very slight, the only possible distinction of interest being that 10% of the British UC compared to 5% of the control group had suffered from either asthma or bronchitis.

A few more of the British UC (3%) than the control group (1%) (but 5% of the workshop group who were *not* Moonies) seemed to have suffered really severe mental breakdowns, but again the numbers were so small that it would be hard to show that, rather than being due to chance, this revealed any significant difference between the mental stability of Moonies and non-Moonies. Only 7% of both the British UC and the control group (but 9% of the non-Moonie workshop group) reported having sought medical help for any kind of psychiatric problem, and nothing in my field research led me to seriously doubt the probable accuracy of this figure. No difference emerged between the groups in the percentage (6%) of those who reported having had some mild problem such as a general feeling of depression without having sought medical aid. What the data did suggest—but this is only tentative and would need further investigation—is that a few of those who go to the introductory workshops might be doing so partly in search of a solution to psychiatric problems, but there was no evidence to support the hypothesis that those who actually joined the UC were any more or any less likely to be the victims of poor mental or physical health than anyone else from a similar background in their age group. All of those from the workshop group who had had any mental health problems and who did join the UC had left the movement by the time of filling in the questionnaire.

Family Backgrounds

By almost any criteria, the majority of Moonies came from what they, and others, would consider to be 'good homes'. Theories of either subjectively or objectively experienced deprivation found no support from the research. Mothers were unlikely to have worked while their children were at school, and were very unlikely to have done so before they went to school (15% compared to 27% of the control group.) Over four fifths of British Moonies saw themselves as having enjoyed average or (for nearly a half of them) above average material well-being (with respect to housing, food, and other material comforts); and roughly three quarters said their spiritual well-being was about (one third), or above, average.

The extent to which UC members tended to come from the upper reaches of society was roughly equivalent in all the national groups studied. As the control group had been *selected* with an equivalent class bias it could not be used for comparison. An interesting point did emerge, however, when the British UC was compared with those who went to the workshop but who did not subsequently join. At first glance it looked as though the class bias was if anything more pronounced among the workshop group who did not join, since just over two thirds of them (65%) had fathers in non-manual work, compared to just under two thirds (62%) of the British Moonies and roughly one third of the population as a whole. However, on closer inspection, it could be seen that only 14% of the

Moonies, but 27% of the workshop group, had fathers in the lower middle class doing comparatively routine work, and that 24% of the fathers of Moonies, but only 6% of the workshop group's fathers, had skilled or manual work with special responsibility (such as being a foreman). This suggested that while the manual/non-manual divide might be a useful indicator of the sort of person who might be curious about or interested in the UC, it could be the degree of occupational responsibility, rather than social class *per se,* which had the final edge in determining who would become a Moonie.

Further support for a tradition of occupational responsibility and, more particularly, of service to others, came from an analysis of the various occupations according to the kinds of values with which they are traditionally associated. Although several were certainly very rich, few of the fathers of UC members were in occupations (such as the stock exchange or "big business") that were primarily concerned with making money, but quite a few of the fathers of the workshop group were. On the other hand, practically none of the workshop group's parents were in jobs caring for other individuals (medicine, looking after the handicapped), but quite a few Moonie parents were. Compared to the control group, both the UC and the workshop group had several more parents in "caring for the country" occupations (the armed services, police force and, especially among the UC, colonial appointments—a tendency which was even more noticeable when grandparents' occupations were considered).

It is possible that parents' occupations may affect the values acquired in childhood, and that these might be more pertinent than values expressed later, in conscious decisions (such as 'to be of service'), reflected in the respondent's own occupation, since a similar analysis of personal occupations at the time of attending the workshop showed no significant difference between those who joined and those who did not join the movement.

There was no evidence that Moonies had had more than a normal quota of parents or grandparents in religious occupations. This was contrary to what might have been expected if one had listened to Moonies in conversation or in interviews, when those who had priestly or missionary forebears tended to make the most of the fact. This may be something that is particularly noticed, and particularly selected for comment, since the Unification Church places high value on having a 'good ancestry'. (Such selective observation has its parallel among members of the anti-cult movements who are likely to make the most of the mentally unbalanced Moonie.)[9]

Given the importance that *Divine Principle* lays on marriage and the family in their role in the restoration of the world, it was not altogether surprising that Moonies currently tended to regard the marriages of those outside he UC to be at best "alright" but, just as often to be, "unbearable" or "miserable". The control group was considerably more optimistic about the state of other peoples' marriages in that it showed a roughly normal distribution around "alright", not infrequently considering them to be quite happy. One might, therefore, have expected the UC members to have reported unhappy experiences of their own parents' marriages, but this was not the case. Their responses had an almost uncannily similar distribution to those of the control group, as can be seen from Table 1.

Table 1

Responses to the question: "How would you describe the marriage of your parents?"

	British UC	Control Group
Very happy	16%	19%
Happy	35%	32%
Alright	26%	26%
Just bearable	12%	11%
Miserable	12%	12%

In other words, although Moonies believed that marriages were unlikely to work very well in contemporary society, this belief did not arise because they had an abnormally high tendency to regard their own parents' marriages as having been unhappy. Moonies did report that their own experiences of marriage (or relatively permanent relationships outside marriage) were not as successful as those of the control group, but it was still the case that the British (and other) UC members who had had such an experience considered that they had been far better off than the norm, nearly half of them saying that it was either happy or very happy, and a further quarter that it was "alright".

There was no evidence of very great misery having been experienced at any time in their lives by any but a minority of the respondents. Two thirds of all the groups described themselves as having been happy (or very happy) up to the age of ten. Between the ages of eleven and sixteen, one third of the control group was unhappy, but, once they had reached the age of seventeen, only 12% reported themselves to be still unhappy, and this figure was reduced to 4% by the time they filled in the questionnaire. Those who were to become British Moonies experienced slightly less unhappiness during early adolescence, but during the six-month period before they met the UC the proportion who said that they were unhappy had risen to a third. The workshop respondents who did not join reported the least unhappiness of all, but what unhappiness the group had experienced had been at its height (23%) just before they went to the workshop: none the less—like those who were to join—one third said that they had been happy at that time (the rest saying that they were "alright"). At the time of filling in the questionnaire, 90% of the Moonies, 72% of the control group, and 48% of the workshop group said they were happy (or very happy).

The various responses to requests for assessments of happiness and other related questions revealed that, in most cases, there had been a noticeable 'dip' at some stage during or shortly after adolescence, perhaps indicating the emotional 'problems of adolescence' which have been so readily recognized throughout the ages. What did emerge, however, was the possibility that Moonies, rather than having a more unhappy childhood than their peers, were more likely—at least in some cases—to have experienced the dip in their development at a later stage than among non-Moonies. This hypothesis received further support from an analysis of replies to a question (not asked of the workshop group) in which respondents provided six key words or phrases with which to describe themselves during various stages in their lives.

Coding the "key words" question for happiness confirmed a fairly sharp dip in the responses of the control group between the ages of eleven and sixteen. The Moonies, as a group, had a slightly less marked dip at this period, and a sharper dip in the six months before attending the workshop, and this was even more pronounced in the responses to "key words" than in the more direct question about happiness. Further analysis of the kind of unhappiness that appeared in the "key words" question showed that, although both groups (UC and control group) were more inclined to internalize their feelings than to report extrovert expressions of either happiness or unhappiness, this tendency was more pronounced in the UC responses. Slightly more than a quarter of the Moonies were very unhappy just before they met the UC, and, at all periods, UC members exhibited more extremes of both happiness and unhappiness.

Several questions dealt with the respondents' relationship to and opinion of their parents. Here again the most noticeable result was the extraordinary similarity in the distribution of responses from the British UC and the control group—both sets of parents, but mothers in particular, receiving far more praise than criticism. There was very little difference between the two groups as to whether the respondent found it easier to relate to one parent rather than the other. There was not much difference between the two sets of responses concerning whether the mother or the father had the stronger personality, nor was there any difference in the corresponding judgments of approval or disapproval for the prevailing state of affairs. If Moonies were being attracted to the UC by its strictures on the 'natural' role of fathers and mothers in the family, this was not to be traced to any special peculiarities in their perceptions of the way in which their own parents had performed these roles.

Asked about their relationship with their parents during the six months before meeting the UC (for Moonies) or before filling in the questionnaire (for the control group), the two groups showed only small differences. Slightly more among the control group said that they had a very close relationship with their mother and slightly more UC members said the relationship was alright but distant. Less than one in ten of the respondents described their relationship with either parent as poor. Three times as many UC respondents (15%) as control groups respondents (5%) had a step-parent—a third of the UC saying the relationship was a poor one, slightly more than a third saying it was good, and slightly less than a third saying that it was "alright".

Educational Background

Coming, as they did, from a largely middle class background, Moonies could be expected to have been better (in the sense of more academically) educated than the population as a whole. This was indeed the case. British members were four times more likely to have been to a fee-paying school, and only half as likely as their contemporaries to have been to a secondary modern or comprehensive school. Two thirds (as opposed to a quarter of their peers) had passed the General Certificate of Education examinations at the Advanced Level; a third had started, and a fifth (compared to one twelfth of the general population) had been awarded a degree (frequently in the sciences or practical subjects). The workshop group was similarly well educated. Not surprisingly, the most impressive results of any group were those of the American seminarians, 81% having given consistently high performance. Among the British UC members, one quarter had had exceptionally good results (A or A and B grades) and only 9% had results that were consistently poor. In comparison to 12% of the control group, only 1% of the British UC could be classified as erratic, while 17% of the Moonies showed improvement over time, with 10% showing a steady deterioration.

As the control group had been significantly matched for educational achievement few useful comparisons could be made in this area, but one interesting factor was revealed in the "key words" question in which, it will be remembered, the respondents were asked to describe themselves at various periods in their lives. Over half of both groups (the British UC and the control group) defined themselves in terms of educational or intellectual achievement at some point despite the fact that the question was completely open. But while such attributions appeared to be at random intervals in the control group responses, in the case of those who were to join the UC a pattern emerged which showed that this kind of self-definition ceased at a particular stage. Sometimes this could be related to the educational system rejecting the respondent, sometimes it was because the system had been rejected by the respondent, and sometimes there was no apparent reason—the respondent simply appeared to be thinking of himself in different terms. It was, incidentally, noticeable that some of the control group who had joined other new religious movements, most notably the Divine Light Mission, did not define themselves by reference to the educational system at all. The UC pattern provides a certain degree of support for the hypothesis[10] that *some* of those who were likely to become Moonies (a) had seen themselves as having an intellectual role to play in society, but (b) had consciously or unconsciously been rejected by the educational system or had themselves rejected it as the means through which this role was to be achieved.

A favourite theory as to why people join new religious movements is that they are drop-outs or drifters who have no ideas about what they want to do, but who aimlessly fall into anything that they come upon. There is a certain sense in which this might be seen as true (as will be discussed below), but it is by no means obvious that those who join the UC are, by disposition, the drifting type: if anything, the reverse seems to be true. It might be added that the "drifting type" were he to have wandered in, would be unlikely to remain in the movement for very long.

Exactly the same proportion of British UC and of the control group (22%) had dropped out of further education for reasons other than joining the UC. The reason given was most likely to be boredom in the case of the control group, and either "not being good enough" or "wanting something else" in the case of the UC. A further 13% dropped out *because* they joined the UC (though by no means all of those who joined did drop out—several continuing in their studies).

Over half of the British Moonies (and 41% of the control group) had, while they were in their final year at school, a very clear idea of what they wanted to do in the future. Only 11% of the Moonies (but 28% of the control group) had no ideas at all about their future. More than a quarter of the jobs the Moonies had wanted to do (and a fifth of those wanted by the control group) were in some kind of helping or serving occupation (most commonly medical (10%) or social welfare (8%)). When those who had finished their formal education were asked what they would like to do if they were to return to study, the majority of both groups gave some kind of knowledge-for-the-sake-of-knowledge reply but the proportion of such answers was higher among the control group, with the Moonies being more inclined to select a training for a skill—either in social welfare or something practical, like plumbing or a secretarial course. Only a very few respondents from either group showed any interest in study that would directly promote a successful lucrative career, and only a few expressed interest in exploring spiritual knowledge (but this might have been thought to have been precluded by the wording of the question).

There was no support among either the British or the European members for the theory that Moonies might have disproportionately pursued non-vocationally orientated disciplines during further education, although the theory might be somewhat justified with respect to the American seminarians, nearly two thirds of whom had degrees in the social sciences, psychology or the arts. (Just over a half of those attending the workshop were qualified for a particular job, and most of the rest were students.)

In general, responses both in the questionnaire and in interviews suggested that the potential Moonie had fairly clear ideas that he wanted to achieve a definite goal—but that he might have found that he had either become disillusioned about the goal that he had originally chosen, or thwarted in his ambitions to achieve it. He was, however, still likely to be wanting to *do* something, although he might not know exactly *what,* or, if the goal had been an idealistic one (which was not infrequently the case), he would not know *how.*

Religious Background

It is when religious background is considered that the importance of the social context, and the alternative offered by the Unification Church, become most strikingly crucial in determining who would become a Moonie. In the Bay Area of California, those who have gone to the workshops have been, at least in the initial stages of introduction to the movement, frequently unaware that the movement called itself a church— indeed that arm of the movement does *not* call itself the Unification Church but is known rather as the Creative Community Project (CCP), sometimes claiming, in small letters stamped on the workshop application form, "Associated with and independent of The Unification Church".

The lectures and the whole atmosphere of the CCP workshop focusses on the idea of doing good for humanistic rather than for religious reasons. During the introductory weekend the name of Sun Myung Moon is not mentioned—and the name of God is scarcely mentioned. *Divine Principle* is "translated" so that the underlying philosophy is justified by reference to social or psychological statements of morality rather than by the Biblical quotations which appear in the published version and which are repeatedly cited in most of the lectures held elsewhere in the West. Many of those who have become Moonies in California were either atheists or very sceptical agnostics at the time of first encountering the UC. They would readily admit that, had they known that it was a religious movement, or if anyone had started talking to them about God, they would not have pursued the matter further. Instead, they were attracted by the fact that the CCP seemed to be offering a practical way of serving the community and of making a better world. Here, they would have thought, was a group of people who were "really doing something". The details of the official ideology would emerge only at a later stage, gradually being unfolded as the new recruit found himself becoming more and more involved with the people and the day-to-day life of the community.

In England (and in Europe and in other areas of the United States), *Divine Principle* has been taught in a far more fundamentalist fashion. If one were not to accept at least a strong possibility that God existed, it would be difficult to become a British Moonie. It would be difficult, if one were not prepared to consider the Bible as a source of divine revelation, to take the UC teachings very seriously. It would be difficult if one were fully committed to a particular interpretation of the Scriptures to take Unification Church teachings very seriously. It might be added that an analysis of those who left the twenty-one-day course showed that the leavers were most likely to be agnostic, atheist, or non-Christian: 12% were Moslem.

While some British Moonies became convinced of God's existence during the course of discussions and lectures, over 80% needed no such persuasion, and most of the others needed very little. By comparison, only a quarter of the control group had no doubts over the existence of God; 29% said that they did not believe at all; the rest were more inclined to doubt than to accept. Those who were in the workshop group were far more likely to believe than were those in the control group—just under half of those who did not join, and just over three quarters of those who did join, definitely believing, and a further quarter of non-joiners (and a fifth of joiners) accepting that God "probably exists". Of the 6% of the workshop group who said that they definitely did not believe, none joined; and of the 16% who said that they did "not really" believe, only two people joined (one of whom had left by the time he filled in the questionnaire).

In answer to an open question about their reason for joining the Unification Church, nearly two thirds of the British members answered in theological terms. Other reasons given referred to the members or to being given a purpose in life, although 7% implied that there was just nothing better available. The Americans were less likely to give theological reasons, the Europeans more inclined to do so. Perhaps it is more telling that, when asked why they had agreed to go to a workshop, just under half of the British members and of the workshop group who joined, but less than a quarter of the workshop group who did not join, said that they had been actively seeking the truth, and were hoping to find it.

Of the particular faiths in which British Moonies have been brought up, Catholicism and Nonconformity (particularly Presbyterians and Methodists) were over-represented and the Church of England was under-represented. This was even more marked among those who attended the workshops. The control group was selected with this bias in mind. Figures for the population as a whole tend to vary according to the different ways in which they have been collected, but the percentages in Table 2 give roughly agreed estimates of affiliation.

Table 2   Religious Background (Percentages)

RC = Roman Catholic
CE = Church of England
OP = Other Protestant
UC = Unspecified Christian
 J = Jewish

ON = Other non-Christian
UB = Unaffiliated: Belief in God
NR = No Real Religion
AG = Agnostic
AT = Atheist

	RC	CE	OP	UC	J	ON	UB	NR	AG	AT	Number of cases
British U.C. +	21	40	25	3	-	-	2	5	3	1	226
Applications * for 21 days w/s	34	21	18	12	-	7	1	5		2	596
Left during * 21 day w/s	23	18	6	18	-	19	1	5		6	102
Applications * for 2 day w/s	35	18	12	16	1	13	2	1		2	1,107
w/s who did + not join, or joined and left	31	30	13	4	1	12	-	9			1012
All UC re- + spondents	34	22	28	4	3	3	-	7			430
Control group +	28	43	12	1	5	4	-	7			109
General U.K. * population	12	66	12	-	1	2	-	7			56 million

 * = "Religion"
 + = "Faith in which brought up"

It is interesting to note that less than 1% of the British UC had been brought up in a non-Christian faith. In contrast with the UC in America where more than 5% are Jews, practically no one from a Jewish background joins the movement in Britain. Most of the small number of Jews who went to a workshop left fairly quickly.

One question that has given rise to a whole series of speculative hypotheses from the very beginning of the study was why it was that a disproportionate number of Moonies came from Catholic backgrounds. As the research continued, however, it began to be clear that the problem is to a substantial degree dissolved once (a) national background, and (b) degree of commitment to previous religion are taken into account.

A large proportion of those who agreed to attend the workshops were from overseas. The British, of whom not quite a quarter were Catholics, comprised only 40% of those attending the two-day workshop, and 52% of those who continued to the twenty-one-day workshop. The percentage of Catholics could be further reduced to 20%, were only those with British fathers to be considered. Among Unification Church members of those who were actually British-born only 12% were Catholics. It should, of course, be remembered that, were a similar exercise to be carried out with the general population, the percentage of Catholics would again drop, though not to the extent that it does for the two sets of respondents from the Unification Church and the workshop groups.

In Britain, "Church of England" tends to be rather a vague label, frequently implying more of a cultural than a religious commitment. In fact, only about 10% of the population are actually members of the Anglican Church. Once one starts to compare the religious background of British Moonies with the distribution of committed, rather than nominal, members of the various churches, the under-representation of the Church of England disappears.[11]

And there is no doubt that Moonies—all Moonies[12]—have tended to come from families with a higher degree of religious commitment than the rest of the population, in so far as this can be judged by such indices as church attendance and the offsprings' assessment of the importance of religion in their parents' lives

(although it should be added that 27% of both the Br
the control group said that religion was not at all impor............
parent). In childhood, Moonies tended to have had greater expo-
sure to organized religion than is the general rule. Quite a few had
been to denominational schools. Up to the age of ten there was a
history of very high church attendance among UC members, 78%
going regularly every week. Of those who attended the workshop, ·
but who did not join the UC, 63% went weekly, while 57% of the
control group did so. The national average for attendance is 16% of
the child population, and 11% of the adult population. During
adolescence a steady and heavy decline had occurred, and by
the time they had reached young adulthood, for each group, UC,
workshop, and the control group, 30% had attended at least once
a month, and 70% had either never gone or had done so on only a
few special occasions during the year. During the six-month period
before meeting the UC half of the workshop non-joiners and two
fifths of the UC never attended church: the comparable figure for
the control group during the six months before filling in the
questionnaire was also two fifths. While 39% of UC members and
25% of the workshop people attended at least once a month
during this period, the comparable control group figure was 29%.
The overall pattern suggests that while those who were to become
Moonies were likely to have had considerable contact with organized religions in the early part of their lives, they were more likely
either to have remained (or become) committed to regular attendance, or to have completely rejected the church than were those in
the control group or (more negatively) the population in general.
This result emerged even though there was little difference with
respect to parental attendance between the Moonies and the
control group: both sets of respondents showed that, when the
respondents themselves were about fifteen years of age, in each
case roughly a third of parents had attended church weekly, a third
had attended occasionally, and a third had never gone at all. Most
parents from both groups accompanied their children to church
up to the age of ten, about a third continuing to do so during the
rest of the respondents' time at home. Church-going among the

American seminarians and their parents was higher than for the British Moonie. European Moonies and their parents were the least frequent attenders.

Since the control group was selected with a bias toward those from more religious backgrounds, it provides little useful comparison on this subject. One difference was that the number of parents who had *different* religious beliefs from each other was greater (43%) among the Moonies than among the control group (33%), suggesting that while the potential Moonie was more likely to have been brought up in a religious home, this home was not necessarily one in which a specific religion was unquestioningly accepted. In other words, it is possible that the Moonie, while taking for granted the importance of religious beliefs, had been more open than others to the possibility of alternative expressions of belief— or, to put a slightly different gloss on the hypothesis, the British Moonie might be looking for a religious rather than a non-religious truth, but might also be confused about which religion represented the truth. Most of those who attended the workshops did not have an unequivocal commitment to any particular dogma, and those who had, tended to leave quickly once they began to learn the content of *Divine Principle.* It might however be added that there have been instances of people who were so completely convinced that they held the key to absolute truth that they went to a workshop or centre with the evangelistic mission of explaining to UC members the errors of their ways and their beliefs—the ensuing battles in exegesis sometimes resulted in the conversion of yet another Moonie.

One of the tendencies to emerge most forcefully from the research was the growing disillusionment that young people were experiencing with the established churches. The word 'hypocritical' (in a variety of exotic spellings) appeared frequently in the questionnaires—Moonie and non-Moonie alike. Asked what faith they held at the time of attending their workshop, respondents might mention a particular faith, but by far the largest group refused to name any particular denomination, saying instead that although they believed in God they rejected, or did not feel able to align themselves to, any particular denomination. Generally speaking, the Church of England elicited the most indifference, the Catholic Church the most forceful accusations of hypocrisy, and the Nonconformists the more mild expressions of ambivalence or rejection. Among the control group, both criticism (from Catholics) and approval (from Nonconformists) were more vocal for the 'six months before' period, Moonies having by then become more inclined to lose interest in the church in which they were brought up and to be searching for some alternative.

The question of religious experience is a complicated one, which cannot be explored here. It should however be reported that in answer to the question, "How often have you been aware of, or influenced by, a presence or power, whether you called it God or not, which is different from your everyday self?", 87% of the Moonies gave a positive answer, referring to experiences *before* they joined the Unification Church (96% saying they had had such experiences since).[13] Half of the experiences were described as awareness (or visions) of either God or Jesus, and most of the other experiences took the form of some kind of realization of a Wordsworthian type pantheism. This high percentage may seem surprising, but it becomes less so when it is added that 67% of the control group also answered positively, and, in other research among male postgraduate students, 72% gave positive responses.[14]

What may turn out to be more crucial than the experience itself is that, despite the fact that the majority of those who have had such an experience say that it altered their lives, either "quite a lot" or "a very great deal", almost half of the British Unification Church members and 36% of the control group had not told anyone what had happened. The reasons for this silence that were given by the Moonies were predominantly that no one would have understood, or that they were afraid of being thought peculiar. The reasons given by the control group were more frequently that they wanted to keep it to themselves or it just did not enter their heads to talk about it.

Not unconnected with the possible implications of this last point are the replies to questions as to whether, with whom, how deeply, and how frequently the respondent had been in the habit of discussing religious matters. There was not a great deal of difference between the Moonies and the control group, although Moonies when grown-up were slightly more likely to have talked often to their parents, and the control group was more likely to have talked to priests or teachers. Both groups talked more to their friends than to parents or professionals. When giving reasons for not talking as much as they might have done, the Moonies were more inclined to say that they had tried and got nowhere (especially with the clergy), or that they thought they would not have been understood (especially with their parents), or that they were afraid the other person would be uninterested or would think them to be rather strange (especially with friends). The reasons given by the control group were more likely to be that they themselves were not interested in discussing such matters, or that they felt that it was something that they had to work out for themselves.

Although most Moonies had never seriously doubted the existence of God, 88% (82% of the control group) did admit to having some worries at some time in their lives. There was very little difference between the two groups, but the Moonies tended to have started doubting slightly later than the control group. Over a third of the Moonies (but only 14% of the control group) gave the existence of evil or suffering as a reason for doubting. The control group was more likely to say they could see no reason *for* belief or to cite scientific evidence, which, curiously enough, was one of the main reasons given by the Moonies for *belief*.[15]

The period before meeting the UC

No one joins the UC under the age of eighteen except in those few cases where the parents themselves are members or are prepared to give their permission. The average age of joining in Britain was 23 years, that for the American seminarians was 25 years, and for the European UC respondents 22.2 years. (The average length of time the British Moonies had been members of the UC was 3.5 years). The average age of those attending the two-day workshop was 27 years, for those going on to the twenty-one-day workshop the mean age was 25.4 years. This difference can be largely accounted for by the number of retired people who go to a workshop weekend and the absence of Home Church members (see below) in the main British UC statistics. The median age remained at 22 years, and the variance dropped from 106 for the two-day workshop to 73 for the twenty-one-day workshop. It was 52 for the age of British Moonies. Those who went to both the two-day and the twenty-one-day workshops were divided in the same ratio of two males to every female which is reproduced in the British UC membership.

It has already been suggested that there is little evidence to suggest that the Unification Church primarily attracts those who are at an occupational loose end. Most of the British Moonies were not only in paid employment at the time of joining, but they were frequently in occupations of fairly high status with reasonably good career prospects. There were 13% in 'higher professional' work, the largest group being engineers. None was in finance, but 10% were in work 'caring for people', such as social work, nursing, and looking after the handicapped, and a further 3% were school teachers. There were 10% doing secretarial or clerical work, and 6% were doing skilled, 4% semi-, or unskilled, manual work. Other occupations included catering, photography, the civil service, and holy orders. Of those not in paid employment, 5% were still at, or had just left, school; 18% were students; and 4% were "travelling" (a far higher proportion of those joining in America are "travelling"). About 4% were registered as unemployed. Over half the British Moonies had been settled in steady employment for over two years, and two thirds for more than one year.

Those who attended the workshops but did not join were far more likely to have been at some transitory stage or unsettled in their careers. The most noticeable phenomenon is that while 41% of those going to a two-day workshop were students, among those who proceeded to a twenty-one day workshop the proportion had dropped to 27%. Less obvious, but none the less interesting, was a drop from 8% to 4% in the proportion of secretaries and clerical workers. The number of *au-pair* (foreign girls working as home helps) girls fell from 14 (1.5%) to 3 (0.5%). These three groups might, in their different ways, provide a fairly good indication of the sort of people who might be lonely and without much to do for an odd weekend, but who might have little or no intention of taking things further (and, incidentally, manage to remain remarkably unaffected by the so-called brain-washing techniques). Nurses formed 5% of both workshop groups, school teachers increased from 2% to 3% and engineers from 1% to 2%. The unemployed also increased from 5% to 10% but were, proportionately, unlikely actually to join.

Over a half of the British members had left their parents' home for more than a year before they met the Unification Church (38% had left more than three years before), while 27% were still living with their parents. Those in the control group were more likely to have left home before or while they were still completing their higher education, whereas the British members were more likely to have continued regarding their parents' house as home until after they had finished full-time education. In other words, while it is not true to say that most Moonies were plucked from their parents, it is true to say that most Moonies had remained within the bosom of the family for longer than many of their contemporaries. This provides further support for the hypothesis that potential Moonies may have enjoyed a protective family environment until a later stage in their development than might be the norm.

The Moonies who had left home were less likely to be, or to have been, married than were either the control group or the rest of their age group. Two thirds (one third of the control group) had no steady boyfriend or girlfriend, and half of those who did have one had no expectations of marriage. Those who attended the workshops also tended to be single, with only a quarter enjoying a satisfactory non-marital relationship, 17% having just ended one, and 39% saying that they had no prospects of developing such a relationship. This accounted for 78% of the workshop group who joined as full-time members.

While most of the control group who were not living with their parents were living either with their spouses or with a group of friends of the same sex as themselves, those in the British UC group were most frequently living alone, usually in a rented room or flat.

All the groups were asked to say whether at various periods of their lives, they were most likely to spend their leisure time alone, with a few close friends, or in a large group. The majority of respondents tended to have spent their time with a few close friends, but one or two patterns were discernible. The control group members were most likely to have spent time in a large group between the ages of eleven and seventeen (more than twice as likely as the UC members at that time.) Those in both the UC and the workshop groups were quite likely to have *changed* from having a few close friends to spending time by themselves in the period immediately before meeting the UC. Only 4% of the control group compared to 28% of the workshop group and 37% of the British UC (and 33% of the total UC response) spent their leisure time alone during the 'six months before' period—the fact that some Moonies were likely to have been lonely before joining the UC may not be surprising. What is perhaps more interesting is that during their adolescence they had been less used to moving in groups (the workshop group were less likely than the control group but more likely than the UC members to have had such group experience at that time).

Just under a quarter of both Moonies and the control group were vegetarians. (The Unification Church as a movement is not vegetarian). British Moonies were more likely to have been heavy drinkers than drug takers, although a third of them scarcely ever, or never, drank, and 80% had never taken drugs. This was in marked contrast to the American seminarians, 43% of whom had never or hardly ever engaged in drinking, but half of whom had taken drugs (usually only soft drugs on odd occasions). The control group was nearer the British UC pattern but less likely to have been heavy drinkers or total abstainers.

Responses to the 'key words' question were coded for indications of self-opinions, and these suggested that the control group tended to be considerably more self-critical than the Moonies up to the age of 17 when they (the control group) became more likely to exhibit mild self-approval. In the coding for 'excessive self-concern', the Moonies scored twice as highly as the control group. Such concern tended to manifest itself in self-disgust or, occasionally, in revealing *mea culpa* self-criticism, or, more frequently, and usually after joining the movement, it might take the form of apparently smug, self-congratulatory remarks. This, in its more extreme forms, exhibited what might be termed the 'bum to saint' syndrome—a pattern that will be familiar to those who have been subjected to the more dramatic version of 'born again' conversion testimonies. Put in rather more sympathetic language, the responses indicated that some, perhaps a quarter, of the Moonies defined themselves in such a way that they were expressing a belief that they had been of no value to themselves or to anyone else before joining the UC, but that they were now of genuine, laudable worth. It should also be noted, however, that, in their self-descriptions, the vast majority of all the respondents at no time exhibited anything other than a mild approval, a mild disapproval, or a mild mixture of both.

There are, of course, difficulties in asking respondents, after they have been in a movement like the Unification Church for some time, about their feelings just before they joined. However much they try to be honest, subsequent experiences affect the selection of their memories in the light of the way they have since learnt to see the world. It is, however, probably worth recording that 16% of the British Moonies (39% of the control group) reported having experienced no discrepancy between their ideals and their achievements during the 'six months before' period; 38% UC (22% of the control group) reported a constant discrepancy; 37% UC (17% of the control group) an increasing discrepancy and 9% UC (22% of the control group) a decreasing discrepancy. Of the Moonies, 28% reported that during that period they were quite happy and satisfied; 24% of the UC (11% of the control group) said they were discontented and passively wanting change; 40% of the UC (10% of the control group) said they were discontented and actively seeking change.

Seekership

A possibility which cannot be quantitatively demonstrated but which might be borne in mind when considering the findings presented in this section is that the cultural conception of the role of the seeker might have importance in inducing many of those who are contacted by the members of a new religious movement to seek to find out more. This applies particularly to those who are contacted in a public place by strangers, but is not so pertinent in the case of those who are first introduced to the movements through an already existing family or friendship network. The concept of the role rather than that of personal seekership is stressed because it is socially rather than individually defined. From both interviews and questionnaires it was often difficult to see much difference among young people in, say, the three societies, North America, Britain, and Scandinavia, in the actual longings for meaning and direction, and dread of the unknown—but that was once one had asked. While the differential uses of social pressure, on the one hand, and of biblical underpinning of the ideology, on the other, emerge as the most important variations in recruiting practices, the most relevant difference between the three cultures themselves appears to be the extent to which the seekership role is socially sanctioned, encouraged, or discouraged. In Scandinavia, one does not publicly discuss questions of ultimate concern. It is not in good taste. Perhaps one might risk it with the closest of friends—but it would be to take a risk. (The Scottish sociologist of religion is tolerated as a professional stranger.)[16] In England, especially among the young middle class, it can be considered rather *comme il faut* to discuss such matters, but it is still necessary to make sure that one is in the right environment with the right set of people. Not everyone could take it. In California, it is almost taken as the sign of a dull mind *not* to question and search, not to expose one's innermost secrets with frank consternation, not to follow all avenues which could possibly provide the answers to the questions on everyone's lips. Someone asking for directions in Fisherman's Wharf is more likely to be seeking the way to Nirvana than to Union Square.

That said, however, it does not necessarily follow that seekers will be finders. While, from answers to a whole series of questions, there could be no doubt that the Moonie saw himself or herself as a seeker far more than did the members of the control group, it was also apparent that several of the workshop group who did not join were, in certain respects, more ardent seekers than those who were to join; and, in certain other respects, those who were to join and then leave were the most active seekers of all.

As might be expected, the American seminarians formed the group with the highest level of cognitive seekers. One in three of them; one in four of the British UC; one in five of the Europeans; and one in seven of the control group said that they were exploring ideologies very actively as a primary interest in their lives during the 'six months before' period. The order was the same for the reading of philosophical books and the investigation of Eastern thought.

But it was not only intellectual knowledge that was being sought. Over half the Moonies, compared to a third of the control group, said that the spiritual side of life was very important to them. Of the British Moonies 57%; of the seminarians 50%; of the European Moonies 46%; and of the control group 30% definitely believed in life after death, compared with, respectively 6%, 2%, 5% and 36% who definitely did not (the rest of the respondents were uncertain).

In view of their apparent discontent with the world as they seem to have experienced it, and their subsequent commitment to restoring the Kingdom of Heaven on earth, it might be thought that Moonies would have been political animals, seeking to change or perhaps reform the world before they discovered the Unification Church. There was no evidence for this at all. If anything, the Moonie proved to be an a-political animal (as opposed to a social idealist). Despite the fact that the Unification Church is renowned for its firm anti-communist stance, I only once came across a British Moonie who said he had joined primarily for anti-communist reasons. Parents tended towards the right in their political allegiance, but given their social background, this was to be expected, and there was only a small difference between the parents of the Moonies and those of the control group. Again, with respect to respondents' own political leanings, only 37% called themselves conservative, and of these only 8% said they were strongly committed. Both the American and the European Moonies were more inclined towards socialism than conservatism. While the Moonies in all the different societies were likely to be about twice as conservative after joining as they had been before (three times in the case of the seminarians), the most obvious fact, both before and after, was how little they seemed either to care about, or to put their faith into, politics. Furthermore, when asked what legislation they would like to implement were they to be made prime minister or president tomorrow, very few of them were able to give any reply at all. This was, indeed, the question that produced more minutes of silence on the interview tapes than any other. When pressed to describe their ideas of what the New Age will be like—and most Moonies insist that they have committed their lives to working for its imminent arrival—the majority of respondents and interviewees conjured up pictures of green grass and little houses with red roofs and smoke coming out of the chimneys, while laughing children played under a blue sky. "The sun will always shine", I was told on several occasions, on one of which I asked how the crops would fare under such conditions. The answer came back with a laugh: "God will arrange for it to rain at night!" More seriously, when I introduced the concept of social structure, which was virtually unmentioned by any but a very few of the rank and file membership, I was told that it was men's hearts, not structures, that had to change—and *then* there would be no need of passports.

All of this is not to suggest that Moonies are fools. They are not. Among their number it is possible to find some of the most intellectually sophisticated and sensitive men and women of their generation. The vast majority of UC members are more, rather than less, articulate and thoughtful than their peers. After six years of talking to several hundred, perhaps a thousand, Moonies, I have yet to meet the stammering, incoherent idiot so frequently described in the media. But this serves merely to emphasise the problem. How could they become Moonies?

The beginning of an explanation started to emerge from the responses by the control group to the question: "What do you personally think the world will be like in the year 2,000?" Reading this was one of the most disturbing experiences of the whole research—and it cannot be denied that several aspects of the research could be experienced as disturbing.

The responses were a complete and absolute contrast to the Moonie pictures of the New Age. Some replies suggested that there just would not be a year 2,000—we would have blown ourselves up; polluted the atmosphere with deadly poison; or exhausted some necessary resource before then. Other pictures were painted: of deformed children; early and painful deaths for a population exposed to nuclear accidents; third world countries taking horrible (and deserved) revenge on their erstwhile masters; mass starvation; over population—abject misery and terror would be the only emotions that would be left to mankind. There was no future, or no future to which these young people could look forward. Not all the replies were in such terms—optimism still existed and for some there was what it might be hoped was a realistically balanced view of the future. Yet the picture, not just of hopelessness but of utter helplessness, that emerged from a not inconsiderable proportion of the control group, coupled with the accompanying expressions of bitterness, frustration, and, perhaps most frequently, resigned apathy, made it clear that the happy little scenes in the Moonie model might appear to some as a compelling alternative where no other seemed to be available.

Respondents were asked to assess a list of nine ideals for the importance they considered them to have in their lives, and the extent to which they were actively seeking them during the 'six months before' period. All the groups (except for those who first joined and then left) put "control over own life" as either the most or the second most important, and as the ideal that they were most actively seeking. (Those who joined and then left put this third

on the list, 'improving the world' being first, and 'spiritual fulfilment' second.)

Given the hierarchical ordering and the authoritarian structure
of the Unification Church, it might appear as a blatant example of
false consciousness or of *mauvaise foi* that the Moonies felt that
they had achieved greater control after joining than they had had
before. Their estimations of the degree of control that they had
exercised before joining over their own lives, over other peoples,
and over the world were strikingly similar to the responses of the
control group, but in all three areas the Moonies believed that their
power had been considerably enhanced (except for the European
Moonies who thought they now had less control over their own
lives). The most striking change came in response to the question
as to how much power they felt they had to alter the state of the
world. Most of the "before" responses of both Moonies and control
group were that they had either had very little or none at all. But
86% of the British Moonies (and a similar percentage of the others)
said that since joining the UC they exercised either quite a lot
(75%) or complete control (11%). It should be noted that several
Moonies explained that it was not so much that they themselves
had power either over the world or over others, but that it was God's
power, and that they were God's instruments.

Returning to the importance and degrees of seekership
associated with the various ideals, some fairly predictable results
appeared. All the groups rated a high standard of living (which
most had enjoyed) lowest on their scale of priorities. Second
lowest for the Unification Church members (fourth lowest for the
control group) came success in their career. This however was
second only to 'control over own life' for those of the workshop
group who did not join. Improving the world was considered
important by all the respondents, but whereas the control group
was more inclined to hope for it, the UC members saw themselves
seeking its attainment. This was also the pattern, though less
markedly so, for an 'ideal marriage'. All the groups considered
better relationships with others to be very important, and were
seeking them. Not unexpectedly, spiritual fulfilment and under-

standing God were high on the list of more Moonies than of control group members, but there was a small number of Moonies who said they were seldom aware of the importance of either.

The most outstanding, and possibly the most significant difference to emerge between the groups came from the response to an ideal suggested to me by a respondent during the pilot questionnaire study. This was termed "'Something' but did not know what". Of the British Moonies 43% classified this as very important, and said that they were actively seeking it; 23% said it was important and they were seeking it; and a further 13% that it was very important but they were hoping rather than seeking. Similar response came from the other Moonies. Among the control group, however, 72% said that it was not at all important, or that they were not often aware of its importance, and they certainly were not seeking it. Just over half the workshop group who did not join gave such a response. While the control group or non-joining workshop group respondent might at this point put a rude comment and a large question mark in the margin, the UC member might put an affirmative 'yes' and add a large exclamation mark.

Home Church membership

We have not yet considered the question, "Who'd be a Home Church Moonie?" A glance at Home Church membership indicates that there were those who, while unable or unwilling to become fully *committed* to the UC way of life, were none the less prepared to declare that they had become *converted* to UC beliefs. By May 1980, there were 140 Home Church members in Britain, most of them having joined during the previous eighteen months. Geographically they were clustered in areas with active centres, a third living in London and the South East, and nearly a quarter in South Wales.

Educational achievement for Home Church members is not as impressive as it is for full-time Moonies, and although 14% had degrees, nearly half had not continued studies beyond school level. This is partly related to the fact that while 80% of the full-time Moonies were under thirty years of age, 80% of the Home Church membership was over thirty, and a half was over forty—although they were least likely to join while actually in their forties.

The most noticeable difference apart from age (although related to it) is that only a fifth of the Home Church members had not been married. Half were still married, 17% were separated or divorced, and 11% widowed. Two thirds had children, frequently quite a large number, and a few were unmarried mothers—12% were originally introduced to the movement by their own offspring.

Rather than being weighted towards men, the sex ratio was 56:44 in favour of women. One quarter put housewife or mother as their occupation, 13% were nurses or midwives. Others were in secretarial, clerical or semi-skilled work. While over a half were in the middle classes, their occupations reflected a lower middle or middle working class bias.

Home Church members often gave the impression that they had been leading lonely or unsatisfying lives. They were anxious to be involved and of help. One of their most frequent complaints was that the Unification Church did not use them enough. Their existence indicated that the Unification Church might appeal to a wider constituency than that from which the full-time Moonie was drawn, but that it succeeded in doing so only as long as it did not demand the kind of unquestioning devotion and sacrificial life-style that the young, unmarried Moonie was prepared to give.

Concluding remarks

Moonies, like most groups of people, exhibit a varied assortment of traits, many of which are more likely to reflect the characteristics of a nation, an age cohort, or a specific social class rather than to be something peculiar to Unification Church members. It is, however, possible to make a few generalizations, some more tentative than others, about the sort of person who'd be a Moonie.

As a group, Moonies tend to be young adults who come from basically secure and comfortable, possibly over-protective, backgrounds. Their parents are likely to have been in positions of responsibility, and it is possible that a tradition of service and the concept of duty will have formed part of the taken-for-granted values of childhood. There is also likely to have been a tradition of a religious orientation towards life, though not perhaps one tied unambiguously to a particular faith. In Britain the potential Moonie may have taken his religion seriously enough to have been disillusioned by its institutionalized expression and, while still accepting that God exists, he is likely to have been interested in finding alternative expressions of his religiosity.

At the time of meeting the UC, the prospective convert might be experiencing many of the problems of life that his peers have faced at an earlier stage of their development. He may have been disappointed in his relationships with others, and he might feel he is neither appreciated nor really understood. He might not be interested in what he considers the superficiality and low standards of the world around him or he might be feeling a certain amount of disgust at himself for having succumbed to the evils of the world. He could be feeling lonely and isolated. He may have defined himself as an achiever at an early age, but could feel uncertain as to how to achieve the goals he feels it is his duty to fulfill. He may not even be very clear as to exactly what the goal is, but he will be conscious of evil and of the suffering of the world, and at some level his goal will encompass "doing good".

In short the potential Moonie's experience of life may have left him with an aching desire to do something even though he does not know what or how. He is looking for someone to give him the chance to give, for someone to help him to help.

FOOTNOTES

1. The research for this study of the Unification Church has been carried out with a grant from the Social Science Research Council of Great Britain to whom I wish to express my gratitude. I would also like to express my gratitude to over 750 members of the public and of the Unification Church who filled in the questionnaires.

2. See, for example, Eileen Barker, "Living the Divine Principle: Inside the Reverend Sun Myung Moon's Unification Church in Britain", *Archives de Sciences Sociales des Religions*, 45, 1, 1978, pp. 75-93; *idem*, "Whose Service is Perfect Freedom: The Concept of Spiritual Well-Being in Relation to the Reverend Sun Myung Moon's Unification Church in Britain", in David O. Moberg (ed.) *Spiritual Well-Being*, Washington: University Press of America, 1979; *idem*, "Explaining the Inexplicable", in Günther Kehrer, (ed.), *Das Entstehen einer Religion-Der Fall der Vereinigungskirche*, Munich: Kosel-Verlag, 1980.

3. *Divine Principle, London:* Holy Spirit Association for the Unification of World Christianity, 1973.

4. David G. Bromley, and Anson D. Shupe, Jr., *Moonies in America: Cult, Church and Crusade*, Beverly Hills: Sage, 1979, p. 174.

5. See E. Barker, "Whose Service is Perfect Freedom", *op. cit.*

6. This is discussed further in E. Barker, "Free To Choose? Some Thoughts on the Unification Church and other New Religious Movements", *Clergy Review*, October, 1980 (Part I), November, 1980 (Part II).

7. Further details are presented in E. Barker, "Confessions of a Methodological Schizophrenic: Problems encountered in the Study of Reverend Moon's Unification Church", *Institute for the Study of Worship and Religious Architecture Research Bulletin*, University of Birmingham, 1978.

8. Several sources have been used, the most frequently cited being *Social Trends* published annually by HM Government.

9. E. Barker, "With Enemies Like That . . . : Some Functions of Deprogramming as an Aid to Sectarian Membership" in James Richardson (ed.), *The Brain-Washing/Deprogramming Debate: Sociological, Psychological, Legal and Historical Perspectives*, New Brunswick, N.J.: Transaction Books, 1981.

10. This is discussed in "Whose Service is Perfect Freedom", *op.cit.*

11. See Robert Currie, A. Gilbert and L. Horsley, *Churches and Church-goers*, Oxford: Clarendon Press, 1977.

12. Nora Spurgin, "Unification Church Profile", privately distributed paper, 1977.

13. This question was first put by Sir Alister Hardy, when director of the Religious Experience Research Unit. See Alister Hardy, *The Spiritual Nature of Man*, Oxford: Clarendon Press, 1979.

14. See David Hay, "Religious Experience Amongst a Group of Post-graduate

Students: A Qualitative Study", *Journal for the Scientific Study of Religion*, 18, 2, June, 1979, pp. 164-82.
15. E. Barker, "Science as Theology: The Theological Functioning of Western Science" in M. Hesse, and A. Peacocke, (eds.), *Sciences and Theology in the 20th Century*, Boston: Oriel Press, 1981.
16. E. Barker, "The Professional Stranger", *Introduction to Sociology*, Open University Course Media Notes for D207: O.U., Milton Keynes, 1980.

YESTERDAY'S CHILDREN:
CULTURAL AND STRUCTURAL CHANGE
IN A NEW RELIGIOUS MOVEMENT[1]

Roy Wallis

New religious movements typically undergo processes of change, both organizational and ideological, in their early years; none more so than millenarian movements which reject the world in which they emerge[2] and expect a radical and imminent transformation of it. Although movements which reject the prevailing social order may differ greatly in many respects, the analysis of the internal changes which have taken place in a single movement may throw light upon the general syndrome, and advance our understanding of the pressures for adaptation faced by new religious movements in contemporary society. In the following pages, I trace cultural and structural changes that have occurred in a new millenarian movement, the Children of God, from its origins to the recent past. Among the more important changes are:

(1) The effective disappearance of leadership between the local unit and the movement's prophet, i.e. from a tightly integrated authority structure to leadership via the mail.

(2) The rapprochement of substantial sectors of the movement with a society and social institutions formerly regarded with intense hostility.

(3) The effective disappearance of a communal life-style.

(4) A differentiation in levels of commitment among those attached to the movement.

The sources of these changes in organization and style are explored in the following pages, together with an indication of their consequences, and a comparison with related changes in other movements (in particular Jehovah's Witnesses and the Cooneyites), leading to some general conclusions regarding the development of world-rejecting movements.

Part I: Developments in the Children of God

The late 1960s was a period of considerable growth in a number of new religious movements which attracted a following among the young in North America and Western Europe. There is little detailed consensus concerning the sources of this social phenomenon, but many observers agree that young people during the 1960s formed a distinctive sociological generation, gathered in institutions of higher education in unprecedented numbers, relieved of the anxieties of survival and securing a job by a buoyant economy which encouraged a belief in the attainability of progress. In this context the resistance presented to the demand for Black civil rights; the escalation of the Vietnam war; and the opposition to the demands of students for reform in the universities, combined to alienate the young from the values and institutions of their society. When subsequent attempts at political reform failed, and the creation of secular alternatives to the conventional lifestyle disintegrated or proved equally unsatisfactory to some young idealists, religious leaders and movements may have seemed to be the only remaining possibility for achieving a transformation of their world.

A number of very different movements grew from this situation. Although many draw upon an alien cultural heritage (Iskcon, 3HO, Unification Church), others had their origins in essentially Western traditions, such as American Revivalism, which proved surprisingly amenable to synthesis with a youth culture shorn of drugs and sex. The Jesus People was a generic label applied to a number of groups and movements which emerged almost simultaneously on the West Coast of America. There is considerable dispute as to which was quite the first to begin an evangelical ministry to the young, employing youth-cultural music and language, and displaying similar antipathies to conventional values and institutions, but certainly among the first was a small band consisting of David and Jane Berg, itinerant preachers, some of their four married children and spouses, and other young people travelling with them. Hearing of the growing population of drop-out young living in the beach towns of Southern California, Berg and his team went to Huntington Beach, where his mother, a retired evangelist, had settled. There they witnessed on the beaches and in the streets, to the lonely and the lost. Although at first they seemed rather weird to the young people they met there, not yet having acquired the dress and language of the counter-culture, the curiosity of a number was aroused. In contrast to themselves, Berg's Teens for Christ, as they were called in 1968, seemed overwhelmingly sincere, intensely committed to something, and above all perhaps, happy. Teens for Christ had acquired premises to which they could invite people who were attracted by their singing and witnessing on the beaches, offering them food and coffee, music and a sympathetic environment. Rapidly adopting the style of dress and language of the young they attracted a steady following, which accelerated in number as Berg and his team committed themselves to a thoroughgoing attack on the prevailing social order of America, castigating it as the Whore of Babylon.

They drew a sharp line between God and the world, between serving God and serving the devil. An early class given to new members was entitled "Is it scriptural to work for money and world riche$?" It argued that

> This idolatrous pastime has about 99.9999% of the people in this country in complete bondage to that great infested lady: MYSTERY, BABYLON THE GREAT. It also gives the same percentage of lukewarm, half-hearted so-called 'Christians' in America an excuse to be out of the will of God! It is the ideal delusion for the snakes, vipers and whited sepulchres of the church system. They find no fault in justifying their 40 hour-a-week worship of Mammon, their weekends of pleasure seeking, and to make up for it all, their 1 hour-a-week worship of the greatest Abomination of all—the false church system. (unpublished manuscript)

They viewed themselves as completely committed disciples,

engaged in full-time service for God, a life incompatible with working at a job in the System.

> We don't have to work on jobs for money because the Lord told us that He would take care of our food, drink, clothing, etc, if we would seek FIRST His Kingdom (Mt. 6:24-34). These things are what the Lord has provided for us bountifully by his "forsake-all" method described in Acts 4:32-37. The Lord does not want us to be hung-up labouring for paychecks, when our most important job is rescuing those "precious stones" (Souls) (1Pt. 2:4-5) from the pit. (Moses David and Joel Wordsworth, *The Revolution for Jesus,* Children of God Publications, 1972:23).

Not only did they reject conventional work and education, they viewed themselves as a Revolution for Jesus against the materialistic and ungodly world, expecting persecution for their stand against its evils, even at times *encouraging* persecution as a confirmation of their righteousness.

Teens for Christ would visit local churches, unkempt and in hippy attire, to sit on the floor in front of the pews, loudly praising and sometimes challenging aspects of the service, a living indictment of what they conceived to be the hypocrisy of Sunday-only Christianity. Occasionally, they would invade a church dressed in sackcloth, bearing yokes and staves, dramatizing their prophetic warnings of the end and their commitment to a life of full-time service to God as witnesses carrying the warning and the message of salvation into all the world. Not surprisingly their self-righteous enthusiasm sometimes precipitated confrontation, ejection, and even arrest.

They campaigned at local high schools and colleges, attacking the godlessness of contemporary education and the "satanic" theory of evolution which conflicted with their fundamentalist interpretation of the creation story. The arrest of a number of followers at one such demonstration led to prophetic revelations for some followers that God would smite those who persecuted his prophets by causing an earthquake which would cast California into the sea. Berg confirmed this prophecy and, jumping bail in some cases and sneaking away from parents in others, Teens for Christ left Huntington Beach and split into groups which moved across country witnessing and demonstrating in warning of the coming of the Antichrist and the return of Jesus.

After some months of wandering across America and Canada proclaiming their warning message of the end and demonstrating in sackcloth and ashes in a number of major cities, they finally gathered, early in 1970, on a property known as the Texas Soul Clinic Ranch (TSC), owned by Fred Jordan, a radio and television evangelist and former employer of Berg. They had by this time acquired the name Children of God from an inventive newspaper reporter, and at TSC they began to implement a way of life in accordance with their beliefs. Berg, now known as Moses or more familiarly as Mo, believed that God's covenant with the Jews was still valid and that before Christ's return the Jews would be converted. The Children of God modelled themselves upon the Jews of ancient Israel and the modern kibbutzim, adopting Bible names, organizing themselves in tribes, dancing in the style of the Jewish Hora, and sustaining a vision of leaving America *en masse* to evangelize the Jews in Israel.

They viewed themselves, at this time, as a separated people. Those who would hearken to the warning message were to be called out of "the Pit", of "the Whorish System", to forsake all, and devote themselves entirely to God's work. To facilitate their efforts, the Children of God, like the early church, would live independent of the system in separated communities, in which they would possess all the skills and facilities needed for survival and for their work. Out of such strongholds guerrilla teams would be despatched to proclaim the message, gather those who hearkened, and return them to the colony. As a colony grew in size, it might divide at an appropriate time, like a Hutterite community, with each new colony possessing all the skills and resources to establish itself independently. By this means the movement would preserve its unity and its witness and remain unspotted by the world. Moses said at this time:

> The strength of a church has always been its unity in the Lord. Its unity in fellowship. (...) ... we are not everybody going to go off and do his own thing ... we are going to stick together ... The only church that is going to

survive is that which is going to survive as a unit, as a commune, as an entity, as a united front, as a colony. ...the only way that God is going to preserve his church is the way he's always preserved his church. Come ye out from among them and be ye separate.... Not just separate and scattered all over the landscape, but separate as a *body*. ("Colonization", February 1970)[3]

Moses damned conventional society as the "Devilish System", and argued that there could be no neutrals, only God's people totally committed to the work of witnessing, or those who were against him.

The most sickening of all people to God is the neutral—the enemy who pretends to be a friend, like most church people today, and the churchy system. ("There are no neutrals", May 1970)

This early vision contained within it an incipient communal introversionism:

God called us a new nation. That means a whole new culture—a whole new nation, a new way of life. We are a sample of the coming Millenium [sic] ("Not a sermon, but a sample!", July 1970)

Moses and his followers were profoundly pessimistic about the future of America, expecting the reaction against youthful revolt to accelerate, even anticipating the emergence of a dictatorship under Richard Nixon, supported by a hardline, reactionary sector of the working class. Later, Mo expected the "Great Confusion" in America to be precipitated by a Black revolt.

Late in 1970, Moses left America to visit Israel and Europe. Israel proved a profound disappointment to him. His vision of converting the Jews and of finding in Israel an environment sympathetic to the Children of God where the kingdom of God could be established was rudely dispelled. He found Israel materialistic and hostile to Christian missionary endeavour. Mo was able to identify far more readily with the Arabs, many of whom were Christian, whom he saw as poor and oppressed and, in Israel, a rejected minority like his young American followers, than with the proud, wealthy and warlike Israelis who showed no inclination to receive the message of Christ.

This experience was of major significance in Moses' thinking. Since the death of his mother, in 1968, he had begun to follow his inclinations away from the earlier puritanical fundamentalism in which she had encouraged him. He had received the gift of tongues shortly thereafter, and had taken on her prophetic mantle, receiving new revelations increasingly at variance with traditional Bible interpretation. He had also begun to pursue a more 'liberated' sexual life, taking a new young wife, and entering into sexual relationship with other close female followers. But the undermining of his theory concerning the Restoration of the Jews was to precipitate gradual, but ultimately extremely radical, changes in the movement's belief and practice. First, Mo came to believe that the Children of God had inherited God's promises to the Jews. He still encouraged his followers to leave America, but now to spread the message into Europe and beyond. Thenceforth they would view themselves as "Gypsies" rather than a contemporary version of the Old Testament Jews. This was in accord with revelations that Mo was receiving from "spirit helpers", in particular Abrahim, a 13th century gypsy leader. The gypsy model may have been one factor encouraging a shift away from large-scale colony-division to that of sending out small teams to witness and establish bases in new areas. In his letter, "The Gypsies" of March 1971, he says:

I am still as much convinced as ever that smaller colonies are the ideal[4]. I am just as much opposed as ever to large churches, over-sized congregations and their cumbersome, burdensome machinery, and their impersonal conglomerate fellowship where leadership loses that *personal* touch, *intimate* fellowship, and *close attention* to the *individual*.

A colony of between twelve and twenty-four was seen as the ideal. The Children of God would follow what was now seen to be the pattern of the early church and of the gypsies by scattering in small, decentralized, "virtually independent...colonies, held together only by His Love, His Spirit and His Word".

Mo also began to modify the early conception of a complete and absolute distinction between the Children of God and "the Enemy". The Children of God, the true disciples, would always remain a tiny minority and, "The indifferent, the luke-warm, the so-called neutrals are really enemies under the skin", but Moses warned his followers:

> This does not always mean that they have to be an actual member, and have already forsaken all, and are already following Him full-time, to be one of us. Jesus and his disciples had many under-cover friends, members of the system... you must remember this, and not curse everyone who does not immediately drop everything and join you. (*Ibid.*)

Hence, while Mo argued that "We've got the only pure christianity I know of in this generation" ("Organisation I", March 1971), the Children of God clearly were not the *only* Christians, the only ones saved. Their *particular* reward was not salvation but membership of a "special elite class of the Overcomers, the total conquerors. Not all the saints are going to get the credit for it—because they failed to do the job.... And we shall rule and reign with Him... a thousand years". ("Personal Answers I", April 1971). There will be those living within the New Jerusalem in the presence of Christ, and the rest of the saved who will live outside "because they haven't been as *faithful* as they should have...". ("Space City", June 1971)

The Children of God expanded considerably during 1970 and 1971 as a result of their evangelistic enthusiasm and the publicity given them in the mass media, which attracted the interest of other Jesus People leaders who had been finding it increasingly difficult to maintain the unity and enthusiasm of their own followers. For many recruited at this time, the large colonies with their mass witness and active evangelism, their fellowship, and the sharp contrast with life in the System were an attraction. Mo was obliged to reiterate frequently his wish that large colonies should split up into groups of no more than twenty or so, to enable them to become more mobile, move into "all the world", and to go underground in the face of coming persecution. This was to be a continuing theme through the following ten years.

Another recurrent phenomenon was initiated in late 1971 when Mo proclaimed a "Homegoing", encouraging members to go home to their families during Christmas, employing this strategy as a means of confounding critics who claimed that the followers were virtual prisoners, and purging the ranks of the half-hearted. This leader has always maintained a "Gideon's Band" view of the movement, that the Lord's work could be accomplished by a small band of the totally committed better than by a multitude of the half-hearted. This vision was important for later developments.

If the Children of God were to be an elite cadre of full-time activists, Mo recognized that they would none the less need the support and protection of others who might be unwilling or unable to "forsake all" for colony life. Early in 1972, he began to advocate that, "we need some kind of recognition and status for friends who can't join us for various good reasons…". ("A wonderful wave of worldwide witnessing", February 1972). In the face of mounting hostility directed towards religious 'cults' by parents' groups and others, the support of conventional members of society sympathetic to the Children of God would be an obvious advantage. Financial support was also valuable, as well as aid in meeting other needs of "the Family" (as members referred to themselves), such as travel, accommodation and the like. By June 1972 ("Other sheep"), Moses was even talking of the Jesus People in civil terms when only a year before he had dismissed them as "nothing but a bunch of System kids and church kids with long hair!"; "sickening, pusillanimous, make-you-want-to-puke-right-on-the-floor, lukewarm, churchianity christians"; and "slaves of the Devil". They were now to be seen as "other sheep" who could be welcomed as an "Associate colony".

> Other Christians may not be the best in the world, and they may not be serving God as much as they should or could, but this does not mean that they're not saved or serving Jesus at all! ("Other sheep", June 1972)

This more tolerant attitude contrasted sharply with the early intolerance and exclusivism and some followers, attracted to the Children of God precisely because of its radical oppositional stance toward society and its thoroughgoing condemnation of all who did not devote their lives and time entirely to God's service, were unable to accept this ideological transition with equanimity. David Hoyt, a leader in another Jesus People movement who had joined the Children of God with a large part of his following the previous year, was one of those to speak against this change as a "compromise", and thereby to precipitate his own ejection from the movement.

During this period, the movement expanded rapidly through Europe, often gaining support initially from ministers or church people who saw it as an embodiment of the Jesus Movement and as a means, therefore, of restoring Europe's young to Christianity. The Children of God was having an impact in Catholic as well as Protestant countries, and this too was an encouragement to moderate the exclusiveness of their pronouncements. It was being received favourably by the World Council of Churches. In September 1972, therefore, Mo announced that

> we have begun to recognise the absolute necessity of having to work with, or even within some of the System to a certain degree in order to try and win some of them. ("Are we Catholics or Protestants?")

Moses was also beginning to appreciate the role of literature as a way of spreading his message and as a source of income. In November 1971 ("Statistics"), Mo had said,

> ...you're not supposed to give a tract or piece of literature to anyone except those to whom you actually witness! We are not tract passers! (...) I'd rather see you witnessing to fewer people and spending more time with each one and getting more real results than stacking up big numbers of those reached! I sent you to reap!

But by August 1972 he had announced that

> Literature is going to become one of our greatest and most widespread witnesses...as well as portending to become one of our major sources of both individual and collective income to finance the work of the Lord....("Monster on the move")

Only six months later his message was that,

> Soul winning is not our major task! Witnessing his wonder working words to the world is our major task. ("Wonder working words", February, 1973)

During 1973, the decision was made that some of Mo's letters hitherto available only to followers, should be printed for public distribution on the street, in return for a donation. (This practice came to be called "litnessing", that is, witnessing through literature.) By June 1973, Mo ("Shiners?—or shamers") was advocating that a quota minimum be set for literature distribution with a percentage of the returns for those achieving the quota, additional rewards for high achievers, and extra duties for underachievers.

Moses was introducing further ideological innovations during this period. He was being aided by a growing, and varying body of "spirit helpers" who gave advice or information, ranging from the "Pied Piper" to "Rasputin". He was becoming increasingly explicit on sexual matters, even circulating, early in 1973, an account of a dream in which he was making love violently with an Indian woman whom he called the Maharishi of Hyderbad ("The Maharishi of Hyderbad", January 1973). His conception of the Children of God as God's new Israel and chosen people for the last days was leading him increasingly towards antinomianism. Moreover, his conception of witnessing and ministering to those whom God wished to reach had changed as a result of his success in bringing into the Family an Italian aristocrat, the Duke Emmanuele of Zoagli and Castelvari, through the latter's attraction towards one of Mo's "wives". He was beginning to realize that physical needs other than food and warmth might have to be met in order to show God's love. In the following months, he would begin to encourage Maria, his permanent companion, to behave flirtatiously with men, even to go to bed with them in order to convince them of God's love for them. As a result of his initial secret experiments, he began to encourage this practice more widely with other loyal female followers and, by 1976, to promulgate "flirty fishing" (F'fing) as a general method of winning souls and allies.[5]

Success at winning a wealthy, upper-class convert like the Duke Emmanuele combined with the negligible growth in size of the movement during 1972 ("Wonder working words", February 1973) was to lead to a further change in direction. The movement's initial constituency of footloose, anti-establishment young, without ties or commitments, and hostile to an impersonal, bureaucratic world, travelling through America and Europe, or congregating in sympathetic youth-cultural enclaves, had begun to disappear. The youth revolt of the 1960s was waning, and in a harsher economic climate fewer young people were rejecting what might be their only chance of securing a well-paid job, comfort and material goods. The young drop-outs who had been the main converts to the movement on the streets, in the capital cities or beach towns of Europe and America, were no longer there in anything like their former numbers. But Mo and Maria had encountered a new constituency:

> The most gospel-neglected class are the rich and the intellectual. (...) It's being stingy and selfish to move out to some remote shanty just to save money instead of souls, because it is limiting the great witness we could have, and our sphere of influence...!
>
> (...) There isn't enough time from now till [sic] the Lord comes to go to every village and reach every little poor peasant! The revolution first captures the upper crust, and they share with the poor.
>
> (...) we are not now reaching the rich as we should.
>
> (...) God wants you to capture leaders!—People who are already leaders. ("Rags to riches", March 1973)

The affluent and influential would not be won over by the same means as the poor and alienated. A more sophisticated strategy was required than street witnessing and Jesus coffee bars, singing at rock concerts or performing skits or "Holy Ghost samples" in public parks. This new constituency would have to be sought in "up-market" hotels, bars and discos, and would need some more concrete demonstration of the love of God than an appeal to their idealism. F'fing was a means to gain access to this new constituency, but not until 1976 would this become general within the movement. As in the past, these changes evoked a certain reluctance on the part of some followers, most noticeable to Mo among leaders:

> Some of our kids have gotten just like the church people: they're scribes and pharisees, self-righteous hypocritical old bottles: "Yea indeed we are the people, and beside us there are no others!—And if you don't do it our way we won't let you do it at all". ("Old bottles", July 1973)

Many resisted the change from soul winning as their first priority to

literature distribution, and Mo had frequently to remind his followers that the purpose of the movement lay in getting out his
message, not in its way of life. Even the earlier commitment to the
communal life and the pattern of the Early Church had been
superseded:

> I'm just waking up to the fact that we're no longer even trying to get back to
> the pristine pattern of the Early Church! We are not the Early Church! We're
> the Latter Church! The *latest* Church and the pattern God wants us to live
> by *today* is not exactly the pattern they lived by 2000 years ago. (ibid.).

Others could not accept the progressive democratization of the
sexual freedom which had hitherto been only an elite privilege little
known to the rank and file. Marriage, once described as "sacro-
sanct", was seen increasingly as subordinate to the needs and
interests of the Family as a whole ("One wife", October 1972). If
God's work would be facilitated by extra-marital sexual relations,
by taking more than one partner, or by abandoning an existing
marriage tie, the conventions of the monogamous marriage could
not be permitted to retard it.

Mo was progressively revealing to his followers the antino-
mian trend of his thinking, the notion that for true disciples, "God's
only law is love"; and many followers who were firmly committed to
traditional Christian moral conventions broke with the movement
over this issue.

The reluctance of some of his early leaders to implement his
policies regarding reduction in colony size, or the dispersal of
followers more rapidly into all the world; to implement his new
policies regarding literature distribution or flirty-fishing; to pass on
without their own interpretation his letters and policies; and to
abandon teaching doctrine at variance with his own; or to restrict
themselves to the authority that Mo had prescribed for them, were
among the major issues which emerged periodically as grounds
for dissatisfaction on the part of the prophet regarding some of his
subordinates. For the first two years or so, Mo governed the
movement's daily operations directly, but later, when he secluded
himself from his followers, and the Children of God spread, first
throughout America and Europe, and then progressively into the

rest of the world, he was forced increasingly to rely upon local leaders to control actual operations. Below him in the hierarchy of authority were the members of his own family: his first wife, now called Eve; offspring Ho, Aaron, Faith and Deborah; and the husbands of the two daughters, Jethro and Joshua. Aaron died shortly after the movement came to Europe; Ho and Faith remained entirely loyal to their father's changing vision; but Mo increasingly found Eve, Joshua, Deborah and Jethro intervening in his decisions, resisting their full implementation, or assuming more authority than he wished them to have.

In September 1974, Mo complained ("Hitch your wagon to a star!")

> "A prophet is not without honour except in his own household and among his own kindred", so some of you therefore have even more faith in me and in the Words that God has already given than some of the RF (Royal Family i.e. his own family and their spouses) have!

In the same month, he admonished Eve:

> Mother dear, you must learn how to work with people as a Queen Mother of any Kingdom should, *under* the authority of the duly constituted Kings and Queens or other officers of the area…it is not your place to usurp their authority and their thrones and start trying to run things yourself, either without them or against them! ("Mo's worldwide family letters Nos., 10, 11 and 12")

Other than through ties of blood or marriage to the prophet, authority not directly delegated by him was available in only a limited number of ways. It could be derived from authority previously enjoyed as leader of another Jesus People group that had joined the Children of God. Such was the situation of David Hoyt, formerly founder and leader of the House of Judah, who was effectively expelled from the movement in 1972. It was also the case with Linda Meissner, formerly a leader of the Jesus People Army who, after joining the Children of God, had been given leadership over the colonies in Scandinavia, and who was then subsequently removed from office in 1975 ("The administration revolution", November 1972). Another source of authority was as a teacher in the movement. Joel Wordsworth and Joab had been early teachers in the movement who acquired great prestige as expositors of the Bible. As Mo's revelations began to move away from conventional understandings of biblical texts, however, their interpretations became increasingly divergent from his own (see "Mo's worldwide family letters Nos. 10,11 and 12", September, 1974) leading to their final and complete excommunication in 1975.

Mo was to wrest control from the hands of those of his family who resisted him, and from those early followers who remained committed to a previous vision of the movement, the "old bottles" unable to take the new wine. In February 1975, he pronounced that,

> ...we still have a few old bottles around who try to exercise too much control from the top instead of inspiring more initiative from the bottom. Some of these old bottle groups have had big organizational meetings recently in which they've been trying to figure out how to run the world without even asking for my suggestions. ("The shake-up")

This smacked of hubris and perhaps even treasonable conspiracy, and precipitated major changes in power-holders. Authority was placed in the hands of those tied to Mo by bonds of personal commitment and affection, who would clearly exercise that authority in delegation from him and not from any presumed 'natural' right or any legitimation. They were often his own former "Spiritual wives" and their husbands, elevated to meet this leadership need. His own family and their spouses were demoted, or left without power-bearing office.

> You might call it a "bloodless coup" to prevent any more usurping of authority by those unauthorised to do so, and to strengthen the King's influence on his Kingdom without interference and contradiction of others. ("The bloodless coup", February 1975)

A structure was created with each subordinate layer nesting within the ones above. So each colony would have its own Colony Shepherd, two colonies would have a District Shepherd, two districts a Regional Shepherd, and so on up through Bishops, Archbishops, Ministers, Prime Ministers and King's Counsellors.

Mo voiced an aspiration to bring the rank-and-file following more into the decision-making process and established a structure nominally responsive to the democratic acquiescence of those below. But he was also making very considerable demands upon members: for income through "litnessing"; for commitment in F'fing; for suffering the rigours of dividing colonies into ever smaller units; and for pioneering new fields.

Moreover, many leaders adopted a style of leadership based on Mo's own autocratic manner, justified for him by the belief that his decisions were guided directly by God and must therefore not be gainsaid. While he permitted his followers to vote on his decisions, even encouraged them to do so, it was with the clear understanding that he was, after all God's prophet, so:

> Of course you don't have to do any of this if you don't want to, and all of this is subject to your own voluntary agreement and consent... I think you *should* because it will be good for you and the Lord's work... I cannot force you to do it, but I hold a few trump cards and those are the Lord's letters which we shall *withhold* from those who refuse to co-operate and from which we shall excommunicate you if you don't obey... So although the choice is yours, if you make the wrong choice and do not obey God's word, you will be excommunicated from the fellowship and the inspiration of His Letters! ("The colony revolution", March 1975)

Mo was prepared to allow absolute freedom of choice, as long as that choice turned out to be what he suggested or commanded in his letters. Mo was beginning to realize, however, that intervening leadership could prove a hindrance in this respect. Mo aspired to a situation in which the "Letters are the Leaders", without any alternative interpretation or intervention, by which his views and wishes would reach the followers unmediated and unamended. Alternative *interpretation* had already been dealt with:

> I'm glad we've gotten away from so many classes. We had so many teachers and some of them were teaching some of the craziest stuff you ever heard. So we just practically cut all that and advised everyone to just read the Mo letters. That way we can be pretty sure that they're getting the right information... ("Ordination", March 1975)

But in the effort to eliminate intervention and interference in his policies and decisions, one extensive chain of command had simply been substituted for another, and within two years it had begun to produce further problems. Local leaders in Latin America, for example, were discouraging F'fing, leading Mo to comment:

> These guys always did want to do their own thing and have their own revolution and not have to follow me or obey me, some groan every time they get a new letter. ("Grace vs. Law!" November 1977)

In the same letter, Mo comments favourably on the unquestioningly obedient among his followers:

> *Most* of our kids don't *know* the old Bible doctrines that well. They don't know that much about the Bible, they never studied or learned about it or had it drilled into them every day like some of these guys with churchy backgrounds.

> So they just take what I say without question, they don't even know any Bible verses to use against the Letters because they don't know the Bible that well. They just trust me and trust the Lord, and love me and take my word for it. (...)

> These poor kids, Lord, could be...getting discouraged because they see that their own leaders are not obeying.

Mo became increasingly concerned about the extensive apparatus of the chain of command (or "chain of co-operation" as it was referred to in the Family). Although apparently straightforward as a bureaucratic command structure, it was expensive to maintain. Support and travel expenses for each level had to be found from income primarily derived through litnessing (i.e. street literature distribution and solicitation), necessitating high quota requirements for rank-and-file followers. Moreover, the chain of co-operation permitted extensive opportunity for intervention between the policy promulgated by Mo and the practice of the mass of followers:

> We found that some disciples were lacking in their needs of proper housing, clothing and so on, and were sent out unbearably long hours under cruel conditions, with leadership demanding impossible quotas...

> We...found that there were many abuses of power.... F'fing was in many instances prohibited or at least discouraged...

> We have heard of quite a few instances where leaders have changed the meaning of my letters by their actions or verbal interpretations. My *Letters*

mean *exactly* what they say, literally and they don't need explaining away, spiritualising or re-interpreting by *anyone*. ("The re-organisation nationalisation revolution", January 1978)

He therefore determined to eliminate the intervening structure of authority, purging old leaders and despatching them to pioneer new areas. "We think the colonies can do better on their own under our direct personal supervision.... I think the *Letters* are going to be the *leaders* and will be obeyed better if they don't have any upper officers interfering!" (*ibid.*) Only the King and Queen's Counsellors were to be retained. A very few "Home Visiting Servants" would be appointed to travel all the time, giving "advice and counsel based on the Mo Letters", but initially at least with no power to command. The colonies, now called Homes, would themselves have purely elective "Home Servants". The movement was to be renamed "The Family of Love". The Servants, i.e. officers in any area, were to be indigenous or at least married to natives; and foreign nationals, particularly the predominantly American leadership, were to move on to new areas. Home Servants were no longer to control finances from litnessing, but were to be dependent upon voluntary contributions from members of the Home.

This "revolution within the revolution" proved particularly traumatic. Experienced American leaders were forced onto the road again, leaving Homes with often only younger, inexperienced locals to maintain them. This disruption paid little regard to the fact that, following Moses' opposition to contraception and encouragement of sexual freedom, many of the leaders forced to uproot themselves had large families of four, five or even more children to support, transport and re-settle in a new home. For a number who felt they had been doing a reasonable job in their former situation to try to meet the demands of those above them, this was a disillusioning experience. The sudden democratization and freedom from leadership control produced a situation of near-anarchy in many Homes for a while. Followers freed from control ceased litnessing, refused to conform to the Home Servant or Visiting Servant's expectations, or to obey their requests, or could not agree on a person to elect as Home Servant in the first place. If they secured funds it now became a matter of personal discretion how much to pass on to the Home. The notion of a community of goods was severely undermined. The role of Visiting Servant was defined in ways that rendered it almost impossible to perform. Visiting Servants were dependent largely upon the charity of the Homes; they were expected to spend almost all their time travelling over large regions to all the Homes; they possessed no right to command, nor any formal authority; but were expected to share themselves, especially sexually, in each Home they visited. The role of Home Servant, while not quite so demanding, was at this time often a thankless task. In terms of authority structure, the movement had shifted light-years away from its early position of absolute obedience to leadership:

> You must obey implicitly, quickly and without question your officers in the Lord, if you wish to remain a member of this Team. ("The revolutionary rules", March 1972)

> God appoints certain members of the body to be leaders of other members (Ps. 75: 6-7).... We are to obey *and submit* ourselves unto these older members because God has put them over us (Heb. 13:17). (Moses David, and Joel Wordsworth, *op. cit.*: 51)

Homes began to fall into debt. Income for the international organization dropped dramatically and, in the course of the following year or two, Homes began to fall away from the movement precepts. In some Homes, members began smoking cigarettes or marijuana, drinking heavily, departing from Mo's prescription regarding the use of healthy food, and in varying ways becoming more worldly. The movement was due for another purge to separate the truly committed. Some who no longer seemed so devoted to the missionary endeavour could be given the opportunity to return home. This included not only those who no longer fully obeyed Mo's precepts, but also those whose large families and mounting years were beginning to sap their enthusiasm for a life of constant movement, without sure financial support.

However, a further consideration militated in favour of changes along this line, which derived directly from Mo's millennial vision. That is, it had always formed part of his view that, as history moved towards its end, God's true witnesses would be increasingly persecuted. An historic event, late in 1978, in the form of the tragedy in Jonestown, Guyana, and the press and public reaction of hostility toward 'cults', confirmed for him that the movement's efforts to spread out, disperse, become nationally indigenous and hence less visible and vulnerable, were sound strategy which should now be pursued even further: "They are really out to *get* us as an *organization*! So one of the best things we can do is to apparently *disorganize*!" ("Where to now?", December 1978).

Those who could no longer support themselves in the field were encouraged to return home, especially the Americans who could make higher wages there than in foreign fields. The progressive abandonment of communal life had resulted in the loss of economies of scale in child-rearing, living costs, assistance in supporting dependents by the unmarried childless, transportation, etc., forcing many household heads back to conventional jobs. Those who returned home were not required to abandon the Family or to sever all connections with it, but could, if they wished, tithe their income to support others in the field, or if their commitment fell below even that level, pay a fixed donation for some of the movement's literature. Even former backsliders were offered the opportunity to receive some of the Letters for a fixed donation for a while, without obligation to commit themselves to the full rigours of life in the Family. By moving back into the System, God's Children could go even further undercover. Some would return home, others would get jobs in the mission field, and all could tithe from their income to support the work. They could witness and litness in their spare time, as well as engage in F'fing. Mo advocated moving into door-to-door witnessing and literature distribution in order to reduce their high visibility on the streets. This would also facilitate meeting people more their own age and in more their own circumstances, for example, families with young children. From such people a little group could be gathered for a "Church in the home" or ("Church of Love"), or a little home Sunday school for their children, to give them the basic elements of their faith. Those followers who remained still more active could sing in bars for support, or on the streets, "provision" assistance (that is secure gifts of goods or cash from friends, relatives, or businesses), litness sufficiently to support themselves, or seek financial aid through a mailing list contacted through prayer letters and the like. The "Gideon's Band" of full-time followers would even, for the most part, continue to live outside the System, preferably fully mobile, travelling from place to place, camping or better still, towing a caravan or a motor home. Thus, there could be a complete spectrum from those still on the margins of society, mobile missionary teams of full-time workers for God, to those who—beyond an interest in the literature for which they sent in a regular donation—could scarcely be distinguished from their neighbours.

Mo drew strength concerning these changes from the history of the Mormons and other new religious movements that had originated as deviant and radical movements in fierce opposition to the surrounding society, only to settle down later, perhaps even abandoning some doctrines or practices in order to survive: "We're going to have to abandon a few things too. 'All things are *lawful* to us, but not all things are expedient' ". ("The maturation of a movement", January 1979)

Part II: Comparative Analysis

In a variety of ways, the Children of God may appear to have undergone a rapprochement with the churches and society of a kind normally subsumed under the notion of *denominationalization.*

The tendency for religious sects to lose their initial evangelical enthusiasm and opposition to the prevailing social order, developing over time a more denominational form, has been documented for numerous cases. The process is normally seen to involve a decline in the requirement of some distinctive standard of merit, knowledge or worth as the criterion of membership, and the employment of largely "formalized procedures of admission".[6]

There is a shift from a self-conception as possessors of sole access to the truth or salvation to one more tolerant of the claims of other groups. The movement's *distinctive* doctrinal position is less stressed in comparison to *continuities* with other groups with which it becomes more willing to work in ecumenical endeavour. There is a tendency for a professional ministry to emerge, along-side formalization of worship, increased emphasis on the education of offspring rather than proselytization, and a lowering of the intensity of commitment of members. The values of the surrounding society are increasingly accepted, and the norms and behaviour patterns of members can scarcely be distinguished from those of the community at large.[7]

The shift toward denominationalism is not simply a consequence of the attitudes and behaviour of members of the group, however, but also of the attitudes of people in general in the surrounding society. As John Wilson[8] has observed:

> ... the shift will not occur at all unless other people tolerate the group and its activities. The public must cease regarding it as a deviant organisation and begin treating it as one group among many, competing equally with other religions.

John Wilson also lays great stress on *bureaucratization* as an important internal element in denominationalization.[9] This seems much less important. While bureaucratization doubtless often does accompany denominationalization for the reasons he advances, it is far from being either peculiar to, or an essential aspect of it. Some sects, such as Jehovah's Witnesses and Scientology, became highly bureaucratized without this leading to denominationalization. Bureaucracy is largely a function of the size and spread of the collectivity rather than of its denominational character. It is, in many cases, a way of *implementing* its denominationalism rather than being *constitutive* of it.

Of more significance for the light it throws on the character of the denomination is the observation of David Martin that:

> ... sacral and intrinsic values do not attach to communal and collective forms but only to the individual, so that these collective forms and arrangements are merely instrumental, and important only in so far as they subserve the individual.[10]

The denomination, Martin stresses, is a "delegated democracy". These insights support the utility of a typology of religious collectivities developed elsewhere[11] to account for the emergence of sects from cults, and suggest—as there adverted although not demonstrated—that a similar conceptualization will account equally well for the transition from sect to denomination. I have argued that the labels applied to religious collectivities need to capture conceptions of the way in which they are viewed both from within and from without. That is to say, whether members view the body as the *only* path to salvation, or as one among a *number* of viable paths seems to be a crucial feature, but so too does the conception of it by the public at large who may view it as *respectable* or as *deviant*.

Typology of religious collectivies

		External conception	
		Respectable	Deviant
Internal conception	Uniquely legitimate	Church	Sect
	Pluralistically Legitimate	Denomination	Cult

In earlier studies, I argued that the central features of the sect can be understood as deriving from its "epistemological authoritarianism", that is the location of authority, for what constitutes either the truth or the path to salvation in some source beyond the individual member.[12] This phenomenon contrasts with the "epistemological individualism" of the cult, which is characterized by having no source beyond the individual's own conception of the way in which truth is defined or salvation attained. It is clear that these principles can also be applied to the other half of the typology. The church in this typology is most readily approximated by such formations as the historic Catholic Church, Calvinism in Reformation Geneva, or wherever a religious monopoly prevails within a society. Such bodies view themselves as the sole repository of the truth, and clearly possess an authoritative locus for attributions of true doctrine and heresy, permitting no substantial articulated dissent from their doctrinal views.

As many accounts of the denomination have emphasized, it is a peculiarly *modern* religious form unable to emerge prior to the spread of religious toleration. The denomination sees itself as only one particular expression of religious truth and is willing to co-operate with others in the pursuit of general goals. Moreover, as Martin had indicated, the denomination is a form of delegated individualism, a representative democracy in which the truth is defined by a broad consensus which none the less tolerates divergences by minority opinion within broad limits. Denominations (Bishop Pike notwithstanding) rarely have heretics, because the majority view of truth rarely commands sufficiently widespread and intense commitment to cast out the deviant behavior.

Hence it follows that the shift from sect to denomination involves not merely the growth of respectability, and not only the tempering of distinctive doctrinal views, and the recognition that others may provide access to the truth or to salvation. It also *crucially* involves the shift from epistemological authoritarianism to a delegated, or representative form of, epistemological individualism, that is to say, the diffusion among the membership at large of the authority severally and collectively to decide what is to be acceptable as truth. Often this is a slow process, following upon the death of the charismatic founder of the sect. The development of a sect from a cult involves the arrogation by leaders of authority once diffused among members. The development of a denomination from a sect involves the recapture of that authority by the members and its redistribution among them.

The Children of God clearly display some signs of accommodation to society. Many members are returning to their homelands, taking jobs, and putting their children into state or denominational schools.[13] They no longer so roundly curse the hellish system and its churches. They have accepted that others, who do not maintain all their beliefs and loyalties, are none the less doing God's will, if only to a limited extent. They have abandoned many distinctive features of their way of life, such as communalism, and seem prepared to abandon others such as blatant antinomianism. Similar changes can be found in other world-rejecting movements. The Jehovah's Witnesses, for example, have also undergone such changes. Jehovah's Witnesses emerged as a body of Bible Students of millenarian persuasion drawn from subscribers to Charles Taze Russell's magazine, *Zion's Watch Tower and Herald of Christ's Presence*. Russell encouraged his supporters to go out and preach and reap the harvest before the end, saying "We believe none will be of the little flock (i.e. the church) except preachers".[14] Russell's pamphlets were distributed by his magazine subscribers, through mailing lists, and by boys hired to hand them out outside church doors. From 1881, he encouraged the most committed Bible Students to take up the work full-time as "colporteurs" (later known as "pioneers"). These colporteurs spent:

> the majority of their time travelling around, usually in pairs, staying a few days in each town or city, and either self-supporting or living off the ten cents a copy commission they received on each paperbound copy of *Millennial Dawn* (Russell's book) they sold to the public for twenty-five cents.[15]

These colporteurs are said to have developed as a self-conscious elite within the movement compared to the other active followers,[16] known as "volunteers" who gave only a few hours each week to literature distribution, etc. In 1894, Russell also established a body of "Pilgrims" (later known as "Circuit Servants") to travel around the various groups of Bible Students in a particular area to give addresses and counsel and ensure doctrinal conformity.

Russell came to view himself as "the chief instrument of God during the initial period of Christ's second presence".[17] His attacks on the clergy led to much hostility for the Bible Students. This sharpened considerably in situations of national crisis, such as war, however, when Witnesses became conscientious objectors; or under totalitarian regimes (Malawi, Hitler's Germany) where the refusal of the Witnesses to acknowledge the state as their first loyalty had led to considerable persecution. The Witnesses' break with conventional society has never been as sharp, however, as that of the early Children of God, and in recent decades, in

Western democratic societies, the movement has generally become tolerated and accepted as little more than an occasional doorstep nuisance.

The active evangelism of the movement has continued, however, and its spread has produced followers with very varying degrees of attachment and involvement. James Beckford has observed that among Witnesses in Britain there are those Publishers (i.e. ordinary members) who remain orthodox in belief but are no longer enthusiastic about the work of doorstep proselytization and literature distribution. Whereas this would once have provoked reprimand and sanction, this is now rare, and there has grown a category of

> lapsed and inactive Publishers who make only occasional appearances at Kingdom Hall...changes in the post-war situation of Western Jehovah's Witnesses have gradually eroded the formerly strict boundaries around each congregation and have facilitated the formation of a kind of "associate membership".[18]

The Witnesses have tempered their attacks on the Catholic Church. They no longer act as if the end were quite so imminent, many congregations having purchased or built Kingdom Halls, suggesting an investment in the future. They now lay less stress on the evils of the world and are no longer quite so ready to exclude those who do not conform closely to movement practices.

A number of similarities can be found in another movement known by various names such as the Cooneyites.[19] William Irvine became an evangelist with the Faith Mission nine years after its founding in 1886. The Pilgrims of the Mission, travelling in pairs throughout rural Scotland and Ireland, conducted evangelistic meetings in local halls and urged those converted to attend both local church and Mission prayer-meetings. Irvine, however, influenced by socialist thought, was becoming hostile to the clergy and churches, seeing them as serving the interests of the wealthy.[20] He became convinced that the path of discipleship involved travelling in complete dependence upon and faith in God, without more than the clothes he wore and without money in the bank; and he began following this regime and preaching it to others, breaking with the

Faith Mission around 1901. Those who accepted Irvine's view sold their possessions, giving the proceeds "to a common fund, left their homes and families and dedicated themselves to live entirely by faith".[21] They were

extremely hostile to professed Christians who rejected their warnings, eventually identified the churches with the authorities who crucified Christ, and cried hell and woe for everyone who refused to sell up everything and become followers of the new way.[22]

Some families resisted the desire of the converts to abandon conventional life, and as would be the case with the Children of God over sixty years later:

It was their goal to divide and disrupt families because their revolution had to break family power over the convert; all such ties were forsaken by young preachers whose where-abouts were often unknown to their parents, and preachers frequently shocked their audience by condemning their family and parents to hell, as Irvine did, on the grounds that they did not follow the pattern of Jesus or his sent ones.[23]

The "tramp preachers", travelling two by two in poverty and chastity, spread throughout the British Isles and to America, Australasia, Europe and Africa. As the movement grew, adherents were gained who were unwilling or unable to follow completely the rigours of the "Jesus Way". Although these adherents were at first harangued by Irvine,[24] and although many preachers considered that their life-style was a departure from the movement's ideal of true discipleship, their willing support of the preachers gradually led to their acceptance. The movement thus began to differentiate into supporters who stayed at home, tramp preachers, and over-seers "who directed the preachers and controlled discipline, order and finance".[25] Irvine began to shift his ideology into alignment with this pattern, expelling those preachers who voiced the now contrary opinion that this was a departure from the commandment of Matthew 10 and the true "Jesus Way". The formation of household churches was sanctioned.[26]

Irvine's beliefs began, in other respects, to conflict with those of leading overseers, particularly with regard to his belief in his own divine anointing and in the end of the age of grace. They began to isolate him from the mass following, refusing to allow him to address conventions of supporters. From 1919, he was effectively excluded from the movement, as subsequently were any followers who maintained allegiance to him.[27] Edward Cooney, an early leading preacher in the movement[28] who continued to oppose its gradual drift towards middleclass respectability, was excommunicated in 1928. Thereafter the movement considerably moderated its strident hostility to the churches and wider society, and the preachers adopted a more comfortable standard of living. The life of poverty and chastity was no longer assumed to be the sole manner of participation.

These three movements, then, show a number of similarities in their development. Radical rejection of the world, and a demanding witness against it, and to rescue souls from its grasp, is followed by a more moderate tone, a rapprochement with conventional manners and mores, and the growth of a periphery of less committed adherents who accept the principal doctrines but who display little enthusiasm for the rigours of the early mode of discipleship. Those changes are accompanied by a reduction in the hostility directed at the movement from without. These developments seem to fall into the pattern of denominationalization even though they may not take the movement quite so far as the comfortable respectability of contemporary Methodism.

Viewed in terms of the typology that we have outlined above, however, the applicability of the concept of denominationalization must seem more doubtful. It cannot be said that these movements have shifted substantially with respect to their view that they stand alone in possessing the complete truth of God's plan. While they may no longer provoke physical assault in opposition to their practices, they continue to be viewed as distinctively deviant. Moreover, they have not yet exhibited any major departure from their authoritarian conception of the source of truth. Rather, in the cases of the Children of God and the Witnesses (adequate information being unavailable for the Cooneyites), differentiation among the membership has produced a periphery of less closely attached individuals, who are less committed to the movement's

norms and values, and who have thus become more accommodated to society. Members of this periphery have implicitly claimed
in varying degrees the right to determine for themselves what is
acceptable in style of life and level of practice, and what is to be
counted as the truth. The core of members, however, maintain their
distance from conventional values and standards, their high degree
of activism in the pursuit of movement aims, and their subordination
of personal choice and evaluation to some central, authoritative
source. Moreover, although I have no information on this in the
case of the Witnesses, it is clear in the case of the Children of God
that the less committed periphery is regarded with some disdain
by the inner movement activists. Peripheral supporters have
complained that:

> ...often I sense a condescending attitude from full time brethren towards
> the (more peripheral supporters) (Member's letter in *Family News Maga-
> zine*, No. 11, November 1979).

And the movement's leader, although at one stage apparently
willing to accept as a permanent feature even an extremely
passive periphery, has more recently begun to insist that it can be
no more than a transitional stage. Tithing and commitment to the
Letters of the prophet are a minimum criterion for membership,
even for the sedentary supporters, working at jobs and living in
their homeland.

Bryan Wilson has used the term *incipient denominationalism*
to refer to the changes that have taken place among the Cooneyites.[29]
This seems to demand a prescience we do not possess concerning the subsequent course of movement development. Future
leaders of these movements may permit greater individual choice
in matters of belief and practice, and thereby fulfill the promise of
"incipiency". On the other hand, it is equally conceivable that the
present core-periphery situation may continue, serving both to
provide a means of attachment even for those who retain some
degree of individual autonomy in matters of belief and practice,
and as a buffer between the sectarian core and the world. Among
the Amish and the wider Mennonite community in America, such a

situation has persisted for some time. Equally possible would be a rediscovery of its pristine virtues and a return to them,[30] particularly when possessed of the "Gideon's Band" philosophy of the Children of God. The latter have clearly not yet come to any firm view about the extent to which the institutionalization of a periphery of the sedentary, of a laity, is an acceptable feature of the movement.

Hence, to my mind, it makes more sense to regard these movements as having undergone changes away from their earlier sharp *rejection* of the world, to a position of greater *accommodation*. This has been accompanied by *differentiation* within the movement. Yet accommodation and differentiation do not, I feel, entail *denominationalization.* Accommodation may merely involve a recognition that the world is stronger rather than that it is right.

In the case of the Children of God, I have suggested that a number of factors were involved in this development which can be detailed as follows:

1. The disappearance of the movement's original recruitment base. This left it the alternatives of shifting from an evangelical towards a more introversionist character, or of locating new potential constituencies.

2. The rising age of the members which created a desire to settle down, to have a more predictable and secure mode of life, particularly among those who had produced a substantial number of dependent children.

3. The difficulties occasioned by growing 'anti-cult' feeling, particularly in the public response to the Jonestown deaths, which encouraged a less visible ministry.

4. The internal dynamic of the movement's view of history. The proximity of the End-Time—the belief that the Antichrist will become world-ruler by 1985—which encouraged dispersal and a less public ministry. Although the Antichrist will initially work with the Children of God, they believe that he will then reject God and them, leading to their persecution. Therefore life is fraught with danger for them during these final days.

Clearly, elements of this history are quite idiosyncratic, but the general form of the changes that have taken place seems to be mirrored in other world-rejecting movements such as Jehovah's Witnesses and the Cooneyites. It seems plausible that this common pattern results from other factors held in common beyond solely their initial rejection of the world. All three are *virtuoso* movements with pronounced *evangelistic* imperative, committed to calling out the faithful or saving souls. The initial adherents were therefore people possessing a high degree of commitment and also highly mobilizable. Their own enthusiasm and success, however, almost inevitably generated the later situation. As they spread their message they recruited among people who, whether because they were less alienated from the world, or because of commitments and ties to it which they could not readily abandon, were less mobilizable than themselves. Thus, they began to develop a structure of membership which differentiated between virtuoso and householder, the peripatetic and the sedentary. In the course of time, even the most actively peripatetic grow older, produce children if celibacy is not enjoined, and thus generate their own ties and commitments which provide reasons for a more settled, less activist mode of life.

On the slight evidence currently available, this pattern also seems to be characteristic of other contemporary world-rejecting new religious movements such as Krishna Consciousness and the Unification Church. The former, for example, is encouraging more limited forms of attachment than the early complete transformation of life required of its young devotees. The Unification Church has begun a "Home Church" programme for those whose interest in or commitment to the church is less total than that of the early disciples. Moreover, the latter has also begun to develop a dialogue with theologians of other, particularly evangelical, faiths, with scientists and social scientists, and to send graduates of its own seminary to liberal theological colleges at major American universities.

H.R. Niebuhr's theory of the transition from sect to denomination argues that this is the result of the appearance of a second and subsequent generations whose life experience has not led them to the zeal and enthusiasm of their parents, and whose improved social circumstances encourage them to accommodate their religious practice to the socially dominant mores. This is undoubtedly the pattern of a number of historical cases. However it is clearly not the *inevitable* consequence of recruitment from the sect's own offspring that Niebuhr believed.[31] Some sects are able to maintain their character apparently indefinitely by insulating their children from the world, by maintaining tests of merit, knowledge or worth, which require the extensive socialization of new recruits and limit the automatic acceptance of offspring as full members, and by preserving a conception of the world as fundamentally evil or dangerous.

Some movements, such as the Unification Church, may be making this transition in the course of their first generation. Reference to the typology provided earlier suggests that a more generalized version of Niebuhr's theory is, none the less, largely accurate. That is, if sectarianization is a strategic response to movement precariousness,[32] denominationalization is a strategic response to social disapproval—i.e., an effort to cultivate greater social respectability. In pluralistic, liberal democratic societies acceptance of a religious movement as non-deviant is considerably encouraged by the movement displaying its tolerance and acceptance of the legitimacy of *other* religious groups. This in turn is encouraged by the emergence within the movement itself of toleration for a diversity of opinion.

The rising hostility to 'cults', and particularly to the Unification Church, is clearly not an insignificant factor in these developments. The Unification Church appears to have adopted a strategic response to the syndrome of the disappearance of its original Western constituency; rising age of members; and social disapproval, of a kind which may presage a relatively early transition to denominationalism. The Unification Church has clearly done more to pursue respectability than the Children of God, and the response to the social circumstances detailed above is therefore evidently a variable mediated by the strategic decisions of movement members. The Unification Church may have gone further along the road to the pursuit of respectability *and* to acknowledging that other groups and churches have access to the truth and salvation as well as themselves than the Children of God, and thus towards initiating the transition from sectarianism to denominationalism.

Changes have taken place in the leadership patterns in all the three movements that were compared above. All have experienced problems related to leadership and authority. These have been resolved in essentially similar ways in the Children of God and the Jehovah's Witnesses, but with a very different outcome for the Cooneyites.

As we saw in Part I, in the Children of God, Moses David has found throughout that intervening leaders have proved to be an obstacle to the complete implementation of his will. His own family and the hierarchy of leaders who were in direct touch with the following have been seen by the prophet as a countervailing force. His response has been to oust the intransigent members in his own family and elsewhere in the chain of command; to elevate to leadership only those with no other basis of legitimation than his approval; and, most recently, effectively to eliminate all intervening leadership between himself and the local communities of followers.

In the movement that later became known as Jehovah's Witnesses, C.T. Russell sought to exercise some control over his following through the Pilgrim service of visitation to local congregations, and by ousting those, including his wife, who challenged his authority, although this initial step toward central control was taken much further by his successor, J.F. Rutherford. Rutherford imposed a test of doctrinal orthodoxy on Elders of the ecclesias (congregations)[33] and sought to constrain their influence on doctrinal interpretation. Beckford notes that:

> ...Elders in the same neighbourhood were forbidden to form "speakers' circuits" in which, during Russell's presidency, the more talented orators had enjoyed considerable freedom of expression and public esteem (and) they were explicitly discouraged from creating their own exegetical or liturgical styles in preference to the pattern of uniform ecclesial meetings that Rutherford was trying to establish.[34]

In 1932, he ended election of Elders, replacing it by appointments made by officials of the Watch Tower Society. Russell, and subsequently, Rutherford succeeded in expelling or forcing the withdrawal of all dissenters, and thereby secured unchallenged central control.

The case of the Cooneyites, however, is significantly different. The movement was directed on a regional basis by an overseer and the preachers in his charge. Irvine, who possessed considerable ability as a speaker, travelled around conventions of such workers and followers, addressing and inspiring them. However, at the first major conflict between Irvine and the intervening leadership, it was Irvine who was ousted.

The principal factor operating here would seem to be that Moses David, Russell, and Rutherford, through their effective control of printed communication to the wider following, had a powerful tool for maintaining and advancing their position, apparently lacking in Irvine, who relied on personal contact and personal letters to convey his views and win support. Each of the three movements was faced with a situation in which its growth beyond merely local confines led the leader to be reliant upon the loyalty and obedience of a body of lieutenants exercising control over local operations. These lieutenants thus had the power to intervene between the leader and mass following, modifying or interpreting his message, or implementing it in a fashion of their own choosing, or able to resist *changes* in his message as his revelation unfolded further. Moses David, Russell, and Rutherford, possessing a printed link with followers, were able to mobilize their support against the intervening leadership in a way in which Irvine apparently was not. In the modern world the printed word, as other sect leaders such as Mary Baker Eddy and L. Ron Hubbard have discovered, is a powerful means of overcoming the centrifugal force of world-wide dispersal and of maintaining central control, and this is a lesson that a sect leader ignores at his peril. We lack the information necessary in the case of the Cooneyites to be quite certain of the pattern, but for the Jehovah's Witnesses and the Children of God it is clear that the undermining of intermediate leadership, and standardization and impersonalization of control have been strategies pursued to maintain and even heighten central authority over issues of belief and practice. They were thus expressly designed to *inhibit* tendencies towards a more negotiated form for doctrine and decision-making in which individual members, either severally or collectively, would be the final repositories of truth, and in which the organization would implement policies arrived at by some form of representative democracy. Whatever minor modifications there may have been in pronouncements about the churches and society, or small accommmodations with the world, and regardless of the growth of a penumbra of less committed members, these movements remain essentially sectarian in virtue of their authoritarian conception of the truth, and there can be little doubt that this has been precisely the goal which their leaders sought in their policies of centralization, standardization and impersonal communication, leadership and control.

FOOTNOTES

1. My researches on the Children of God and related new religious movements have been generously assisted by research grants from The British Academy, the Leverhulme Trust, the Social Science Research Council, and The Queen's University of Belfast. I am grateful to all such sources for their invaluable support, and to Dr. Bryan Wilson for his helpful comments on this paper in draft.
2. Roy Wallis, *Rebirth of the Gods? Reflections on the New Religions in the West*, Belfast: The Queen's University, 1978; see also, "The elementary forms of the new religious life", *The Annual Review of the Social Sciences of Religion*, 3, 1979, pp. 191-216.
3. Unless otherwise indicated all references to Children of God sources are from the letters of Moses David printed for distribution to his followers. These letters are identified here by a title and the date of initial promulgation.
4. Although Mo says he is "as much convinced as ever" about this, I have been unable to locate any prior explicit statement of this view.
5. Roy Wallis, *Salvation and Protest: Studies of Social and Religious Movements*, London: Frances Pinter, New York: St. Martin's Press, 1979. See especially chapter 5.
6. Bryan R. Wilson, "An analysis of sect development", *American Sociological Review*, 24, 1959, p. 4.
7. *Ibid.*, pp. 4-5.
8. John Wilson, *Religion in American Society*, N.J.: Prentice Hall, Englewood Cliffs, 1978, p. 142.
9. *Ibid.*, pp. 150-168.
10. David Martin, "The denomination", Appendix to his *Pacifism*, London: Routledge

& Kegan Paul, 1976, pp. 208-224. Originally published in *British Journal of Sociology*, 13, 1, 1962.

11. Roy Wallis, *The Road to Total Freedom: A Sociological Analysis of Scientology*, London: Heinemann Educational Books, 1976 (Columbia University Press, New York, 1977).

12. *Ibid.*, pp. 11-18.

13. In earlier years, the Family maintained "school colonies" for their children primarily providing basic knowledge and skills, Bible study, etc., using Montessori methods. They also developed a considerable range of educational aids so that each Family group or colony could carry all it needed to provide educational fundamentals for their children. Education beyond twelve years of age was considered unnecessary.

14. Timothy White, *A People for His Name: A History of Jehovah's Witnesses and an Evaluation*, New York: Vantage Press, 1967, p. 26.

15. Alan T. Rogerson, *A Sociological Analysis of the Origin and Development of the Jehovah's Witnesses and their Schismatic Groups*, unpublished D.Phil. thesis, University of Oxford, 1972, p. 81.

16. *Ibid.*, p. 82.

17. T. White, *op. cit.*, p. 64.

18. James A. Beckford, *The Trumpet of Prophecy: A Sociological Study of Jehovah's Witnesses*, London: Blackwell, 1975, p. 88.

19. Douglas S. Parker & H.M. Parker, *The Nameless Sect*, unpublished manuscript, no date. I am grateful to Mr. & Mrs. Parker for permission to draw upon this unpublished study.

20. *Ibid.*, p.4.

21. *Ibid.*, p. 6.

22. *Ibid.*

23. *Ibid.*, p. 7.

24. *Ibid.*, p. 11.

25. *Ibid.*, p. 11.

26. For some limited observations on this sect in more recent times, in the Pacific Northwest of America, see Keith Crow, *The Invisible Church*, unpublished masters thesis, University of Oregon, 1964.

27. Parker & Parker, *op. cit.*, pp. 19-20.

28. The movement which has no generally agreed name is often referred to as the Cooneyites.

29. B.R. Wilson, "Preface" to Parker & Parker, *op. cit.*

30. Such a pattern was observed for English Quakers by Elizabeth Isichei, "From sect to denomination among English Quakers" in Bryan Wilson (ed.), *Patterns of Sectarianism*, London: Heinemann, 1976, pp. 161-181.

31. B.R. Wilson, *op. cit.*, 1959; *idem Sects & Society*, London: Heinemann, 1961.

32. R. Wallis, *op. cit.*, 1976.
33. J. Beckford, *op. cit.*, p. 31.
34. *Ibid.*, pp. 31-32.

THE RISE AND DECLINE OF TRANSCENDENTAL MEDITATION

William Sims Bainbridge
Daniel H. Jackson

Transcendental Meditation is a simple spiritual exercise practiced at one time or another by a million Americans. Purveyed
through an organized social movement headed by an Indian guru,
Maharishi Mahesh Yogi, "TM" was said to be a scientifically
validated means for improving personal satisfaction and effectiveness. Although TM was derived from Hindu religious tradition,
allegedly it was not a religious practice. However, the inner core of
the movement took on a distinct religious quality, and, in 1977, a
New Jersey court ruled that TM was religious and therefore could
not be taught in public schools. In this essay, we chart the rise and
decline of TM in America, using quantitative as well as qualitative
data, with particular attention to the movement's evolution toward
religious status.

What follows is a basic ethnographic description of the movement, which is a necessary context for understanding the two
major trends in its history. The first of these trends is precisely
measurable: the recruitment curve rises from zero in the mid-1960s
to the peak year of 1975 when 292,517 new meditators were
initiated, and then falls rapidly. The second trend is more subtle but
equally important—an initial emphasis on specific compensators
and conventional rewards changing to an emphasis on general
compensators and religious deviance.

A Secular Magic

Our research is guided by the Stark-Bainbridge theory of religion which offers deductive explanations for the main features of cults as well as of more conventional forms of religion.[1] The theory notes that all humans seek *rewards* and that many rewards are scarce or nonexistent. In the absence of desired rewards, humans often accept *compensators* instead. Compensators are postulations of reward to be attained in the distant future or in some other nonverifiable context. We analyze TM as a *composite* of reward and compensator.

Perhaps few people in modern society feel free to rest during the day. American culture sets a rapid pace of activity and accomplishment, with no mandated afternoon tea or siesta. Because Transcendental Meditation was supposed to accomplish important social benefits rather than being sheer self-indulgence, it gave meditators authority to stop and rest. Thus, the *reward* gained through TM (rest) was facilitated by the assertion that the technique was something *more* than a means to that reward.

As we shall see, the *compensators* that were associated with TM ranged from the claim that the practice would increase the meditator's mental clarity and energy to the grand hope that widespread meditation would utterly transform human society. In the Stark-Bainbridge theory, *magic* can be distinguished from *religion* by the narrower scope of compensators it offers. TM's more modest claims are not religious in nature. They promise specific benefits, capable of empirical test, and enter the realm of magic. The more grandiose claims—some shared by core members of the movement from the beginning, others publicly announced only recently—fully qualify TM for the status of religion. They promise the most general and astonishing benefits.

TM's greatest public relations success was not the movement's endorsement by the Beatles musical group or other celebrities, but the large number of articles published in scientific journals, apparently proving TM's claims or at least giving them scientific status. "Physiological Effects of Transcendental Meditation," by the TM leader Robert Keith Wallace, appeared in *Science,* in the issue of March 27, 1970. Writing with another TM enthusiast, Wallace published "The Physiology of Meditation" in the February 1972 issue of *Scientific American.* These articles proclaimed to a wide scientific audience that TM produced a new state of con- sciousness, distinguishable from the waking state, sleep, or the hypnotic state. Although the very concept of "state of conscious- ness" remains of dubious scientific value, at the end of the 1960s, many scholars accepted it, and lay people assumed that it was a valid part of respectable psychology.

By early 1973, a TM booklet listed eighty-eight more-or-less scientific publications apparently supporting the Maharishi's asser- tions that TM provided an entirely new experience for the mind, and was capable of curing drug addiction; improving work efficiency; facilitating education; increasing life satisfaction; raising athletic performance; and awakening creative abilities. Some of these items were private TM documents, but others were articles pub- lished in respectable scientific journals. The movement used to good propaganda effect this apparent endorsement by the scientific community, distributing reprints of the most favorable articles and citing them at every opportunity. Only after TM had achieved its greatest expansion did a number of debunking articles appear in magazines and journals, suggesting that the original findings had been false or exaggerated.[2]

Further capitalizing on its putative scientific status, the move- ment staged many well-publicized conferences, often sponsored by respectable institutions, such as universities or business groups. TM received many kind words from state and local governments— recognition that was very useful in the cult's publicity. One TM handout listed seventy-six government proclamations, mainly dating from 1973 and 1974, which supported the value of the Transcen- dental Meditation program. Statements from the offices of eight governors and forty-seven mayors were included. The cult particu- larly distributed copies of a resolution adopted by the House of Representatives of the state of Illinois in 1972. This effusive docu- ment urged state agencies to look into the potential of TM as a tool in solving a variety of problems and listed as facts a number of the cult's claims.

The growth of TM in the United States was based to a great extent on its appeal to students and, no doubt, its presentation as an intellectually respectable but novel technique of personal development was especially important with this group. Although the Maharishi had visited the United States briefly in 1959, the real organizational beginning came in 1965, when a favorable response from students at UCLA prompted the formation of the Students International Meditation Society (SIMS), the aegis for much of the later recruitment. In 1967—the first year in which new American initiations could be counted in the thousands—the Maharishi spoke at UCLA, Berkeley, Yale, and Harvard. In 1970, the movement distributed a book of testimonials from 128 meditators who had practiced the technique for an average of 14.5 months. Their average age was 23.3 years, which implied that they began meditating at an average age of twenty-two. Fifty-three percent gave their current occupation as student.

The United States was the most fertile ground for TM. In mid-1971, the German magazine, *Der Spiegel,* reported that 70,000 Americans and nearly 20,000 West Germans had learned TM. *Time* magazine, in 1975, estimated that the U.S. total had risen to 600,000, augmented by half that number elsewhere, including 90,000 in Canada and 54,000 in West Germany. Before we analyze initiation figures more closely, we must understand the practices of the TM movement.

Entering Transcendental Meditation

The sequence of learning Transcendental Meditation is as follows. First, the newcomer attends two free lectures to hear the conceptual basis of the technique and the claims for its value. The student is then invited to enroll for meditation instruction, paying the fee which, in 1977, ranged from $65 for a junior high school student to $165 for a non-student single adult. The actual instruction is carried out in private between the newcomer and teacher. A

Transcendental Meditation "Information Packet for Researchers" described the session:

> The teacher first performs a brief, traditional ceremony of gratitude to the tradition of knowledge from which the TM technique comes. The student witnesses but does not take part in the ceremony; however, he does provide fruit, flowers, and a handkerchief, which are some of the traditional ingredients. Then the new student learns the technique and practices it, first with the instructor and then by himself. He discusses his experience with his teacher, and is given further instructions based on those experiences.

The instructor, be it noted, undertakes the ceremony, while the student merely observes. The ritual is the possession of the core members of the movement—not of the mass of meditators. The ritual is supposed to remind the initiator of the tradition he transmits and to ensure that he do his job precisely as required. But it appears to contain *religious* elements as well. Many teachers saw these as essentially *philosophical* concepts merely expressed through the esoteric language of Hinduism, but the sacred and supernatural qualities of the metaphors were always available for emphasis. The official teacher bulletin, "Explanations of the Invocation," states:

> The Lord of Creation has to maintain all levels of creation—both gross and subtle. Therefore he cannot be limited to any level of time or space, for the Lord is omnipresent—the omnipresent level of life is his abode. The recital of the words helps us to gain Transcendental Consciousness and establish the eternal truth of gaining purity in the inner and outer fields of individual life . . .
>
> The truth of Brahma, the Creator, born of the lotus, rooted in the eternal Being, is conventionally and traditionally depicted by a picture where Lord Narayana, lying in a restful pose, has the stem of a lotus emerging from his navel, and Brahma, the Creator, is seated on that lotus. So the wisdom of Transcendental Meditation, or the philosophy of the Absolute knowledge of integrated life came to the lotus-born Brahma from Lord Narayana.

After the teacher completes his ceremony, he gives the initiate a personal *mantra,* the word that is the "mental vehicle" that permits the person to do Transcendental Meditation by focusing on its sound for each 20-minute session. Meditators were told to keep their mantras secret even from their closest friends. Supposedly, each mantra was carefully selected to harmonize with the individual's nervous system and would not be suitable for other persons. In fact, the mantras were assigned purely on the basis of the new meditator's age, and were taken from a list of just sixteen Sanskrit words.

The day after initiation, the new meditator attends the first of three "checking" meetings, where he and others share their experiences and have their meditating fine-tuned. Over the months and years that follow, the meditator may occasionally visit the local TM Center for free, individual checking. But after initiation, most meditators go their private ways, perhaps continuing to meditate but no longer in contact with the movement. Thus, for the majority, TM was a simple technique learned in a few visits to the local Center. To experience Transcendental Meditation as a religion, one had to become more fully involved.

The next step for someone drawn all the way into the movement might be to attend one of the many Residence Courses that are given throughout the country. These weekend retreats were said to produce gains equalling those of months of twice-daily meditation. They included videotape lectures, group discussions, and yoga exercises. An enthusiastic meditator might attend several such meetings. From October 2, 1975, through May 9, 1976, a total of eighty Residence Courses were scheduled in the Pacific region alone. According to official TM statistics, meditators had spent a total of 110,000 days at Residence Courses in the United States by the end of 1972.

While the introductory lectures leading to instruction in meditation were designed to appear secular and scientific, higher levels of indoctrination contained explicitly religious elements. Advanced Lectures were based on the Bhagavad-Gita, and sought to apply principles from this holy book to problems of modern life. In 1972, the Maharishi videotaped what was said to be the first complete recitation of the Rig Veda in the West, and he also completed an English translation of the Brahma Sutras.

The movement's involvement in formal intellectual education culminated in the establishment of Maharishi International University, an institution of higher indoctrination for TM teachers, first conducted in 1972 in rented facilities at Santa Barbara, California. Later, the campus of the defunct Parsons College in Fairfield, Iowa, was purchased for the university.

The MIU program did not merely include TM training as an additional subject among ordinary academic courses: rather it introduced a new version of each basic college subject, reinterpreted in terms of the movement's ideology, the "Science of Creative Intelligence." Already by its second year at Santa Barbara, MIU offered twenty-four "interdisciplinary" courses, including World Literature and the Science of Creative Intelligence, Art and SCI, Technology and SCI, Music and SCI, Psychology and SCI, Biological Sciences and SCI, and Physics and SCI.

The Science of Creative Intelligence was presented to students through a basic SCI course consisting of color and video cassette lessons based in great measure on the Bhagavad-Gita. The content was an elaboration of claims for Transcendental Meditation, laced with parables and metaphysical postulates, rather than anything that can be recognized as conventional *science.* Like Scientology and Christian Science before it, the Science of Creative Intelligence used the name of science in a scientific age to express its boundless pride. An MIU report explained, "The TM technique enables students to experience directly the pure field of creative intelligence within their own minds, thereby providing a personal basis for the verification of the intellectual concepts presented by the study of SCI." Further study, ascending to ever higher levels of enlightenment on the basis of meditation, supposedly allows the person to see beyond petty political and intellectual disputes to achieve a unification of human knowledge and to turn all energies to the good.

The Movement

Only a minority of meditators took the extra steps toward full movement membership and became teachers. But even one or two percent of a million is a large number. There were only 17 American TM teachers at the end of 1966, but by the end of 1972 a total of 2,555 people had taken the teachers' course. *Time* magazine estimated there were about 6,000 teachers by the middle of 1975, and a movement report claimed that, by January 1977, "over 10,000 teachers had been trained."

The growth of TM was to some extent the spread of small businesses across the landscape.[3] One or more trained teachers would establish a Center, perhaps by renting office space or, more cheaply, by offering introductory lectures and meditation training in schools or homes. After 1972, initiation fees were supposed to be paid to the National Center, with half the amount, less personal income taxes, being returned to the teacher responsible for each new meditator.

In 1972, the standard fee was $35 for a high school student, $45 for a college student, $75 for a non-student adult, and $125 for a non-student married couple. Thus, the amount returned to a teacher for each initiation might be as little as $17.50 (less income tax) or as much as $37.50. Out of the returns, the initiator was supposed to pay his share of maintaining the local Center, including even the cost of publicity materials and of TM's own data forms. It is clear that an initiator needed to handle a very large number of initiations to make a living at this work, but at least there existed a prospect of financial success.

Even in times of peak growth, after the very beginning, there was hardly enough initiating work to go around. In 1973, when 132,634 Americans were initiated, on average only one new client was available each week per trained teacher. Many Centers intentionally distributed the work among their several teachers, rather than allow one or two teachers to predominate while others went without the gratifications (including status in the movement) of being a professional initiator. Teachers, and those in training to be teachers, performed many kinds of unpaid work around the Centers. They put up posters, arranged for lecture rooms, gave promotional speeches, maintained the Center, and gave checking sessions. To the extent that they were unpaid volunteers, all these people were members of a social movement rather than of some kind of profit-making spiritual service corporation.

In many respects, Transcendental Meditation is a *millenarian* movement, promising the radical transformation of society. This message was proclaimed in the booklet, "To Create an Ideal Society."

> The quality of life in society is determined by the quality of life of individual citizens. If citizens are enjoying enrichment of body, mind, and behavior then the whole community will be characterized by peace, harmony, and progress. The Transcendental Meditation program of His Holiness Maharishi Mahesh Yogi provides the technology to develop the full potential of the individual thereby improving the quality of life and creating an ideal society...
>
> Thus, the Transcendental Meditation program is a scientifically validated program to create an ideal society and to usher in and perpetuate the Age of Enlightenment. The ideal society will be a reality sooner as more individuals the world over begin to practice the Transcendental Meditation technique.

In 1972, this millenarian spirit was expressed in the World Plan, a program to bring TM to all the world's people. Members bought World Plan Bonds and contributed to a World Plan Fund. The central organization planned a system of 3,575 future Centers around the world, including 203 for the United States, 241 for the Soviet Union, 543 for India, and 745 for China—a Center for every million people throughout the world. Few of the projected World Plan Centers materialized, but this grand scheme expressed TM's intention to expand until it encompassed all humanity.

Statistics on the Growth of TM

In 1965, the TM organization began keeping fairly careful, and eventually computerized, records of initiations in the United States. Data made available to us report the cumulative total of persons initiated, month by month, from January 1967 through December 1977, a total of 918,281 meditators. Figure 1 summarizes these numbers by year. Other sources indicate that nearly 1,000 Americans had been initiated before 1967, about three-quarters of them in 1966. The growth curve is not smooth. We see initiation declines in 1969, 1974, 1976 and 1977. The peak came in 1975, when nearly 300,000 learned TM. In percentage terms, 1967 was the boom

Figure 1: Annual Growth in TM Initiations in the United States

Year	Cumulative Total at the End of Each Year	Increase in the Year Number	Percent
1966	about 1,000	-	-
1967	5,500	4,459	450%
1968	15,300	9,847	180%
1969	24,800	9,474	62%
1970	45,200	20,444	83%
1971	96,400	51,192	113%
1972	182,700	86,332	90%
1973	315,400	132,634	73%
1974	436,800	121,420	38%
1975	729,300	292,517	67%
1976	869,600	140,273	19%
1977	919,300	49,689	6%

year with a 450 percent growth, while most later years fell far short of 100 percent. Understandably the greatest percentage growth occurred early, since an influx of relatively few neophytes produces rapid percentage growth if the base number of members is low. But these observations ignore the question of *how* persons are drawn to the movement.

Recruitment to deviant religious movements tends to occur through personal relationships—through social bonds.[4] TM itself believed that social bonds were more important than mass media appeals. One set of instructions for public lectures told the recruiter, "Be friendly. Remember, most people start TM because they hear about it from their friends who are strong meditators and are getting good results." If new recruits are brought in by old recruits, then one might postulate the possibility of constant percentage growth. If each meditator brings in just one new meditator each year, then the total will grow by more than 100 percent annually.

This simple model ignores four facts. First, it fails to subtract the number of people who stop meditating or otherwise drop out of the movement—former meditators who may even spread negative sentiments toward TM. Second, it assumes that people make friends at random across the entire population, when in fact many latecomers to the movement are prevented from recruiting anyone because all their friends are already meditators. Third, this model assumes an infinite pool of potential recruits, when in fact meditators may come from certain limited subgroups in the population, perhaps composed of individuals with very special backgrounds . and needs. Fourth, it neglects the competition TM faced—other movements recruiting in the same market—including cultural tendencies that gained prominence after TM's rise.

A more detailed picture of the rise and decline of TM recruitment is shown in Figure 2, a chart of initiations per month for the eleven years 1967-1977. The curve rises fairly steadily to a peak at the beginning of 1974, when February saw 19,121 initiations. Then followed nearly a year of slow decline, until the figures leapt upward again early in 1975. In May of that year 31,443 were initiated, while the all-time high was 39,535 in November. The

TRANSCENDENTAL MEDITATION INITIATIONS PER MONTH

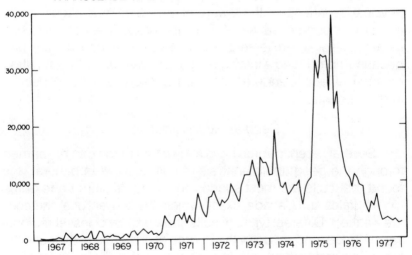

Figure 2: The Rise and Decline of Transcendental Meditation in the United States.

curve then plummets, with only brief halts, to a low of 2,735 in November 1977, only 7 percent of the figure two years earlier. Not only was 1977 the lowest total year since 1970, as Table 1 reported, but November 1977 was lower than any month since December 1970. We have been told informally that, since 1977, initiations have dipped below 1,000 a month.

We cannot attempt here to explain the shape of TM's growth curve, although a few comments can be made. One might simply describe TM as a fad with no inherent staying power. First, the rumor went out that TM was valuable. Many people tried it. Then, perhaps from disgruntled former meditators, the rumor went out that TM was not valuable. When the second rumor caught up with the first, the fad stopped.

The time of catastrophic decline corresponds roughly with a rise in the fee for initiations and a rise in competing fads. For example, in a 1976 book, William Glasser said that *running* is a better way of achieving the same goals sought by TM, and the less organized and cheaper jogging fad may have gained recruits at the expense of TM.[5] Like TM, jogging provided a pleasurable physical experience—the reward of emotional realization—packaged in the compensator-claim that the procedure was a virtuous means of self-improvement. But TM is more than a past fad, because it produced a lasting religious movement with committed members willing to endure but forced to react to a period of decline in recruitment.

Geographic Distributions

Several recent papers have shown that much can be learned through the geographic analysis of cult activity.[6] In general, it is found that cults are most successful in the Western parts of the United States and Canada, exactly where the conventional churches are weakest. Different types of cults show greater or lesser regional variation, dependent upon the degree of *deviance* of the cult. The Stark-Bainbridge theory distinguishes three types of cults, characterized by the difference in degree of radicality of the alternative to conventional culture which each type offers. *Audience cults* display little or no formal organization, are usually carried through the mass media, and provide little more than romantic mythology.[7] *Client cults* range in organizational structure from loose networks of private practitioners to formal service corporations, limit relations with customers to short-term exchanges with relatively narrow aims, and provide specific magic. *Cult movements* are fully-fledged deviant religions in high tension with their sociocultural environments, seeking to monopolize their congregations' spiritual energies.

Transcendental Meditation confronted the world as a mixture of client cult and cult movement. For most meditators, it provided only a brief educational experience. For teachers and other committed members, TM became an all-encompassing cult movement.

Figure 3 is a pair of maps of the United States, showing rates of TM activity per million urban inhabitants in each of the nine geographic regions. Data for the first map comes from a TM training manual printed in October 1972, which lists 1,977 teachers working at 135 Centers across the country, in 43 states and the District of Columbia. The geographic distribution is almost identical to the patterns previously found for other cult movements. The Pacific region has the highest rate, while the Mountain region comes second, and the East South Central region is lowest. The chief departure from past findings about cult movements is the somewhat elevated New England rate. These figures show the cultural receptivity to religious deviance in different parts of the nation.

The second map shows rates of initiations per million urban inhabitants, the data being derived from the very complete membership files made available to us by the TM organization. We tabulated the number of persons initiated from 1967 through 1977, whose homes were in 5,629 urban areas, and which constituted a total of 735,280 meditators. While the distribution of meditators reflects that of teachers, there are significant differences. Now the Mountain region achieves the same rate as the Pacific, and for the first time in our geographic studies, the New England rate is highest. A special receptivity to client cults that do not appear religiously deviant has already been noted for the New England

TEACHERS PER MILLION, 1972

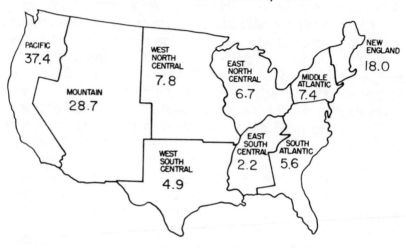

INITIATES PER MILLION, 1967-1977

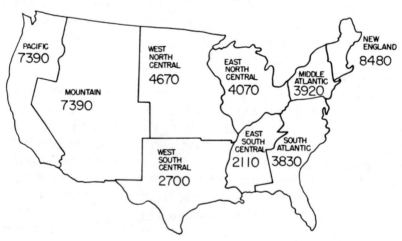

Figure 3: Geographic Distribution of the TM Movement.

region, and apparently TM was especially able to exploit this market from its strong base at Yale, Harvard, and other universities in this region.

That Transcendental Meditation was a socially acceptable client cult for meditators but a deviant cult movement for teachers, is seen not only in the gross pattern of the two maps, but also in comparison of the intensity of variation between them. In 1972, 15.6 percent of the nation's urban population lived in Alaska, Washington, Oregon, California and Hawaii, the states of the Pacific region. But 24.3 percent of the meditators and fully 45.7 percent of the teachers lived in this region. Thus, the Pacific region had somewhat more than its share of meditators, who participated only as *clients,* and much more than its share of teachers, who were fully *members* of the movement. New England, more receptive to client cults than to cult movements, had 6.0 percent of the urban residents, 10.7 percent of the meditators, but just 8.4 percent of the teachers. For meditators, the highest region had 4.0 times the rate of the lowest region, while for teachers the ratio of highest over lowest was 17.0!

Examination of the growth of TM in the nine regions, year by year, reveals that national trends predominate. In each region, the number of initiations rises from 1970 to 1971, 1971 to 1972, and 1972 to 1973. But then, in each of the nine regions, the number drops very slightly from 1973 to 1974, before leaping up to the peak year of 1975. The figures for 1976 drop by half across the board, and plummet still further for 1977, the lowest year since 1970. Although there are great regional differences in *rates* each year, the *trends* are remarkably synchronized. This suggests that regional differences are not simply a matter of geographic backwaters that are out of communication with cultural centers. Rather, standards of judgment vary across the nation, and new trends are communicated rapidly but received differently.

Figure 4 examines the geographic distribution of urban initiates in a final way—through measures of the *variation* across states and the *correlations* across states for pairs of years. The first column of figures reports the coefficient of variation for each of the

*Figure 4: Rates of TM Initiation for the Fifty States
and the District of Columbia*

Year	Coefficient of Variation	Correlation (r) with: 1970	1977
1970	1.14	1	.86
1971	0.95	.89	.83
1972	0.85	.85	.86
1973	0.77	.88	.87
1974	0.59	.81	.87
1975	0.58	.74	.81
1976	0.57	.85	.93
1977	0.78	.86	1

years. High coefficients of variation mean big differences in the rates of initiation in various states. Low coefficients of variation mean smaller differences from state to state.

The coefficient of variation drops steadily from 1970 when it is 1.14 to 1974 when it is 0.59. This shows the broadening acceptance of TM as a relatively non-deviant client cult. Despite the fact that the total figure more than doubles from 1974 to 1975, and drops by more than half to 1976, the coefficient of variation is nearly constant for these three years: 0.59, 0.58, and 0.57. This establishes a limit to the evenness of distribution which TM was able to achieve when most popular and least deviant. In the final year, the coefficient rises again to 0.78, a fact to which we shall later return.

The second and third columns in Figure 4 give the correlations (Pearson's r) linking state rates for 1970 and 1977 with the rates for other years. Of course, there is a tendency for the rates in any one year to correlate most highly with rates for adjacent years: 1970 correlates most highly with 1971, and 1977 most highly with 1976. Each has the weakest association with 1975, the peak year of initiations. But the most striking feature of the correlations in Figure 4 is that all the rest of them are almost identical, falling in the narrow range from 0.81 to 0.87. The correlation between the extreme years, 1970 and 1977, is one of the highest, 0.86. This means that the pattern of rates remained about the same over the eight years, even while the rates and their spread moved over wide ranges. Again, we see evidence that the reception TM received from state to state was a function of differential regional responses to religious deviance rather than being merely a result of slow communication of the TM fad into cultural backwaters.

The Decline and Transformation to a Cult Movement

The Stark-Bainbridge general theory of religion predicts that when people are denied access to desired *rewards* they are apt to accept *compensators* instead. This is facilitated if the people involved already exchange compensators of some level of generality, and need only increase the emphasis on compensators as rewards become unavailable. Applied to the case of TM, a movement that always had a religious aspect for inner members, the theory predicts *an intensification of the supernatural element as a response to the decline in initiations.*

We have seen that the decline in initiations was extreme, a drop of 93 percent from November 1975 to November 1977. By the beginning of 1977, 10,000 people had been trained to perform initiations, but only 49,689 meditators were added to the movement in 1977. Thus, on average the teachers could have initiated only *five* new meditators each in the entire year! Of course, many teachers had already quit the movement. But others, losing their main source of material and status rewards within TM, must have been open to the offer of new and more powerful compensators.

One reward that many teachers lost in 1977 was quite tangible— credits toward Advanced Training and Refresher (ATR) course tuitions and expenses. According to the system in effect at the end of 1973, a teacher would earn credits for each new meditator he taught. Each initiation was worth 1 percent of the $535 fee for the six-week course in Switzerland, plus 1 percent of the transportation costs up to a total of $250. A letter to all initiators from the World Plan Executive Council, dated July 21, 1977, wiped out all such credits, citing the decrease in initiations as its justification. Not only did members lose a promised return on investment, but they had good reason to feel cheated by the central organization that now failed to meet its obligation to them. By offering what appeared to be greater rewards, TM might restore the dedication of members.

Millenarian movements never succeed in recruiting all potential members, and they have developed various tactics for convincing their adherents to keep up their hopes. One is the idea that success, rather than requiring the recruitment of the whole population, can be achieved by a small but critical number of members. An article published in 1973, in a TM handout directed at the military, quoted the Maharishi as saying, "If only one-tenth of the adult population of the world were regularly to meditate for short periods every day...war would be impossible for centuries to come." After recruitment dropped precipitously, and that one-tenth seemed out of reach, TM claimed that society would be improved radically if only one-hundredth of people were meditators. A 1977 flier for Maharishi International University claimed that crime and other social problems diminished greatly when this more modest level of meditation was reached. The 1977 MIU catalog went even further, asserting that world peace could be achieved when only one-thousandth of humanity meditated.

A decisive change in the TM movement came with the announcement of "a new breakthrough in human potential," the *siddhis*. MIU's 1977 catalog says, "The siddhis are performances of higher states of consciousness described in the yoga system of Patanjali, one of the six systems of Indian philosophy which elaborate the knowledge of the Vedas." Among the attendant qualities are "the ability to know the past and future, knowledge of other minds, the ability to become invisible, passage through the sky...." An addendum pasted into the catalog described siddhis as "supernormal powers," and announced, "Students entering MIU in the fall of 1977 will be among the first to qualify for these historic new courses and raise their capabilities to the level of the *siddha* (superman): command over material nature by mere intention of the mind." A handout advertising a public lecture on this breakthrough listed among the new results of TM: "levitation, invisibility, mastery over nature, fulfillment of all desires and aspirations, creation of an ideal society in the Age of Enlightenment."

Some of the siddhi qualities could be construed as subjective feelings of peace and rapture that were given exaggerated or poetic names because they were unusually splendid. "Levitation" might be a metaphor for a sensation of intense relaxation, while "invisibility" might mean a freedom from social anxiety. Whatever the Maharishi meant by those terms, the movement took them literally. In so doing, TM took *the final step from client cult to cult movement* and entered the realm of supernatural religion.

Supernatural claims were published alongside more modest brain-wave studies in the booklet *Enlightenment and the Siddhis,* issued by Maharishi European Research University in Switzerland. One testimonial reported an experience of clairvoyance, while another described levitation:

> A friend has lost a pen. He said it was in the hotel kitchen that he had lost it and when I did the technique I saw it in my mind under some boards by the stove. When I went to look for it later, I found it exactly where I had seen it while practicing the technique.

> I was sitting on a couch meditating at the time. I felt a tremendous amount of energy go through me and simultaneously I had a vision of my spine and my chest being just white light and a form in the air some place and then my body moved up and down on the couch about three times. I thought, 'Oh, what is that?' and the next experience I had was of hearing my body touch the floor. I say 'hearing' because I didn't feel it until after I heard it. It touched down, very, very softly. There was very little feeling of contact. I moved about a six foot distance at that time.

Not only was such levitation supposed to be the *subjective sensation* of floating through the air, but *physical* suspension and movement as well. The Siddhi booklet was accompanied by a photo labeled, "Canadian Christiana Quarton flies while sister-in-law Gail and her baby look on." It shows a woman apparently floating cross-legged in mid air. The levitator seems to be six to ten inches above a large mattress upon which another woman sits, holding a small child. There can be no question; the picture purports to show real, physical levitation.

Separately, clairvoyance and levitation are feats of magic. But the Siddhi program promised so many extreme magical benefits that it was a full package of specific compensators comprising the general compensator of true religion.

Public announcement of the Siddhi program was made in April 1977. By mid-May, lecture teams were giving public talks that disappointed many by failing to demonstrate levitation while asserting that it had been achieved. The national television network news programs derisively reported TM's astounding new claims, and suggested that gymnastic meditators might have learned to hop aloft for an instant using their knees or a sudden thrust of their backs. Indeed, the photo of Christiana Quarton could be attributed to just such an athletic accomplishment. She appears to be lightly built. The mattress might provide some trampoline bounce. Her face and flying scarf are blurred as if by rapid movement, although her legs and her hands which are held between them are in sharp focus. Perhaps she had launched herself upward by muscle power, and was caught in the middle of a short bounce by the camera.

Unflattering public attention continued to be directed at TM's levitation for several months. *Newsweek* commented, in its June 13 issue, that the Maharishi had forbidden public demonstrations. In its August 8 issue, *Time* suggested an hypothesis to explain the new turn in TM's career: "What is a maharishi to do when sales start to grow sluggish. One answer; announce a shiny new product."

The most active month of 1977, in terms of initiations, was March when 7,963 newcomers learned to meditate. This figure was far below that of the peak month of November 1975, when there were 39,535 initiations. The introduction of the siddhis certainly did not help the recruiting trend. April, when news of levitation began to leak out, saw only 4,437 initiations, a drop of 44 percent from the previous month. May was down 62 percent from March, at 3,025 initiations. The average for the last seven months of 1977 was 3,169. We cannot be sure that bad publicity about levitation reduced the influx of initiates, since the trend had been downward for more than a year already, but the conclusion is not unreasonable.

Simultaneously with its experiments in levitation, and its public evolution from client cult to cult movement, TM struggled to *avoid* the legal label of *religion*. As we have seen, although TM was based in a religious tradition, for a long time its more religious teachings and practices were revealed only to the inner core of members while ordinary meditators were offered an apparently nonreligious practical technique. Even so, some observers had accused TM of being a religious cult expediently masquerading behind a false scientific mask.[8]

In March 1976, a group of parents, clergy and other interested persons took TM to court in New Jersey, seeking to stop TM programs in the public schools. The plaintiffs charged that TM was religious in nature and had assumed secular camouflage in 1967 or 1968 in order to reach a wider audience. Late in 1977 (after TM had launched levitators but unaffected by this development), a judge of the Federal District Court in Newark halted the TM school programs and announced that he had found that both the courses and the initiation ceremony were of religious character.

The movement's World Plan Executive Council informed the American Centers that it would not appeal against the New Jersey court decision, quoting the Maharishi as saying, "If the law of the country will demand from us that we teach in the name of religion, then fine, we will abide by the law and feel nearer to God." In our view, a successful appeal would have required not only much money for legal fees, but also a transformation of TM's ideology and practices to make them seem more secular. After some indecision, TM did appeal the case, without first reasserting secular status. Early in 1979, the United States Court of Appeals in Philadelphia supported the lower court's ruling that TM was religious in nature.

Conclusion

Transcendental Meditation's emergence as a religious cult movement is related to the fall in initiations documented earlier. Two alternate hypotheses might try to explain the connection.

(1) Transformation into a religious cult movement caused the

drop in recruitment because the general public rejects deviant cults.

(2) The drop in recruitment caused an intensification of the religious element.

The first hypothesis is entirely reasonable, but does not fit the facts. The decline in recruitment began more than a year before levitation and nearly two years before the adverse court decision. Perhaps the changes of 1977 prevented a recovery in recruitment, or forced the figures below what they might otherwise have been: but they could not have caused decline throughout 1976.

The second hypothesis fits well. After recruitment had fallen off, the supply of material and social rewards available for movement members was severely restricted. Furthermore, the decline discredited some TM compensators, notably those that hinted at growing status and other rewards that were to follow as TM became an established cultural force and influential institution in the United States. Loss of expectation of these rewards might be *compensated* by an increase in more extreme postulations of future rewards. That is what happened. No longer able to promise the material and social resources of many new recruits, the movement promised instead magical benefits symbolized by the defiance of physical nature through levitation. Taken together, the promises added up to an almost boundless promise, the general compensator of religion.

The decision of the court was based on the religious aspects of Transcendental Meditation that had always been shared by inner members, not on changes after 1975; but a successful appeal against its ruling might have been achieved through modification of the program for training meditators. The references to Hindu religious texts could have been dropped from the Science of Creative Intelligence courses, and the initiation ritual could have been purged of devotional elements. But a dramatic shift toward greater secularism would have undercut the shift toward greater and more general compensators for inner members. The needs of dedicated TM teachers pressed toward more religion, not less.

Once Transcendental Meditation was publicly branded as a radical cult, public reaction to religious deviance may indeed have reduced recruitment still further. Figure 4 showed a significant rise in the coefficient of variation for recruitment rates across states, from 0.57 in 1976 to 0.78 in 1977. Since this measure had achieved a stable level in 1974 and remained steady for a significant rise and then for a drop in recruitment, this increase for 1977 is probably meaningful. It probably indicates that increased deviance in TM's status was reflected in more varied reaction in different states. We conclude that at least part of TM's 1977 loss was due to an increase in the movement's cultic deviance.

Transcendental Meditation did not die in 1977. The decline left a solidly organized religious cult movement, undoubtedly one of the largest new religions in America. Recruitment continues, if at a greatly reduced rate. Now that highly supernatural magic and general compensators have become the cult's main business, we cannot expect another period of rapid growth. But if it establishes a firm social base in the community of current members, TM may achieve less explosive but more lasting conversions. In its short and brilliant history, Transcendental Meditation shows how the failure of rewards and modest compensators may lead to intensification of the supernatural, and to an evolution from client cult to cult movement.

FOOTNOTES

1. Rodney Stark and William Sims Bainbridge, "Of Churches, Sects, and Cults: Preliminary Concepts for a Theory of Religious Movements," *Journal for the Scientific Study of Religion,* 18, 2, June, 1979, pp. 117-131; *idem,* "Towards a Theory of Religion: Religious Commitment," *Journal for the Scientific Study of Religion,* 19, 2, June, 1980, pp. 114-128.
2. See John White, "A Critical Look at TM," *New Age Journal,* January, 1976, pp. 30-5, *idem,* "Second Thoughts: What's Behind TM?" *Human Behavior,* October, 1976, pp. 70-1, Robert R. Pagano, Richard M. Rose, Robert M. Stivers, and Stephen Warrenburg, "Sleep during Transcendental Meditation," *Science,* 191, January 23, 1976, pp. 308-10, Don Allen, "TM at Folsom Prison: A Critique of Abrams and Siegel," *Criminal Justice and Behavior,* 6, 1, March, 1979, pp. 9-12.

3. See the entrepreneur model of cult formation proposed by Bainbridge and Stark, "Cult Formation: Three Compatible Models," *Sociological Analysis*, 40, 4, Winter, 1979, pp. 283-295.
4. John Lofland and Rodney Stark, "Becoming a World-Saver: A Theory of Conversion to a Deviant Perspective," *American Sociological Review*, 30, 1965, pp. 862-875; William Sims Bainbridge, *Satan's Power: Ethnography of a Deviant Psychotherapy Cult*, Berkeley: University of California, 1978; Stark and Bainbridge, "Networks of Faith: Interpersonal Bonds and Recruitment to Cults and Sects," *American Journal of Sociology*, 85, 6, 1980, pp. 1376-1395.
5. William Glasser, *Positive Addiction*, New York: Harper & Row, 1976.
6. R. Stark, W. S. Bainbridge, and D. P. Doyle, "Cults of America: A Reconnaissance in Space and Time," *Sociological Analysis*, 40, 4, Winter, 1979, pp. 347-359; Bainbridge and Stark, "Superstitions: Old and New," *The Skeptical Inquirer*, 4, 4, Summer, 1980, pp. 18-31; *idem*, "Client and Audience Cults in America," forthcoming in *Sociological Analysis*.
7. For at least superficial quantitative analysis of several audience cults see Bainbridge, "Biorhythms: Evaluating a Pseudo-science," *The Skeptical Inquirer*, 2, 2, Spring-Summer, 1978, pp. 40-56; *idem*, "Chariots of the Gullible," *The Skeptical Inquirer*, 3, 2, Winter, 1978, pp. 33-48, *idem*, "In Search of Delusion," *The Skeptical Inquirer*, 4, 1, Fall, 1979, pp. 33-39.
8. See George E. LaMore, "The Secular Selling of a Religion," *The Christian Century*, December 10, 1975, pp. 1133-7.

Additional Bibliography

Bloomfield, Harold H., Michael Peter Cain, Dennis T. Jaffe and Robert E. Korey, *TM—Discovering Inner Energy and Overcoming Stress*, New York: Dell, 1975.

Denniston, Denise, Peter McWilliams, and Barry Geller, *The TM Book—How to Enjoy the Rest of Your Life*, New York: Warner, 1975.

Forem, Jack, *Transcendental Meditation*, New York: Dutton, 1973. Maharishi International University, *SCI Teacher Training Course*, MIU Press, 1972.

Wallace, Robert Keith, "Physiological Effects of Transcendental Meditation," *Science*, 167, 1970, pp. 1751-4.

Wallace, Robert Keith and Herbert Benson, "The Physiology of Meditation," *Scientific American*, 226, 2, February, 1972, pp. 84-90.

MUST ALL RELIGIONS BE SUPERNATURAL?

Rodney Stark

The most basic intellectual dispute in the scientific study of religion has long been over how to define our subject matter. What phenomena will we classify as religious, and what as something else? The conflict has been whether a supernatural component must be present in a belief system for it to be classified as religion. Many prominent social scientists suggest not,[1] but I have always lined up with the majority, and argued that it creates confusion and a loss of theoretical economy to classify as religions, belief systems that embrace the supernatural as well as those that even may militantly reject it.[2]

In past essays, I have argued that to lump together supernatural and naturalistic faiths is to make it needlessly difficult to explore conflicts between the two or to pursue the rather different capacities present in each. Now I am prepared to go much farther. As Durkheim correctly proclaimed, there can be no church of magic.[3] I maintain that there can be no wholly naturalistic religion: a religion lacking supernatural assumptions is no religion at all. I shall argue here that our definitional dispute does not come down to a matter of taste. I shall try to show that the differences between supernatural and non-supernatural or naturalistic systems are so profound that it makes no more sense to equate them than to equate totem poles and telephone poles.

159

I pursue my thesis at two levels. First, I shall consider theoretical results. Given a few modest axioms about what humans are like and how they behave, and adding some elementary definitions, I shall try to show the manner in which supernatural belief systems have unique capacities, and thus are vitally different from belief systems lacking supernatural premises. From these theoretical results, I shall deduce a number of empirical conclusions, among them: the decline of liberal denominations; secularization as a self-limiting and unstable phenomenon; new religions as the expected response to secularization of older faiths; and I shall contend that radical regimes will remain unable to root out religion, and that the harder they try the more they may invigorate religious opposition. I shall also try to explain why many organizations that begin by being wholly secular evolve into religions. For each of these conclusions I assess available empirical support.

Theoretical Considerations

The conclusion that a supernatural component is the unique aspect which permits religions to sustain enduring organizations has emerged from a newly developed deductive theory of religion.[4]

We start with the mundane axiom that humans seek to gain rewards and to avoid costs. However, when we inspect this human tendency more closely, two important things can be seen:

1. Many rewards are *quite scarce* and are *unequally distributed.* Substantial proportions of any population have far less of some rewards than they desire or than some other persons actually possess. Scarcity, both absolutely and relatively, is a social universal.

2. Beyond the facts of inequality and scarcity, we may note that some greatly desired rewards *seem not to be available at all.* No one can demonstrate whether there is life after death, but it can easily be seen that immortality can not be had in the here and now, in the natural world available to our senses. But simply because the reward of eternal life is not directly available has not caused a diminution in the desire to obtain it.

Noting the strong desires for rewards that are unavailable to many, and for those not directly available to anyone, we can recognize another characteristic human action: the creation and exchange of *compensators*. We do not use the word *compensator* in any pejorative sense. We use it simply to recognize that when highly desired rewards seem unavailable directly, humans tend to develop explanations about how this reward may be gained later and/or elsewhere. Compensators are a form of I.O.U. They promise that in return for value surrendered now, the desired reward will be obtained eventually. Often people must make regular payments to keep a compensator valid, which makes it possible to bind them to long-term involvement in an organization that serves as a source of compensators. Put another way, humans will often exchange rewards of considerable value over a long period of time in return for compensators, in the hope that a reward of immense value will eventually be forthcoming in return.

It is by no means the case that compensators are exclusively religious. They are generated and exchanged throughout the range of human institutions. When a radical political movement instructs followers to work for the revolution now, in return for material rewards later, compensators have been exchanged for rewards. The party receives direct rewards, the followers receive an I.O.U. Similarly, when a parent tells a child, "Be good, work hard, one day you will be rich and famous," a compensator-reward exchange is proposed. Sometimes, of course, compensators are redeemed. But, unless or until they are redeemed, they figure in exchange processes as compensators: that is, they are easily distinguished from the reward itself.

In our system, we identify compensators as forming a continuum from the specific to the highly general. Specific compensators promise a specific, limited reward. The most general compensators promise a great array of rewards and/or rewards of vast scope. A shaman's promise, that, if certain ritual procedures are observed, a person will be cured of warts, is a specific compensator. The promise of a happy life is a general compensator. Elsewhere, we have found this distinction vital in distinguishing between magic and religion, which in turn makes it possible for us to deduce Durkheim's proposition that there can be no church of magic.

When we examine human desires and common varieties of compensators, we can see that humans often desire rewards of such magnitude and scarcity that only by assuming the existence of an active supernatural can credible compensators be created. For example, humans seem not only to want to know the meaning of life, but to desire greatly that it *have* meaning. But, for life to have a great design, for there to be intention behind history, one must posit a designer or intender of such power, duration, and scale that he must be outside or beyond the naturalistic world. Or, for humans to survive death, at least thus far in history, it is necessary to posit supernatural agencies. Indeed, to believe that earthly suffering imposed by scarcity is but a prelude to everlasting glory is to embrace the supernatural. While I am able to deduce this point from our theory, surely the point can stand on its own merit: some desires are so much beyond direct, this-worldly satisfaction that only the gods can provide them. This simple point has profound implications.

So long as humans intensely seek certain rewards which are of great magnitude, and which remain unavailable by direct actions, they will be able to obtain compensators only from sources predicated on the supernatural. In this market, no purely naturalistic system can compete. Systems of thought that reject the supernatural lack all means to promise such things as eternal life, in any fashion. Similarly, naturalistic philosophies may argue that questions such as, "What is the meaning of life?" or, "What is the purpose of the universe?" are meaningless utterances. But they cannot provide answers to these questions in the terms in which they are asked.

This profound difference in compensator-generating capacity provides the basis on which we have chosen to define religions as *systems of general compensators based on supernatural assumptions.*[5] Our intention is to isolate those systems of thought that have the capacity to deal with human desires of maximum scope, intensity, and scarcity, from those systems lacking such a capacity.

The fact that this definition parallels what common sense has always meant by religion is convenient and probably not accidental. Social scientists are not singularly qualified to recognize fundamental features of human society. Indeed, it is hard for people not trained in social science to fail to notice that religions are a unique source of maximum compensators.

Furthermore, our theoretical analysis leads to some rather dramatic conclusions. Consider this one: ideologies lacking supernatural assumptions cannot successfully compete, over the long run, in generating commitment when confronted by ideologies that accept the supernatural. To be more specific: so long as humans persist in desires that cannot be directly satisfied, the eventual fate of wholly "demythologized" churches, for example, is sealed. Or one may conclude that while modern-day communism is in conflict with religion, it is not itself a religion and remains permanently vulnerable to religious competitors, especially once communist regimes come to power.

To sum up: these theoretical results hold that not only is the notion of a non-supernatural or naturalistic religion a logical contradiction, but that, in fact, efforts to create naturalistic religions will fail for want of that vital resource that has always been the *raison d'etre* of religion: *the gods.*

Empirical Evaluation

A considerable array of empirical evidence, both old and new, can be used to test specific deductions from these theoretical results.

The first obvious empirical implication is that *for religious organizations to move markedly in the direction of non-supernaturalism is to pursue the path to ruin.* For a variety of reasons not relevant here, a number of major Christian and Judaic groups have discarded their traditional system of compensators, and today offer such compensators in only a very weak form. Their conception of the supernatural has receded to a remote, inactive, almost non-existent divinity. We find bishops and theologians who not only reject the divinity of Jesus, but who suggest that notions of a god "up there" are simple-minded and superstitious. They say little about whether a god who is not "up there" has anything potent to offer the dying, the poor, or those who seek purpose in the enigma of existence. Our theoretical results force the conclusion that to the extent a religious organization "demythologizes" and moves toward naturalism, it will fail to kindle the levels of commitment obtained during a more supernaturally-oriented period. I think we have abundant evidence that this is so.

While there is some disagreement about how much better off the more conservative Christian denominations are at present, there is agreement that the liberal churches are in organizational decline.[6] Membership is down. Indeed, in the 1960s, there was widespread evidence of apathy and dissatisfaction in the pews of the more liberal denominations. The majority of members of these denominations agreed that their religion did not provide them with satisfactory answers to the meaning and purpose of life.[7]

These signs of decay are not limited to the rank-and-file. In a subsequent study, we found that the then much-publicized "New Breed" of clergy held little hope for regenerating these bodies. They had discarded nearly all traces of traditional supernaturalism to embrace this-worldly political and moral rhetoric and concerns. But these were insufficient to sustain even their own commitment to the church, let alone those of the laity—a conclusion which follows from the fact that the majority of the "New Breed" liberals doubted they would become clergy again if they had the choice to make over.[8]

If it is the loss of supernatural resources to provide strong compensators that is the cause of the declining vigor of the liberal churches, then it should follow that *people who drift out of these churches do not do so primarily to embrace secular humanism.* While such people may become unchurched, they should not be considered irreligious in the sense of having rejected supernaturalism. Again, there is much evidence to sustain this conclusion.

In the late 1960s, Charles Glock and I were, as far as I know, the first persons to examine empirically the phenomenon of denominational switching.[9] Our data were quite puzzling. There was more switching from the conservative to the liberal bodies than in the reverse direction. Nevertheless, the liberal bodies were not growing, while the conservatives were. At the time, we failed to grasp the whole picture. We did note that the most conservative groups attracted large numbers of people who reported they had grown up without a religion. Thus, we saw that some people who may drift out of the liberal churches into an irreligious condition may eventually be drawn to a more traditional faith. We should have guessed, also, that even if those who drop out of the liberal churches never reaffiliate, *their children tend to do so* and to display a preference for the more conservative churches. Moreover, many who drift out of the liberal churches and do not reaffiliate are not, as Glock and I supposed, primarily irreligious in terms of belief.

Let me review a considerable body of more recent facts in support of these generalizations. When we examine geographic patterns of church membership we find little variation over much of the country.[10] The South does not have higher rates of membership than the Northeast or the Midwest. But the Far West differs immensely from the rest of the nation. In an unbroken belt, running from San Diego through Anchorage and including Hawaii, church membership is very low. While elsewhere in the nation membership runs at almost two-thirds, along the Pacific it runs at only one-third. A similarly large difference between the West and the rest exists with respect to church attendance.

Despite the weakness of the organized churches on the West Coast it would be wrong to describe this region as a bastion of secularity. People there are only unchurched, not irreligious. When we examine poll data on religious beliefs, the contrasts between the Far West and other regions are quite minor. For example, the proportion of atheists and agnostics is 2 percent for the South, 3 percent for the Midwest, and rises to only 7 percent in the Pacific region. Belief in life after death runs at about 80 percent in the rest of the nation, and is affirmed by about 70 percent in the Pacific region. These are differences. But compared with church-membership and church-attendance differences they are slight. Moreover, they indicate that although the average person on the West

Coast is unchurched, he or she continues to accept the supernatural. As we shall see, this combination contributes much to the religious volatility of the region. Even more telling evidence, that defection from the major denominations is not evidence of the growth of secular humanism can be found in the many studies that have pursued further the phenomenon of church-switching.[11]

What is the least stable religious background in the United States? The secular home! Analysis of merged national samples from the annual General Social Surveys find that of Americans who described the religions of their parents as "None," less than 40 percent remained without a religious affiliation. Thus while the many religious groups in the nation typically retain 70 percent or more of their born-members, the majority of those who are raised without religions convert. Although the press thought it news recently when Madalyn Murray O'Hair, the militant atheist leader, was denounced by her son who has become a "Born Again" Christian, this was not really unusual. Instead, as witnessed by the national data, irreligiousness seems very hard to transmit from parent to child.

The instability of secularism ought not surprise us. We recognize that offspring of radical sectarians often tend towards a less severe faith because they do not wholly inherit the extreme life circumstances that impelled their parents' faith. We ought equally to recognize that the children of the irreligious will tend towards faith because they do not wholly inherit the usual life circumstances that made their parents feel comfortable without religious compensators.

If these various facts mean what I think they do, then American patterns of denominational switching are part of a dynamic process that might be seen as a moving equilibrium. Despite member shifts away from the more conservative churches, the liberals decline because of even heavier losses into the ranks of the unchurched. The conservatives continue to grow because they are able to offset their losses by attracting people back from the ranks of the unchurched. And the truly secular proportion of the population grows little, if at all, because the majority of the unchurched remain believers, and the majority of the sons and daughters of the truly secular part of the population return to religion.

The question is, to what religions will they return? We have already seen that many return to denominations offering stronger rather than weaker compensators. But that is not all that is going on. Secularization is a self-limiting process. Major religious organizations may turn towards secularism and crumble. But that does not necessarily imply the demise of religion. Instead, to the extent that religious competition and innovation are not suppressed by the state, *new faiths will arise offering a stronger version of the supernatural.* These new faiths will prosper as the old ones fade. We have made a number of quite powerful tests of this proposition.[12] If organizational weakness of dominant faiths prompts religious innovation, then we ought to find that new religions (which we identify as cults) will flourish where the churches are weakest. Having recently developed means to assign church-membership rates to the nation's cities, counties, states, and regions, we needed only good measures of cult activity to test this proposition. A number of measures of cult prevalence and activity could be constructed.

Our first measure is based on our coding of 501 current cult movements in the United States.[13] Dividing the number of cults located in a state by the state's population produced a rate per million. When we examined the joint distribution of state cult and church-membership rates, the correlation was found to be -.61—a powerful relationship indeed. Because our cult membership rate had certain built-in limitations, we turned to many other measures. One of these is based on 1,345 New Age centers and communities listed in the *Spiritual Community Guide* (1974). This rate is correlated with church membership at -.52. We constructed another measure, based on a national list of New Age bookstores, foodstores, and restaurants. The observed correlation was -.58. We also coded three decades of letters published in *Fate* magazine by readers reporting personal mystical experiences. Each letter included the writer's city and state and thus with 2,086 letters to work from we could construct a fairly reliable rate for states. The correlation with church membership: − .58. The publishers of *Fate* were kind enough to give us state-by-state circulation figures. Using these data based on more than 80,000 subscribers we again created state rates and found these rates to be correlated − .68 with our church-membership rates. A further measure of cult activity was based on more than 200,000 initiates into Transcendental Meditation for the year 1975. These rates were correlated − .51 with church membership. Finally, from the nation's *Yellow Pages,* we created state rates of astrologers with a business listing. The correlation with church membership was − .35.

In addition we have a data set based on coding the nation's existing sect movements. Sect formation is strongly negatively related to cult activity. Sects flourish where the churches are organizationally stronger. They may well reflect efforts by the churched to remain churched, while cults seem better described as efforts by the unchurched to become churched.

These data expand our understanding of the unique power of supernatural compensators and reiterate the proposition that secularity is an unstable rather than an absorbing state. When I wrote *American Piety* I failed to realize this. Recognizing that substantial numbers of people must be dropping out of the liberal denominations, I assumed that they had joined the ranks of secularists, and that there most of them would stay. For a secular person, immersed in university life, that is, of course, rather easy to believe. But it seems not to be so. People tend not to remain in secularity and, more important, secularity travels poorly down the family tree.

Perhaps even more important is that merely to state one's religious preference as "None," is a poor measure of what we understand by secularity. In a recent study of occult interests and beliefs among college students, the group with much the highest level of belief and interest were those who gave their religious affiliation as "None."[14] (This was confirmed by our computations performed on Robert Wuthnow's data for his Bay Area youth sample.) Too often, when one notices that about 20 percent of university students (as was true in our sample) say they have no religion, one takes that as another sign of the rising tide of secularization. But one must surely think again on discovering that 73 percent of these secularists believe there is probably great value in Yoga, Zen, and Transcendental Meditation; that 62 percent of them express some interest in "occult literature;" and that 22 percent of them express faith in astrology. Lest one dismiss this as rampant student silliness, be advised that only tiny proportions of students who claimed to be "Born Again" Christians held similar views. Indeed, the "Born Again" were by far the most resistant of religious groups to pseudo-science and popular occultism. Thus, we must question whether demonstrations of variation in the proportions of populations claiming no religious affiliation in fact tell us anything significant about variations in the strength of secularism. Unless one wants to push the definition of religion to such restrictive limits that only standard brands are to be counted, then these supernaturally-oriented "Nones" are not irreligious.

I must mention additional evidence that secularity is an unstable state. Several studies have found Jews to be very over-represented in some of the leading new religions such as the Unification Church and the Hare Krishna Movement.[15] Indeed, data that I have processed for J. Gordon Melton (1980), which he collected by questionnaire at a Midwest convention of witches and ritual magicians, showed that 6 percent reported their religious background as Jewish. Not only is this far out of proportion for the nation as a whole, it is even more disproportionate for the area from which these people come. But the most revealing new fact available in these data is that *not one* of these ex-Jews reported their background as Orthodox.

For various recent historical reasons, non-Orthodox Jewish origins are probably a proxy variable for having been raised in a secular family. There are strong indications (including Jewish over-representation in radical politics) that, a generation ago, Jews were more likely than non-Jews to have turned to secular humanism. If so, today's Jewish young people have a higher probability of a secular background than do people of other ethnic backgrounds. Given historical reason for which Jews might feel reluctant to adopt Christianity if they seek a new faith, and if secularity is hard to pass on to the next generation, Jews ought to be even more predisposed towards the new religions than are people from Christian backgrounds. It may be noted in passing that Jews played the leading role in attempting to establish Ethical Culture as a naturalistic alternative to supernaturally-based faiths. This not only underlines the vulnerability of Jews to secularism in previous generations, but demonstrates that the attempt to create religions without gods results in religions which are inherently lacking in appeal.

To argue, as I do, that naturalistic meaning systems are at a relative disadvantage in dealing with the biggest and most persistent human desires also leads to the conclusion that *there will be a tendency for organizations that attempt to grapple with such problems to shift from naturalistic to supernaturalistic premises.*

This sort of organizational transformation has become increasingly common in recent years, and Bainbridge and I have tried to outline key elements in this process.[16] Here it may be helpful briefly to review several cases of groups that began as purely secular and evolved into full-blown religions. The best documented of these is a group identified as The Power by Bainbridge in his extensive ethnographic study.[17] The group was founded as a purely secular therapy service by a young Englishman and his wife in 1963. He recruited a number of his old schoolmates as clients. But soon the group abandoned the individual therapy model for group sessions. The sessions grew increasingly longer as the group became ever more committed to more ambitious goals. Soon they demanded nothing less than to become wholly wonderful people able to construct an utterly satisfying world around them. But, as time continued to pass, available means failed to yield these intensely shared demands. And, through one tiny step after another, the group became magical and then began to construct a novel and complex theology involving a four-fold divinity. Soon, they collectively withdrew to a deserted stretch of beach in Mexico where they prompted one another into all manner of mystical experiences, perfected their new revelations, and then returned to the world to spread the new faith.

Striking similarities can be found in the case of Synanon as analyzed in a recent series of studies by Richard Ofshe.[18] Synanon began as an organization that aimed to cure drug addiction, and gained rapid fame when its unwarranted claims (irresponsibly confirmed by professional social scientists) of a high cure rate were widely publicized. The actual low rate of success was apparent inside the group, however. In an effort to achieve better results the group moved towards a communal, life-long membership model meanwhile elevating its aims to levels that can only be described as Utopian. As time passed, and these aims also proved elusive, mystical experimentation set in. The Ouija board was introduced into Synanon encounter sessions and messages from the dead gave religious significance to Synanon's mission and to the founder's authority.[19] Soon the mysticism became dominant. Synanon declared itself a religion, and its founder, Charles E. Dederich, was declared the highest spiritual authority of the group.

In both these instances an overtly secular psychotherapy group found itself reaching for those vast and utterly scarce rewards that have always exceeded the human grasp in this world, and, rather than pull back from these desires, the group evolved a novel compensator system to sustain them.

This pattern is also displayed by Scientology.[20] It, too, started as a secular therapy, Dianetics, which attracted literally tens of thousands of followers in the 1950s. It, too, committed itself to impossible goals of human fulfillment. Specifically, L. Ron Hubbard promised that his new therapy would enable people to become "clears," to erase all their psychological scars and blocks, and thus gain superhuman powers, including total recall, an extraordinary IQ, freedom from ailments such as the common cold—in short, they would be to normal people as normal people are to the severely insane. As Bainbridge and I argue, failure to achieve these aims caused a number of departures and innovations.[21] Chief among these were the introduction of supernaturalism in the ideology, and the construction of a host of compensators for the rewards the therapy itself could not deliver. Although some Scientologists continue to believe that their organization is a science posing as a religion for legal reasons, the truth is that Scientology long has been a religion posing as a science.

A list of therapy movements that have been transformed into religions could be extended to great length. Indeed, a movement toward mysticism seems to characterize the human potential movement generally. Like Jung, whose pursuit of the psyche led him to the supernatural, *est* and other leading human potential cults seem fated to evolve into religions. However, the evolution from secular to supernatural is not limited to psychotherapy settings. In the nineteenth century, for example, there was a marked tendency for prominent American and British socialists to take up Spiritualism as their initial high hopes of political triumph were extinguished by events.[22] And, of course, during medieval times, it was typical for political grievances to burst forth as millenarian movements.[23]

From a safe distance, I recently charted the transformation of a group that began as a militant lesbian commune. My ability to follow this group stemmed from the fact that the leader was a compulsive spray-can slogan painter with a very distinctive hand. When I first began to notice her proclamations in the mid-1970s (they festoon buildings and underpasses along routes I routinely travel) she merely proclaimed the superiority of women and of exclusive feminine association. But she soon became more strident. One of her favorites was to draw a circular target and write "Put all men and boys here. Is that clear enough for you?" Other frequent slogans were "Amazons will win" and "Kill for a World Without Men." Third-hand reports indicated the group believed that soon thousands, and then millions, of women would join the cause and that the Amazons *would* win. Instead, very little happened. Recently the slogans have changed dramatically: "Off Jesus, Up the Mother," "The Blood of Witches is on Christian Hands," "Wica Will Win," "Amazons of Wica." These first appeared on the walls of a Protestant church near the commune. What can be read on the walls of Seattle is the transformation of militant lesbians, filled with dark talk of arms and ammunition and boundless hopes of triumph, into a coven of witches.

Why these transformations? Each case is no more than an elaborate collective enactment of one of our basic theoretical derivations: that in pursuit of goals of immense value which cannot be obtained through direct means, humans will tend to create and exchange compensators. This is, of course, no more than an extension and reworking of Malinowski's fundamental proposition that people use magic when other means are unknown or unavailable. The point must be emphasized once more. Not only do naturalistic organizations lack the resources for great compensators which are present in religions, but, when they get too close to the matters with which only religion can deal, they tend to become religions too.

It is obvious, of course, that not all radical political movements do get transformed into religions: that is, they do not embrace supernatural assumptions. Indeed, most recent radical movements have not turned to the supernatural. Moreover, for a variety of historical circumstances they militantly oppose religion. Our theoretical results force the conclusion that *if naturalistic organizations such as radical regimes attempt to supplant religious organizations they will be chronically vulnerable to religious opposition.* Yet, there sit a number of communist parties, secure in their control of the state, and militantly opposed to all traditional forms of supernaturalism. Doesn't that call our theoretical results into question?

Let me point out that the ability of radical movements to drain off the relative deprivation that otherwise might have sustained sect movements,[24] and the effort of radical regimes to supplant religions are among the main reasons for our definitional troubles. It has seemed appealing to evade questions about the interplay between religions and radicalism by expanding the definition of religion to include radical movements. Since the whole burden of my argument is against such a definition I am required to show how my analysis can deal with these matters.

It is certainly true that militantly anti-religious radical movements have come to power in a number of nations, especially Russia and China. Once in power, they have launched long and vigorous campaigns to root out religion, and they have not hesitated to resort to intense persecution to achieve these aims. Indeed, being in control of totalitarian states, the communist elites have had extraordinary resources to draw upon against religion. In my judgment, however, these efforts have been a stunning failure. Moreover, I am even prepared to argue that the religious impulse of the populace may have even been strengthened by these repressive measures.

It is clear that the Soviet government is frightened of religion. At Christmas and Easter, for example, they deploy huge numbers of police to turn back people from entering churches—allowing only elderly, regular attenders to go in. The important point here is that the crowds that must be turned back are huge, that despite the high probability of having one's name taken, so many people try to go to church anyway. And for everyone who tries to go to church, how many scores of others remain religious in more circumspect fashion? No wonder the present Pope seems to scare all the regimes of the Soviet bloc.

China too presents a fascinating study in the failure of a communist regime to root out religion. Over the past several decades, fashionable historical revisionists have fostered the notion that not only were Christian missionaries in China agents of imperialism and of Western ethnocentrism, but also that they were unsuccessful. We are told that they could attract only "rice Christianity." If this is so, what are we to make of recent statements by the Chinese regime that it is going to ease its repression of Christians, and the acknowledgement that large numbers of Chinese persist in Christian belief? Thirty years without missionary rice, and in the face of draconian repression, and still Chinese Christianity persists. Moreover, the traditional religions of China are acknowledged still to have a firm grip on masses of Chinese.

Our theoretical analysis does not lead us to predict that religion will triumph over secular and repressive states. It merely argues that such secular states cannot root out religion, and that, to the extent that they try to root it out, they will be vulnerable to religious opposition. The reasons for this seem clear enough. Before the revolution, radical parties can issue credible compensators concerning many scarce rewards. They can promise that, come the revolution, relative deprivation will be assuaged. After the revolution, however, marked stratification and thus relative deprivation remain. Moreover, the party lacked from the start the capacity to provide plausible compensators for the most unavailable rewards that lead people to religion. Lenin's body may be displayed under glass, but no one supposes that he has ascended to sit on the right hand, or even the left hand, of Marx. And, dams along the Volga do not light up the meaning of the universe. Moreover, repressive states seem to increase levels of individual deprivation and, in so doing, to fuel the religious impulse. In making faith more costly, they also make it more necessary and valuable. Perhaps religion is never so robust as when it is an underground church. I must conclude that unless or until communist regimes turn supernatural and become religions they always will be outmatched in their conflicts with religion.

Conclusion

The primary point of this essay is simple. The truly priceless compensators can come only from the gods. Therefore wholly naturalistic systems of thought lack the capacity to fulfill the primary functions of religions. Therefore they are not religions.

But, having argued that we ought to restrict our definition of religion to phenomena that include a supernatural element does not mean that I think the social scientific study of religion should be limited to studying religion. To do so would be to work in a stultifying vacuum. Thus, for example, there is every reason to suppose that many fundamental elements of a theory of sect formation would apply rather well to political sects, indeed to schisms within any kind of formal organization. Furthermore, to isolate the unique properties of schisms within religious organizations requires careful comparison with non-religious organizations. Or, to look in another direction, it is impossible to study sect or cult formation without some elements of a theory of the state. For example, we deduce from our theory that religious pluralism is the natural state of the market—that religious monopolies are only possible (and then only to a certain extent) when the coercive powers of the state are utilized. But we cannot explore the interplay between religion and the state if we mistakenly equate the two. And that is my concern here. If we are to make progress in understanding social life, we need to have adequate conceptual tools.

FOOTNOTES

1. See, for example, Thomas Luckmann, *The Invisible Religion,* New York: Macmillan, 1967, Robert N. Bellah, "Christianity and Symbolic Realism," *Journal for the Scientific Study of Religion,* 9,2, 1970, pp. 89-96, J. Milton Yinger, *The Scientific Study of Religion,* New York: Macmillan, 1970.
2. See Rodney Stark, "A Sociological Definition of Religion," in Charles Y. Glock and Rodney Stark, *Religion and Society in Tension,* Chicago: Rand McNally, 1965, pp. 3-17, Rodney Stark and William Sims Bainbridge, "Of Churches, Sects, and Cults," *Journal for the Scientific Study of Religion,* 18,2, 1979, pp. 117-131; *idem,* "Towards a Theory of Religious Commitment," *Journal for the Scientific Study of Religion,* 19, 2, 1980, pp. 114-28; see also, Jack Goody, "Religion and Ritual: the Definitional Problem," *British Journal of Sociology,* 12, 1961, pp. 142-64; Melford E. Spiro, "Religion, problems of definition and explanation" in Michael Banton (ed.), *Anthropological Approaches to the Study of Religion,* New York: Praeger, 1966, pp. 85-126, Peter L. Berger, *The Sacred Canopy,* New York: Doubleday, 1967.
3. Émile Durkheim, *The Elementary Forms of the Religious Life,* London: George Allen and Unwin, 1915.
4. Our set of axioms and some initial derivations have just appeared in R. Stark and W.S. Bainbridge, "Towards a Theory..." *op. cit.*
5. R. Stark and W.S. Bainbridge, "Of Churches..." *op. cit.*
6. See Dean Kelley, *Why Conservative Churches are Growing,* New York: Harper & Row, 1972.
7. Rodney Stark and Charles Y. Glock, *American Piety,* Berkeley and Los Angeles: University of California Press, 1968.
8. See Rodney Stark and Bruce D. Foster, Charles Y. Glock and Harold E. Quinley, *Wayward Shepherds,* New York: Harper & Row, 1971.
9. R. Stark and C.Y. Glock, *American Piety,* op.cit.
10. Rodney Stark and William Sims Bainbridge, "Secularization, Revival, and Cult Formation", forthcoming.
11. See C.K. Hadaway, "Denominational Switching and Membership Growth," *Sociological Analysis,* 39, 1978, pp. 321-37; W.C. Roof and C.K. Hadaway, "Shifts in Religious Preference in the Mid-Seventies," *Journal for the Scientific*

Study of Religion, 16, 1977, pp. 409-12; James R. Kluegel, "Denominational Mobility," *Journal for the Scientific Study of Religion,* 19, 1980, pp. 26-39.

12. R. Stark and W.S. Bainbridge, "Secularization..." *op. cit.*
13. R. Stark, W.S. Bainbridge and D. P. Doyle, "Cults of America," *Sociological Analysis,* 40, 4, 1979, pp. 347-59.
14. R. Stark and W.S. Bainbridge, "Secularization..." *op. cit.*
15. See J. Stillson Judah, *Hare Krishna and the Counterculture,* New York: Wiley, 1974, J. Gordon Melton, "The Origins of Contemporary New-Paganism," a . paper read at the meetings of the Popular Culture Association.
16. R. Stark and W.S. Bainbridge, "Of Churches..." *op. cit.*
17. William Sims Bainbridge, *Satan's Power,* Berkeley and Los Angeles: University of California Press, 1978.
18. Richard Ofshe, "The Social Development of the Synanon Cult," *Sociological Analysis,* 41, 1980, pp. 109-127; *idem.* "Synanon: The Failure that Founded a Tradition" in A. Gartner and F. Reissman (eds.), *Mental Health and the Self-Help Revolution,* New York: Human Sciences Press, forthcoming.
19. Anthony Lang, *Synanon Foundation: The People's Business,* Cottonwood, Ariz., 1978.
20. Roy Wallis, *The Road to Total Freedom: A Sociological Analysis of Scientology,* New York: Columbia University Press, 1976.
21. R. Stark and W.S. Bainbridge, "Towards a Theory..." *op. cit.*
22. J. H. Noyes, *History of American Socialisms,* Philadelphia, 1870; T.D. Seymour Bassett "The Secular Utopian Socialists" in Donald Drew Egbert and Stow Persons, (eds.), *Socialism and American Life,* Princeton: Princeton University Press, 1952; Logie Barrow, "Socialism in Eternity: The Ideology of Plebeian Spiritualists, 1853-1913," *History Workshop,* 9, 1980, pp. 37-69.
23. Norman Cohn, *The Pursuit of the Millennium,* New York: Harper & Row, 1961.
24. R. Stark, "Class, Radicalism, and Religious Involvement," *American Sociological Review,* 29, 1964, pp. 698-706.

APOSTATES AND ATROCITY STORIES: SOME PARAMETERS IN THE DYNAMICS OF DEPROGRAMMING*

Anson D. Shupe, Jr.
David G. Bromley

Social movements, including new religious movements, evoke responses from the wider society, and these reactions themselves become significant influences on the way in which movements develop. Those movements that seek rapid, total change in social structures and/or individual personality structures through non-coercive means, and which we elsewhere have termed "world-transforming" movements,[1] never fully realize their publicly stated goals. Indeed, in general, the more sweeping the change a social movement envisions, the lower the probability that it will be achieved, rendering the total transformation of an entire society an histori-cally rare event.[2]

Despite a very low rate of success by virtually any standard, many social movements start out with great expectations and grand designs. The factors that account for the discrepancy between stated goals and ultimate achievements may be broadly grouped into those internal to the movement (i.e., developing organizational requisites) and those external to it (i.e., varying degrees of social control levied on emerging movements by established organizations and institutions), although these are not entirely independent of one another. Much of the sociological literature on social movements, including particularly the church-

---

*This paper is the product of a joint effort. The order of authorship is random and does not imply any difference in the importance of contributions.

sect literature, has dealt largely with internal factors such as the changing composition of membership and pressures toward organizational stability and bureaucratization.[3] Largely because of the type of social movements typically used as data, even the recent resource mobilization approach has emphasized internal factors.[4] Clearly such internal factors are of critical importance in understanding the development of social movements; in our own analysis of one particular religious movement we have emphasized the pressures toward routinization of charisma, bureaucratization, and accommodation of individual career interests as factors deflecting that movement's pursuit of its publicly announced goals.[5]

At the same time, however, external factors are at least of equal importance in determining social movement trajectories, but these received less attention until more politically oriented theories of social behavior began to inform social research in the 1960s. Many issues in this area, therefore, still remain unexplored. Our present concern lies in one specific aspect of the societal reaction to social movements: the construction and dissemination of atrocity stories by apostates from these movements. These individuals have played a key role in shaping the public perception of and reaction to the new religions. Apostates have also played a major role in discrediting earlier "new religions" such as the Roman Catholic Church, the Mormons, Shakers, and Jehovah's Witnesses. It is the historical re-creation of this role at those times when the established social order perceives a threat to its interests that lends sociological significance to the analysis of apostasy and the atrocity stories that apostates relate. While we do not here attempt to present a comprehensive theory of defection or apostasy from social movements, we take a first step in that direction, at least with respect to the current new religions.

It is difficult to overestimate the influence which apostates have had in shaping the course of the new religions. Most individuals in American society have had little personal, direct contact with members of the new religions apart from perhaps an occasional, transitory encounter with a member engaged in proselytization or fund-raising activities. Virtually all of the public "knowledge" about the new religions, therefore, has been obtained indirectly from accounts in the media, a substantial proportion of which was initiated by opponents of the new religions in general and apostates in particular. Because these individuals have often been readily accorded credibility by the media, they have had a disproportionate influence in setting the agenda for public discussion of the new religions.

In order to place the activities and impact of apostates in context, it is important to consider briefly, first, the sources of strain arising from the new religions and, second, the nature of the familial institution and the character of deprogramming as a uniquely parental solution once parents face the problem of children who have been converted to one of the new religions. We then consider the social context of apostasy and atrocity stories and conclude with a brief evaluation of their impact on the new religions. Our data are drawn from our several year study of the Unification Church and its affiliated organizations, which we have referred to as the Unificationist Movement (UM).[6]

Our main thesis is that the recounting of atrocity tales by apostates constitutes a major mechanism of social control which historically has altered the development trajectories of numerous social movements. Because apostates have played such a key role in the repression of social movements, we shall examine the process of their emergence and their impact as one step toward identifying factors influencing the course of development of social movements.

Strain Between Families and the New Religions

There were two major sources of strain between families and the new religions: a challenge, first, to the family's authority structure and second to its goal of preparing offspring for participation in the economic order. Families devoted much of their socialization activity to producing offspring capable of achieving socially and economically successful careers and life-styles. Success in this effort was both a source of parental feelings of fulfillment and accomplishment and a major basis for societal support for the family as an institution. Parents therefore attempted to rear their children so that the latter were able to play highly specialized roles, possessed self-interested motivation, were free from ideological constraints on role performance, and held instrumental (as opposed to affective) role orientations.

Membership in such groups as the Unification movement, by contrast, involved assuming a very diffuse role in a communally organized group. Indeed, these communal organizations specifically sought to suppress self-interested motivation by limiting personal possessions, individually controlled wealth, and even distinctive grooming or clothing which might serve as a basis for structured social inequality. Particularly among novitiates a great deal of time and energy was expended in learning to free oneself from the "constraints" of ego and possessions, placing the good of the group above their own personal needs and desires, and pursuing spiritual rather than material ends. Further, members were expected to reject the calculated reciprocity characteristic of instrumentally-based role relationships for what they termed "heartistic" relation-ships, that is to say affectively-based relations predicated on the fictive kinship system of the Unification movement, in which other members were literally treated as one's "brothers" and "sisters." All of these requisites of communal life received strong support both from peers and from the movement's ideology, which located the source of most of mankind's most serious, persistent problems in selfishness and the pursuit of individual goals. Thus communal solidarity, rather than developing the requisites for conventional careers, was the preeminent concern: the socialization process of the Unification movement offered virtually no preparation for inte-gration into the contemporary American economic system.

The threat to the authority structure of the family emanated from the fact that although parents socialized their offspring to assume autonomous adult roles, they anticipated that adult inde-pendence was not inconsistent with continued loyalty to the family unit or to their own continued titular leadership of its members. However, the Unification movement's communal style of organization required, initially at least, full-time involvement and continuous geographical mobility on witnessing and fund-raising teams. Parents tended (sometimes correctly) to view decreased visitation and communication as evidence of reduced loyalty to the family. Even more disconcerting to parents, however, was the perception that their roles as father and mother were being appropriated by Moon and his wife. Indeed, within the UM's fictive kinship system, Moon and his wife are designated as "true parents," clearly differentiated from members' biological parents, and unto them members accorded superior moral status. They ceded to Moon the authority to make extraordinary claims upon them personally, and assumed the status of disciples. The prospect of Moon playing a major role in decisions that parents otherwise felt should rightfully be the family's (if not the offspring's alone), such as career, marital, and child-rearing plans, was threatening to parents.

While the sources of strain between families and the new religions can be analytically located in the challenges to familial interests and authority, these were experienced in particular cases in terms of a series of incidents and issues sometimes spanning a period of weeks, months or even years. Typically this sequence began with the offspring's decision to attend one or a series of workshops lasting from a few days to several weeks. If parents were "informed" about the new religions in question, they usually warned their offspring and protested against this "useless and dangerous" venture. A commitment actually to join a new religion was even more threatening, for it was followed by such decisions as dropping out of college, deferring long-planned careers, giving up romantic or marital relationships, eschewing personal possessions, and, of course, reducing communication with and commitment to the family. Later in the sequence (if membership lasted more than one or two years) even more basic and threatening commitments were forthcoming, such as development of a career within the movement, marriage within the movement (with the time and the partner being decided upon at least with the approval of movement elders), and child-rearing within the movement, sometimes in a communal context.

As parent-offspring conflict developed over these emerging commitments, for a variety of reasons parents began to perceive that their offspring were unable to respond to them in what they regarded as an appropriate fashion. First, the communal organization of the new religions frequently provided novitiates with powerfully confirmatory experiences. The interpersonal harmony, caring, and mutual support characteristic of communal groups offered a sense of acceptance and security. Since the communal group was relatively independent in meeting a wide range of individual and collective needs, members did not have to concern themselves with personal possessions or money. A member could literally possess no money and yet feel no sense of anxiety or deprivation. Given the highly individualistic, competitive, achievement-oriented, and self-sufficiency orientation of the larger society, to many novitiates the climate of the communal groups seemed (at least initially) exhilarating and almost utopian. Parents, by contrast, usually experienced the new religious movement through their theologies, which were bizarre or even heretical when viewed from the perspective of conventional Christianity; through media interpretations, which were decidedly negative; through anti-cult movement publications, which were seriously biased and sometimes bordered on the hysterical; or through their own deteriorating relationship with their offspring, which aroused anxiety about the latters' health and well-being. As a result of these diametrically opposed interpretations of the novitiates' experiences, responsive communication was at best difficult to achieve.

Second, exchanges between alarmed parents and offspring were often threatening to both parties. Novitiates' knowledge of the group's theology was often very limited.[7] Therefore, when called upon to defend their beliefs new members responded either with less than articulate, knowledgeable statements or with a rather stilted parroting of major elements of the ideology. While their inability to communicate adequately the entire gestalt of their experiences in the new religious movement was frustrating for new members, it was extremely threatening to parents. The latter, proceeding from the assumption that change in belief precedes change in behavior (an assumption that is somewhat dubious in light of much social psychological research)[8] concluded that conversion could not have taken place. Communication thus foundered because, for many novitiates, details of the theology were not central to their commitment, while for parents their offspring's inability to articulate their beliefs in comprehensible terms negated the possibility of true conversion. Parents, then, began to consider alternative explanations.

Third, while parents were preparing their offspring for adult autonomy, they nonetheless customarily maintained some measure of control over them. This authority emanated from shared career and domestic goals toward which both parents and offspring had worked, monetary support during the extended educational process, and basic loyalty to the family unit. When offspring joined a new religious movement, the salience of each of these mechanisms of control declined dramatically. Confronted by a developing commitment to a new religion to which they were unalterably opposed, parents typically turned to appeals to family loyalty, reminders of sacrifices made for common goals and, ultimately, to emotional and/or monetary sanctions. The failure of such measures to dissuade the convert served only to increase parental fears and apprehensions that something was drastically wrong.

At some point in the process of their offspring's developing commitments to a new religion, many parents concluded that something far more sinister than religious conversion was involved in their offspring's changing behavioral orientation because the transformation seemed relatively rapid (although in actuality this was not always the case); was not preceded by any overt expression of religious interest; involved a bizarre theology; and was not amenable to discussion, parents frequently concluded that their offspring were being deceived and/or in some way coerced. Over time, as parents of converts began to discuss their common experiences, a brainwashing ideology developed within the anticult movement, which both explained converts' otherwise unintelligible behavior and legitimated the use of coercive tactics to restore these brainwashed individuals to their normal, healthy states. The major elements of this ideology included the following:[9]

(a) The Unification movement (and other "cults") were pseudo-religions which had adopted the cloak of religion solely to gain tax-exempt privileges and insulation from legal regulation. These pseudo-religions were, in reality, profit-making ventures operated by ego-maniac charlatans for their own personal aggrandizement.

(b) The youths who innocently became involved in the Unification movement did not undergo a true conversion but rather were victims of deceptive, seductive, and/or manipulative processes that destroyed their free will (labeled "mind control" and "brainwashing").

(c) The "programming" process and the resultant subjugation of members was considered both physically and mentally deleterious to them. In addition, the purposes for which these "automatons" were used were socially injurious to a number of institutions (e.g., the family, Judeo-Christian religion, and American democracy).

(d) Since the free will of members had been suspended by the "programming" process, they were considered incapable of voluntarily leaving these groups; hence the only hope of their resuming conventional life-styles was to "deprogram" them.

The Dynamics of Deprogramming

Deprogramming processes are diverse and multifaceted phenomena and it is important to realize this in order to understand the role that the deprogramming process and deprogrammed individuals played in discrediting new religious movements. Our most fundamental observation is that deprogramming represented an exertion of parental power. In its least coercive, or voluntary form, deprogramming was referred to by proponents of the anti-cult movement as "re-evaluation." It involved verbal persuasion by families, counselors, and friends, and it permitted some genuine exchange of views between the offspring and parents, implying only a moderate imbalance of power. Conversely, the most coercive form, and the form of which most people thought when discussing deprogramming, involved a ritualistic, and sometimes violent treatment of members of new religions, often resembling, in many striking details, medieval exorcism, which implied clear and dramatic imbalance of power between offspring and families. Furthermore, in this case, any attempts to resist family influence by the offspring were perceived, and responded to, as defenses "obviously" symptomatic of his "programming" (a situation similar to that of the mental ward).[10] These two forms of deprogramming— re-evaluative and coercive—may be treated as two polar types.

The dynamics and eventual results of any given deprogramming appear to have depended on three primary factors:

(1) The adversaries, parents and deprogrammers, on the one hand, and the "cultic" offspring, on the other, brought to the deprogramming confrontation their own respective personal motivations and interests, of which there existed many possible types and extremes, and these in turn influenced in emergent fashion the way in which the offspring responded to the deprogramming. Thus we reject the simplistic assumption of deprogrammers that an offspring's responses were predetermined by a standard brainwashing process producing a stereotypical "zombie" personality syndrome. Rather, we argue that persons displayed differential, *individualistic* receptivity to deprogramming methods, and manifested nothing like the uniformity of consciousness attributed to them.

(2) The potential scenarios which could unfold during deprogrammings were many. Any one of a variety of factors— including the interactions of characteristics of the parents; offspring; particular religious movement in question; and other mundane parameters—might influence the course of events.

(3) Throughout the deprogramming process and up until the end, a variety of outcomes were possible, ranging from escape and return to the religious movement; to short resistance, capitulation, and simple exit; or to the aggressive assumption of the role of apostate. Which of these outcomes materialized can be best understood as the product of the balance of power and interests of the two parties concerned, as well as (from the offspring's perspective) the desirability of various possible roles into which the young person might move if he or she disavowed the role of "cult" member.

Thus, contrary to the deprogrammers' claims, there was not a reliable, standard "therapeutic" deprogramming procedure which invariably "restored free thought" and which restored offspring to their families. So-called successful deprogrammings, according to our interpretation, were rather the emergent products of parents communicating to children their sincere, heart-felt fears, concerns, and love; the offsprings' empathic reactions to parental emotion, as well as to their own preexisting doubts about various aspects of their particular new religion; and the deprogrammers' intuitive abilities to pick up on and exploit these factors during the volatile parent-child confrontation. It is worth exploring the dynamics of the process underlying this alternative interpretation in greater detail.

Members of new religions entered the deprogramming situation possessing not only various levels of commitment to their religious roles but also backgrounds of very different experiences and kinds of involvement in such groups. Thus, for their part, offspring did not begin a deprogramming with any homogeneous orientation.[11] We discovered that UM members had been drawn to the movement by such factors as, the idealistic purpose offered by the group; the alternative life-style explicit in its communal organization; the personal attraction of specific missionaries; or the broad range of problems and issues addressed by Unification theology. Some individuals, under group encouragement, broadened their bases of initial involvement almost immediately while others retained their original interests or expanded these only gradually.

Moreover, members' feelings of involvement and commitment, not to mention the normal range of doubts concerning theology, hierarchical authority, and self-identity that accompany membership in any religious organization, varied over time. Many members of the Unification movement and other persons joining communal groups felt great personal fulfillment in the support and interdependence with other group members, and experienced liberation from the social, sexual, and economic competitiveness of the larger "profane" society. These feelings probably continued over time and generated intense feelings of commitment. They were a two-edged sword, however, since many long-term members eventually had to confront the necessary realization that their chosen religious course would involve indefinite self-sacrifice for the good of the movement, obedience to group leaders, suppression of ego and continued postponement of conventional careers, and the complications of social commitments (e.g., marriage and child-rearing within the group) which rendered any future change of course increasingly problematic. The realization that self-abnegation was an ongoing, endless, lonely struggle, which called for more ruthless measures as finer vestiges of egoism were attacked, caused some individuals to reflect on their commitment. The long-range implication of the demands of this all-consuming commitment, in other words, were difficult to ignore. In addition, over time, the less lofty aspects of the group became noticeable: despite proclaimed ideals of equality and sacrifice, there emerged in the new utopia, in however muted and subcultural a form, structured inequality (in the familiar sociological form of privileges, prestige, and power), invidiousness, and competitiveness. Awareness of the ignoble side of group life, of course, raised for members the question of whether the group's ideals were actually attainable on any level. Thus, there were differences in theological sophistication and commitment which offspring brought with them to deprogrammings.

Likewise, parents entered a deprogramming with a number of concerns, fears, and attitudes regarding the offspring's decision to defect from the family's traditional religion and life-style, and to enlist in a radical new religious movement. More mildly concerned parents were likely to express their disappointment, confusion, or even anguish, confronting the young person with the consequences of his or her defection for the family. Parents could argue that the stigma of participation in this type of social movement might follow the offspring for many years after the latter "came to his senses" if membership was not soon terminated; that there were alternative avenues to express idealism; that whatever social and personal benefits were expected from participation in the movement should be weighed against costs and drawbacks; and that this present idealism and sense of fulfillment might end in despair and bitterness when the offspring learned that the movement's utopian goals were impossible to achieve. Parents who were more embittered lashed out in fear and anger that lifelong sacrifices and invest- ments for conventional careers were being wasted, that the family as a whole suffered embarrassment, and that the offspring's health and well-being were in serious danger.

Whatever predispositions and perceptions the parties brought to the deprogramming situation, the format of the exchange was determined by the relative power of the two opposing camps. When both parties interpreted the deprogramming as a re-evaluation, the deprogrammee possessed a greater degree of influence in the ensuing exchange. Although in agreeing to a re-evaluation, the offspring tacitly acknowledged some remaining parental authority, the fact that he or she was free to leave implied that the exchange of points of view proceeded on a relatively equal basis. In the coercive deprogramming situation, however, the deprogrammee possessed virtually no influence in the ensuing exchange. In this case, the process resembled more a one-sided attempt to "edu- cate" the deprogrammee, and any resistance on his part was interpreted and disparaged as "proof" that he was indeed under the influence of mind control.

In both re-evaluations and coercive deprogrammings, new (negative) items of information about the movement in question were frequently put before the deprogrammee. This is understandable since individuals joining communally organized religious groups such as the Unification movement immediately began assuming a full-time consuming role that required few substantive skills or detailed ideological knowledge. Most movements did not regularly attend to the mass media, and UM, like other groups, discouraged attention to "negative" media reports about their group. Thus it is no coincidence that the sooner the parents attempted a coercive deprogramming after their offspring had joined a new religion, the more successful was it likely to be. Such "cult" members, ignorant about the allegations against their gurus and movements, were not likely to be well-versed in refuting them. Fairly new UM members, for example, might be confronted with media reports about Moon's wealth, political and financial aspects of the movement which contrasted with the way it portrayed itself, and even with more esoteric elements of the ideology to which they had not yet been exposed, any of which could prove disconcerting, shake their faith, and feed previously existing doubts and misgivings.

The deprogramming situation was one of intense emotions among persons with fundamental bonds to one another. Whether the deprogramming was coercive or a re-evaluation, offspring confronted enormous pressure from parental emotions running the gamut from deep concern and marked apprehension to uninhibited outpourings of fear and grief. Fathers wept openly and siblings made expressions of love normally left unspoken in contemporary middle-class nuclear families. The mere fact that several family members might have left their own familial and occupational activities to travel long distances, and gave vent to tears and distraught behavior, often impressed the deprogrammee. Where parents had permitted forcible abduction, the shock that they had felt compelled to take such drastic action often overshadowed the offspring's own anger, and led him to reconsider his position.

Finally, the deprogrammee often faced a real problem in satisfactorily explaining a variety of inconsistencies, the awareness of which could be more easily suppressed within the context of the powerfully confirmatory communal group but which stubbornly persisted (with the help of parents and deprogrammers) in the deprogramming situation. For example, issues such as the use of deceptive practices in fund-raising and witnessing in contrast to the group's lofty ideals, the repeated disconfirmation of Moon's theological predictions; and Moon's highly publicized opulent life-style as compared to that of his average follower, were invariably raised by parents and deprogrammers. These charges such as the glaring inequalities between leaders and followers, and deceptive fund-raising were difficult for many offspring to refute, either because some were true and deprogrammees had seen them occur or even engaged in them, or because they did not possess enough organizational and theological knowledge to argue otherwise. Faced with numerous press reports, with former UM members who appealed to them as "one who has also been there," and with other information which unanimously condemned the group as a pseudo-religion and money-making operation, many offspring found their faith severely weakened.

The predispositions which both sides brought to deprogramming interacted with the dynamics of this process, yielding numerous possible and not easily predictable outcomes. Thus, deprogrammees might: (1) return to the movement against parental wishes (perhaps feigning profound effect from their arguments) or even with their reluctant consent; (2) agree to a period of trial separation from the movement; (3) leave the movement and resume former career or educational activities; (4) reject both family and the movement; or (5) after rejecting the movement, join the anti-cult movement. For example, if the convert's commitment was strong and the parents' concern only moderate, the former could successfully "hold-out" during a re-evaluation session's emotional and/or intellectual onslaught, and insist on returning to the group. Should the offspring accede to more serious doubts or ambivalent emotions, a trial separation might ensue or even a total disaffiliation from the movement. On the other hand, stronger coercive steps taken by the parents might convince the offspring that membership in the communal groups was not worth the cost of inflicting further pain on his family, or create in him the conviction that something indeed must be terribly wrong for his parents to have taken such serious action. Thus, whether deprogramming was "successful" in any individual case was not (as the deprogrammers maintained in their crusade to cast themselves as a legitimate profession) a function of applying certain standard therapeutic procedures (such as confronting converts with invariate litanies of allegations about "cults"), nor was it (as the liberal champions of civil liberties charged) largely the result of the coerciveness of the situation. Rather, the "success" or "failure" of a specific deprogramming was always an interactive, emergent product of the factors listed above. When deprogrammings were successful, they were so not for the reasons claimed. "Successful" deprogrammers were simply able, through intuition and from experience, to apply a crude thumb-nail sense of group dynamics to pick up on and "run with," the predispositions, perceptions, and interests of the situation as held by both parents and converts, which were also found within the coercive/non-coercive parameters of the confrontation situation.

The Necessary Emergence of Apostates

Let us now turn to one particular pattern of exit from a new religion which we term *apostasy*. As operationally defined here, apostasy consists of leaving a new religious movement, and then of joining an organized counter-movement. In this case, apostates from the Unification movement and other new religions joined an already existing network of regional and local parents' groups that we have elsewhere termed the anti-cult movement,[12] and subsequently played a key role in discrediting new religions through recounting sordid anecdotes which we have labeled *atrocity stories*.[13]

The emergence of apostasy as one avenue of exit from a given new religion can best be understood by contrasting two distinct scenarios. In the first scenario, one of re-evaluation, when parents raised only moderate opposition to their offspring's membership in a new religion, and when the latter determined, either because of doubts raised (or reinforced) during the re-evaluation or from parental pressure, to foresake his membership, exit was easily managed by both families and individuals. The parents were satisfied that the young person had agreed to leave the group, and the exchange was one of little coercion so that the offspring did not define the situation as one of forced choice. Whether expressed in terms of cognitive dissonance or attribution theory from social psychology, the implications of the lack of forced choice for an offspring's interpretation of the decision to leave are obvious. In this case everyone (parents, offspring, community) could define the deprogrammee's decision to leave and renounce the new creed as simply a "mistake" and a blunder of "misplaced idealism." Under such conditions, parents might possibly even acknowledge in the magnanimous spirit of reconciliation that there were after all some positive qualities about the movement which would have attracted any basically idealistic person.

The second scenario, when parents vehemently opposed the offspring's membership in a new religion and went to the trouble of arranging a coercive deprogramming, saw apostasy as a likely avenue of exit. In this case, negotiation between deprogrammee and captors was negligible: the latter usually told the former they were prepared to wait indefinitely until the new religious faith was renounced. In the context of a stubborn stand-off, colored with minor violence and high emotions, this second scenario resembled a zero-sum game, with little chance that compromise suitable to both parties could emerge. The deprogrammee was left with the options of reassuming the world-view held by parents and deprogrammers, or of resisting by sheer will or trickery until the opportunity to escape arose. (Deprogrammees whom we interviewed, or whose affidavit accounts we read, who successfully resisted this process employed a range of escape techniques, from feigning illness or self-inflicting injuries in order to be taken to medical authorities, to overcoming captors in a physical burst for freedom, to lulling deprogrammers into over-confidence before departing. Once returned to their groups, such members assumed a heroic stature, and their accounts of such experiences at the hands of deprogrammers resembled the atrocity stories told about religious movements by apostates.[14]) Here we consider only those individuals who did choose to capitulate to the perspective of parents and deprogrammers.

For those who felt ambivalence about their experiences in a given religious movement, and who carried this feeling into the deprogramming situation, *or* who had doubts raised or confirmed during deprogramming, and/or who confronted the onslaught of parental harangues, severing their ties with the movement often represented a reasonable decision. However, in many cases there had been an ongoing dialogue between family and offspring before the abduction or deprogramming took place, in which the offspring typically defended the decision to stay with the group. In those instances, one might ask, how was it that the deprogrammee could suddenly and so radically change allegiances, as if instead of shifting apparently profound commitments and identities, he were merely shifting hats? *And* how could he be immediately welcomed back into his family after all the turmoil that had occurred? The answer is that to admit that they had made a mistake, and to declare no further interest in the given movement was not enough. Consider that their parents had been humiliated by the offspring's often hostile and sometimes thorough rejection of parental life-style and goals in the time preceding deprogramming as well as at least during the initial phases of the deprogramming itself. Consider the often substantial fees paid for deprogramming and the trouble to arrange it. Consider also the possible risk of civil and even of criminal prosecution that all—parents and deprogrammers alike —faced. These factors dictated that the price of re-entry into conventional society had now risen, and only public admission of having been brainwashed as well as testimony about other allegations of heinous cult outrages would suffice to pay it. Thus, public contrition for having abandoned parental values became the cost of re-admission into the mainstream community.

"Successful" deprogrammings had two major effects: first, they lent apparent validity to the basic brainwashing ideology; and second, they helped to support the case for establishing deprogramming as a legitimate occupation. From the parents' standpoint, "successful" deprogrammings assured them that they possessed a valid, confirmed explanation for their offspring's hostility and rejection (i.e., that he was literally "not himself"); a stigma-free accounting for their offspring's membership in a deviant religious movement through the mechanics of mind control, as perpetrated by malevolent individuals; and a label (*i.e.*, "cult" member) which did not require a long period of incapacity or recovery to remove after deprogramming.

There is admittedly a certain contrived sense about such a solution to the problem of exit. That is, the explanation has a conspiratorial ring to it, in which all parties consciously connive to exonerate the youthful members of any blame. However, we remind readers that even *before* deprogrammings young cult members often already entertain very real doubts and ambivalence, and these are perhaps much more prevalent either than the surface solidarity of communal organizations would suggest or than anti-cultist and brainwashing model advocates would admit. In other words, the seeds of defection were more often present than popularly supposed. Once—with the encouragement of their families, friends, and deprogrammers—a member began a process of retrospective interpretation, the shift in roles from committed "brother" or "sister" of the communal group, from which he was now absent, to a former ideal status as dutiful, loving child or sibling, could conceivably take place quite rapidly. Whatever its interpretation by those who experience it, or by observers, the numerous anecdotes are convincing proof of the rapidity of this de-conversion experience. It is mislabeled as a moment when the mind "snaps" back to reality and freedom of thought.[15] The deprogrammer, Ted Patrick puts it in a colorful simile:

> Then there'll be a minute, a second, when the mind *snaps back* and he comes out of it. The only way I can describe it is that it's like turning on the light in a dark room or bringing a person back from the dead. It's a beautiful thing, the whole personality changes, it's like seeing a person change from a werewolf into a man.[16]

Of course, not all individuals who capitulated to the parents and deprogrammers' perspective developed into apostates. In general, those who became apostates were motivated, often out of feelings of anger and a desire for revenge, to speak out against the danger of others falling into the same "trap," or they were encouraged to issue some statement publicly before gatherings of the media, for example, to the effect that they were indebted to their parents for "rescuing them" from a destructive experience. Some anti-cult associations, with which we have not dealt here, deliberately recruited and promoted such persons for the apostate role. However, there were only a limited number of such status positions and platforms for such role-related messages. After a brief period of basking in the limelight of newpaper articles, local radio, and television talk-shows, and occasionally national-circulation magazine articles, most apostates returned to pick up the pieces of interrupted or shattered abandoned career trajectories. Most faded into obscurity. A minority became deprogrammers themselves or leaders of anti-cult associations, enlisting in the anti-cult movement full-time. Thus, Barbara Underwood, for example, wrote with her mother a book on her experience in the Unification movement, entitled *Hostage to Heaven*,[17] and married a Moonie apostate, Gary Scharff, a major figure in the deprogramming wing of the anti-cult movement during the late 1970s. Allan Tate Wood also wrote an apostate's account of his UM experiences, entitled *Moonstruck*,[18] engaged in frequent speaking appearances, pursued a graduate degree in counseling psychology at a southwestern university, stating it to be his proclaimed goal to treat "cult victims." In any event, there is no question that the most injurious consequence of deprogramming with respect to the wider social repression of religious movements was the creation of apostates and the dissemination of the anecdotal atrocity stories which they told. It is to these stories that we now turn.

Atrocity Stories as Genre

Apostates' testimonies provided much of the drama which captured public attention and helped the anti-cult movement to obtain a degree of public credibility which might well have been otherwise unattainable. One persistent problem faced by the anti-cult movement was an inability to penetrate the new religious movements and gather first-hand evidence to support their allegations (although some young journalists did make brief forays into workshops, seminars, and meetings for this purpose). Yet because both the charges of brainwashing and the proposed solution of deprogramming were so extreme, convincing evidence was vital to their case. While the anti-cultists could allege that brainwashing occurred, and could describe the brainwashing process as they contended it happened to others, none of them had actually been brainwashed or seen brainwashing taking place. It was the apostate who could offer this "smoking gun" quality of evidence. Apostates could authoritatively state that they had been brainwashed, describe the process in detail, recount the irresistible nature of the process, and even elaborate on how they themselves had brainwashed others. Further, they described their personal exploitative fund-raising practices and uncontestably political activities as well as the authoritarian, regimented life-style which was intended to separate children from their parents. The effect of such testimony was to discredit the claims of new religious movements that they were religious, and that their members were in fact voluntary, committed converts.

It is this testimony that constitutes what we shall refer to here as atrocity stories. By an atrocity story we refer to the symbolic presentation of actions or events (real or imaginary) in such a context that they are made flagrantly to violate the (presumably) shared premises upon which a given set of social relationships should be conducted. The recounting of such tales is intended as a means of reaffirming normative boundaries. By sharing the reporter's disapproval or horror, an audience reasserts normative prescription and clearly locates the violator as being beyond the limits of public morality. In the case at hand, atrocity stories were constructed so as (1) to portray affiliation in new religious movements as the product of coercive, manipulative practices rather than of voluntary conversion, and (2) to portray new religions themselves as vehicles for the personal, political, and economic aggrandizement of a few leaders at the expense of the well-being of members, their families, and the public at large.

Atrocity Stories: Brainwashing

Apostates' atrocity stories uniformly conveyed a standard, even a statistically predictable, set of anecdotes that portrayed their joining a given new religion as preceded by an overwhelming onslaught on their senses that swiftly eroded their (normally) critical reasoning facilities and left them highly compliant to pressure for conformity.[19] These personal accounts were characteristically filled with references to zombie imagery: apostates characterized themselves as "robots," "automatons," and "mental three-year-olds" in occasional orgies of self-recrimination. The UM apostate, Kathy Knight, said shortly after her deprogramming that she believed her mind to have "been in a strong box for the past three years." (*The News Sentinel,* Fort Wayne, Ind., 11/20/76). All apostates implied, if they did not directly suggest, that there was a malevolent, manipulative force that deliberately orchestrated the destruction of their free will. To the extent that such public accounts were accepted, of course, they undermined the idea that the membership of the new religions was converted in the conventional sense of the word.

An apostate from the Unification movement, Richard Greenwald, for example, related a classic tale of having experienced a series of befuddling processes, drawing on themes of hypnosis, sexual seduction, drugging, and thought reform:

> I think I was hypnotized at first. Basically by the girl that met me because she kept staring into my eyes and I kept being attracted to her eyes. Then, during the meal, it's very possible for some sort of drug to make me more susceptible to the lecture. Then after that it was brainwashing because I was hooked. I wanted to stay there. I wanted to learn what they had to say. There was repetition all the time. Very appealing. The more I heard the more I rejected my family, the outside world. (*The Sun Messenger,* Cleveland Heights, OH 10/16/75)

Another UM apostate, Dennis Carper, recalled how the group allegedly combined sensitivity-training techniques and group dynamic strategies with the rather mysterious method of "spot hypnosis":

> I became involved by going to a dinner and a few of their lectures, but, by attracting you and using spot hypnosis, placing suggestions in your mind on a person-to-person basis, using their hands a lot and telling you anything you are wanting to hear, they draw you deeper and deeper into the church and into the cult. (*The Pioneer,* Smith Center, Kansas, 12/4/75).

Other stories highlighted the mechanisms of inculcating guilt and fear, and of reducing recruits to subservience and child-like dependence during indoctrination. Many UM apostates in particular recounted details of regimented daily routines characteristic of that movement's seminar training and the operation of its field units, and condemned the alleged inability to act and reason autonomously within the context of the communal group. A UM apostate, Larry Gumbiner, for example, recalled of his workshop orientation:

> There were 14 hours of lectures interspersed with singing and games. The whole time I was never left alone. I went off to the bathroom and was reprimanded for being inconsiderate and breaking group unity. (*The Arizona Daily Star,* Tucson, Ariz., 7/1/76).

Others emphasized the movement's techniques of rote memorization and its one-sided discussions with novitiates. Another UM apostate, David Geisler, said "We had to answer word for word from the lecture.... There was no freedom of thinking, dialogue, or originality allowed." (*Columbus Evening Dispatch,* Ohio, 8/20/76). Such indoctrination techniques, apostates claimed, damaged their ability to think either critically or independently about what they were being told. While it was not actual physical imprisonment that kept members within the group, they nevertheless maintained that they did not feel free to leave, thus retaining in these anecdotes the coercion element necessary to make their stories analogous to prisoner-of-war brainwashing studies. Apostate Terry Sherven, for example, referred to what he termed a "psychological force" holding him in the Tony and Susan Alamo Foundation, a sectarian offshoot of the Jesus Movement:

> The brothers would form a ring around you and through the Scripture they would badger you, ask you how you believe, where you could find it in the Scripture that told you now that you were saved and in the house of the Lord. (*The Spotlight,* Washington, D.C., 10/18/76).

Much of this "psychological force," apostates were quick to affirm, resulted from the guilt and fear engendered by a movement's doctrines, for example, concerning the satanic or demonic world outside of the "cult" group, the individual's own sexuality, or the misfortunes awaiting those who left the movement. For example, Scott McQuin, a UM apostate told of the emotional conflict caused him by such techniques:

> I was happy inside the Church but not totally happy because I missed my wife. I was torn between my real family and my Moon family, and they told

me that it was a choice between Satan and God. I would leave the church for a while and go home, but I never felt safe there because of sin. I was convinced that the only place that I would be really safe was the Unification Church. (Schweikhart, 1976:9).

Larry Gumbiner, another UM apostate, speaking to the Oklahoma Bar Association, recalled: "We were told that if we worked against the movement our grandchildren would dig up our bones and spit on them." (*Anadarko News,* OK., 12/2/76). Another UM apostate, Michael Englebert, claimed even more bluntly: "I fear for my life. I was told repeatedly that if I left the Church I would be killed." He ominously recalled one anecdote:

Allan, I can't remember his last name. He was starting to speak out against the church. For some strange reason he was killed a few days later. I had seen him three days before he died. (*The New Haven Register,* Conn., 7/30/76).

An additional, frequently cited element included in apostates' accounts of how individual free will was "broken down" was by physical deprivation, and particularly by violations of values concerning proper nutrition, sufficient rest and sanitation, and physical safety. The implication was that such deprivations (having *prima facie* outrage value to a presumably well-read, rested, and secure reader) helped to debilitate "cult" members, or created in them a disorienting sense of insecurity that contributed to suggestibility and an undermining of free will. In the article above, Alamo Foundation apostate Terry Sherven recounted:

I was always compelled to sleep on the floor, including the winter. There were no adequate sanitation supplies. For instance, one or two toilets would periodically back up for as many as 100-200 males.

Ex-Moonie, Diane Devine, likewise related a tale of unwholesome living conditions during an indoctrination seminar:

Over a hundred girls were crowded into the basement of a recreation hall, some on bunkbeds covered with two-inch foam rubber pads, others on the floor.... All sharing two toilets, two showers, and four sinks. (*Columbus Evening Dispatch,* Ohio, 8/20/76).

The most extreme allegation of physical deprivation was

that individual resistance was critically lowered by a lack of even minimally adequate nutrition. For example: "There was very little protein in the diet. The food was almost totally carbohydrates (cookies, ice cream, coke, peanut butter and jelly sandwiches.) On Sunday you might get a drumstick." (*The Patent Trader,* Mount Kisco, NY, 8/5/76). Likewise, Reed Heller, a UM Apostate, described a similar absence of proper nutrition: "We were kept busy 18 to 20 hours a day and restricted to two low-protein diet meals daily." (*The Dallas Morning News,* 12/4/75).

The result of such deprivations left "cult" members, in the words of another apostate, Robert Buda, (*The Daily Argus,* Mount Vernon, NY, 10/4/75), "zonked out." Buda claimed: "I had lost 20 pounds, had pneumonic cough and was staring strangely into space with a big smile." Christopher Edwards, an ex-Moonie, in his book *Crazy For God* (1979: 51), recounted a dramatic moment of horror when, during his indoctrination at the Unification movement's Boonville ranch on the West Coast, the deleterious physical and psychological effects, including child-like regression, of such a life-style became apparent to him:

> I glanced into the mirror as I brushed my teeth. Back and forth, up and down.... Suddenly, my hand froze. Foamy Crest tooth-paste dribbled down my chin as I stared into the glass. I hardly recognized myself! My face was red and perfectly smooth. My eyes were wide as a child's as round as oranges. My eyelids, which normally partially hooded my eyes, were now glued to the skin above them.... I had the same glassy stare as all the others! I must be deeply spiritual after all, just like they'd said. Amazed and slightly frightened, I headed back to the Chicken Palace to retire. Slipping off my jeans, I climbed into my bag and zipped it up to my chin.... As I lay there drowsily, childhood dreams and fantasies mingled in my mind with images of chocolate-chip cookies and warm milk. I finally drifted off, carelessly running my fingers back and forth across the top of my bag, just as I used to do with my blanket as a child.

Apostates reported that after conditioning by such brain-washing processes they then went out in vampire-like fashion to "infect" others in the same sinister, plague-like way. A UM apostate, Richard Greenwald, offered a classic example of this pattern:

> I learned to hypnotize people and went out to witness, bring in new people.

In Berkeley we were bringing 30 new people every day. And they were hooked by that first supper and lecture.... (Greenwald claimed he hypnotized them when he would) walk up to them, stare at their eyes, get their attention and hold their attention. Talk about things to form a common base with them. I would draw out from them things that they were interested in and then play on those. And I would suggest things to them that they wanted to hear so they would want to come over and see what this is all about. We were trained to do as our leaders did. It was very easy to pick up. (*The Sun Messenger,* Cleveland Heights, OH 10/16/75).

Atrocity Stories: Fraudulent Religion

Anti-cultists, and in particular apostates, employed three primary themes to discredit the claims that the new movements were indeed legitimate religions: (1) deliberate estrangement of family members; (2) economically exploitative practices, and (3) overtly political activities. One of the most common allegations maintained that new religions deliberately sought to separate a young convert from his or her biological family in order to maximize their control. Earlier we alluded to the strains which arose in affected families; here it suffices to point out that such strains and growing estrangement were staple themes of atrocity stories. Thus Dennis Carper, a former member of the Unification movement, told a newspaper reporter:

[Upon joining] You...begin to cut off your other outside connections. First of all, things are not so affected like your school or your friends, then more and more you cut off your friends, your possessions, then your family.

It seems like the more you cut off, the cult becomes more and more demanding and you become more dependent on this small group of people inside the cult. They are the only ones that you have any close relations with and they begin to control you more...until you can't make your own decisions.... I cut myself off from all my family.... (*The Pioneer,* Smith Center, Kansas, 12/4/75).

Others, such as the UM apostate, Michael Englebert, alleged deliberate attempts to interrupt communications between parents and offspring:

They claim that parents are all Satanic because they don't approve of the church. I wrote to my Dad and he never got one of the letters. And when he sent me a message that he was coming to Yankee Stadium I never received it. (*The New Haven Register,* Conn., 7/30/76).

The ultimate indicators of alleged estrangement and of a total reversal of filial obedience may be found in the sensational claims by apostates that they would have willingly committed murder, particularly patricide, on Moon's command. Thus Dennis Carper affirmed: "Had I been asked to kill my parents I would not have hesitated." (*The Sun,* Colorado Springs, Col., 11/23/75). Janis Feiden, also a Unification apostate, concurred: "I would have killed for him. I would have done anything Moon said." (*The Dallas Morning News,* Texas, 10/19/75).

An allegation by apostates was that in the new religions youthful idealism was perverted and exploited for economic ends; "cult" members engaged in fund-raising practices and behavior which they would formerly have defined as dishonest and reprehensible. Stories of these practices generally reflected three sub-themes; (1) that vast amounts of money flowed into the coffers of "cult" leaders through the efforts of their duped followers; (2) that "cult" members deceived and exploited the public to obtain donations; and (3) that members themselves were exploited by ruthless "cult" leaders. For example, apostates complained that the Reverend Moon and other Unification leaders enjoyed a luxurious life-style at the expense of members who lived and worked in spartan communal groups and who were deliberately manipulated. On this theme, ex-Moonie Michael Englebert stated:

The average Moonie out fund-raising on the streets is not responsible for himself... [But] Regional directors and people above them, their senses are all right. (*The New Haven Register,* Conn., 7/30/76).

Such allegations were commonly made of other groups besides the Unification movement, however. Terry Sherven, an apostate from the Alamo Foundation, voiced a similar allegation of economic exploitation of members.

The pay was $1 a week for the first month and after that members were asked to forgo payment. For the last approximately four months that I worked there, I never saw any of the money that I made. (*The Spotlight,* Washington, D.C., 10/18/76).

Likewise, both Edwards[20] and Underwood[21] reported in detail their rationales and deceptive activities as fund-raisers for the Unification movement, as did Ellen Rosemara and other apostates at the 1976 "Dole hearing."[22] Cynthia Slaughter told the various officials present at that hearing (p.24):

> ... I fund-raised 18 hours a day ... I was kicked out of office buildings three times and came back bragging. And we really got a lot of reinforcement from our leaders.... I also fund-raised in bars at 11:00 at night. I was told to use my "fallen nature" to get money. I'm sorry if I sound this way, but I just feel I was exploited. And did do deceitful things, which is against my general character.[23]

Other apostates provided "seedy" testimonies that discredited the agencies which, presumably, had socialized and encouraged them to engage in these activities. The UM apostate, Dennis Carper, told one reporter, in detailing his fund-raising exploits: "I can't remember how many times I took the last dime from a bum." Likewise, another UM apostate, Richard Greenwald, reported:

> I pulled in $700 or $800 a week, selling flowers. You go to businesses, commercial places, industrial places. You sneak in. I was pretty good at it.... I could get money from anyone now. I know how. I got the last penny from a bum on the street. (*The Sun Messenger,* Cleveland Heights, Ohio. 10/16/75).

Indeed, exploiting the poor for allegedly lofty spiritual purposes was a standard atrocity sub-theme of apostates. For example, Terry Murray, also a UM apostate, recalled:

> We went door to door in the poorest section, telling the people we represented an organization called the World Crusade and were selling flowers to raise money to help rehabilitate people who were in trouble. The girl told me, "Any line you can use is a good line." So the line I adopted was "We're opening drug centers all over the United States and we're planning to open one in the Albany area and would appreciate your "financial assistance."
>
> I was lying, of course, but I figured that if God wants me to lie, it's OK. (*The Knickerbocker News,* Albany, NY, 6/16/76).

In the same vein, explaining how she was engaged in "heavenly deception" to earn between $80 and $200 a day for the Unification movement as a street solicitor, an apostate, Ann Gordon, said:

> I went door to door selling peanuts.... It was incredibly easy. I was told how to put ten cents worth of peanuts in a bag and sell them for a dollar. Later, we sold unshelled nuts because there were fewer to a bag. All I did was smile and say, "Hi, I'm with the Unification Church and we're raising money for a drug program!" Or, "We're trying to bring families together and people to God, won't you help us!" We'd say it real fast, and people never asked questions. Of course, we never *had* a drug program." (Crittenden, 1976: 92).

Another atrocity tale theme, which was designed to damage the image of "cults" dealt with the alleged political aspirations of their leaders. This charge was levelled, usually at the UM, by apostates who claimed to have been involved in lobbying and/or other explicitly political activities in direct assignment from leaders of the movement. Such practices by religious denominations and other legally recognized religious groups, of course, were specifically illegal. These allegations of political infringement were often presented together with vitriolic excerpts from some of Moon's "insider" speeches (e.g., the *Master Speaks* series) to UM members in which he spoke out directly of his vision of a world-wide theocracy that would be created in part by such lobbying activities. Particularly good illustrations of such stories can be seen in 1976 at the first "Dole hearing," and again during 1976-78 when U.S. Representative Donald Fraser chaired a House Subcommittee on International Organizations in an investigation of the UM's possible role in the "Koreagate" scandal (hereafter the "Fraser Committee"). In 1976, for example, a UM apostate, Ann Gordon, gave a detailed personal statement before Senators Robert Dole, James Buckley, and others, in which she named both prominent legislators and the respective UM members assigned to lobby their offices as part of the "capitol hill ministry," i.e., an effort to promote pro-South Korean foreign policy (particularly American economic and military aid). She told officials:

> In August of 1975 I was sent to Washington D.C., at Moon's personal

request, to do public relations work on Capitol Hill for him and for South Korea. The Washington P.R. Center has approximately 20-25 young men and women working full-time in this capacity. I, like all the others, was assigned a list of Senators and Congressmen which were to be my own contacts exclusively.... P.R. members were to make gradual acquaintances and friendships with staff members and aides and eventually with the Congressmen and Senators themselves, inviting them to a suite in the Washington Hilton rented at $54/day (although the normal rate should have been around $120/day), where dinner and films or short lectures on Moon's ideas and "accomplishments" would be presented. All this effort is sort of an on-going program by Moon to get political support for himself and the Park Chung Hee dictatorship in South Korea. (CEFM, 1976, II: 3-5).

Similarly, in 1976 Allan Tate Wood, the apostate former president of Moon's anti-communist Freedom Leadership Foundation, testified to the Fraser committee about the "true" political aims of Moon.[24] This account of establishing American Youth for a Just Peace, a UM-based pro-Vietnam war lobbying group, was typical of the anecdotes in which he sought to discredit the UM.

Mr. Wood. We set up the American Youth for a Just Peace to be a legitimate partisan political lobby organization to carry out pro-war activities.... We used Unification Church members. I called up all the heads of the Unification Church in May 1970 and invited them to come to Washington and bring with them as many members as they could. We gathered about 70 or 80 people, and we lobbied for a week, going out in teams of three to all Congressmen's and Senator's offices.

Mr. Fraser. I asked you earlier about American Youth for a Just Peace. I understand they lobbied to support the Cambodian invasion. When that took place, was the Unification Church asked to help in some fashion?

Mr. Wood. It was Unification Church members who carried out the lobbying. I was president of the Freedom Leadership Foundation, and I was co-chairman of the American Youth for a Just Peace. Every staff member in that office was a member of the Unification Church, except Charles Stevens.

Mr. Fraser. Were there instructions on that particular lobbying effort coming from Church authorities?

Mr. Wood. Yes.

Mr. Fraser. From whom?

Mr. Wood. Again, coming ultimately from Mr. Moon.[25]

Chris Elkins, another high level Moonie who carried on the activities of the apostate role for some time after leaving the

Unification movement, recounted for the Fraser committee details of the way in which he had been assigned by the Unification movement to participate in (among other activities) work for congressional candidates perceived as favorable to pro-South Korean policies:

> Mr. Fraser. Now you referred to the fact that you were assigned to work in a political campaign. When did that take place?
> Mr. Elkins. This was in October 1974. ... I was sent up to New York to participate in campaigns.
> Mr. Fraser. Who gave you the instructions to go to New York?
> Mr. Elkins. Neil Salonen. [President of the UM in America.]
> Mr. Fraser. Did he give them to you directly?
> Mr. Elkins. Yes.[26]

Elkins also testified as to general lobbying activities of the Unification movement:

> Mr. Fraser. Let me ask you about this. You say that you, yourself sat up at night working on the automatic typewriter typing letters?
> Mr. Elkins. Yes.
> Mr. Fraser. These would be directed to members of Congress?
> Mr. Elkins. Yes.
> Mr. Fraser. The subject matter was what?
> Mr. Elkins. Was concerning military aid.
> Mr. Fraser. Military aid to—?
> Mr. Elkins. South Korea, particularly Southeast Asia, particularly if there was a build up.
> Mr. Fraser. Where were these typewriters located?
> Mr. Elkins. 2025 "I" Street which were FLF headquarters at that time.[27]

The Impact of Apostasy and Atrocity Stories

Apostates, and the atrocity stories that they recounted, had an enormous impact on the new religions because these stories influenced both general public opinion and the perceptions of institutional officials who controlled resources important to the new religions. The effects of apostate activities were so pervasive that only those dealing with the media and political institutions can be considered here.[28]

As we noted earlier, public perceptions of the new religions were based largely on media accounts. The American media tended to accept in rather uncritical fashion apostates' recountings of their experiences in the new religions as well as their portrayals of the leaders and organizations of these movements. There were three primary reasons (among others that might be identified) for this uncritical posture. First, apostates offered precisely the kind of dramatic articles and spectacular headlines which made for "good copy"—for example, themes such as "lost" children, sexual and economic exploitation, megalomanic leaders, foreign conspiracy and political subversion, brainwashing and deprogramming, and tearfully reunited families. Second, media representatives tended to share the value orientations of apostates and their parents, and hence it was not surprising that they empathized with parents and applied similar ethnocentric and/or conservative standards of comparison in evaluating the radical changes in dress, attitudes, behavior and life-styles of new religions' members. Third, it was difficult for media representatives to believe that apostates and their families would expend so much time and energy if there were not a real crisis. Because they appeared to have little to gain by seeking publicity for publicity's sake, the apostates and their families were presumed to be sincere. They were, after all, fairly ordinary, reasonable, middle-class people for the most part, who elicited ready sympathy in their statement of grievances.

The consequences of the routine publishing of apostates' allegations were devastating to the new religions. Apostates' stories were printed in literally hundreds of local newspapers across the country as the sample provided above suggests. Newspapers also frequently reprinted stories by apostates from other newspapers, creating the impression of larger numbers than was actually the case. In addition to these newspaper accounts, major magazines that appealed to family or youth readerships ran similar articles. For example, during the late 1970s, magazines such as *McCall's* (Rasmussen, 1976), *Seventeen* (Remsberg and Remsberg, 1976), *Good Housekeeping* (Crittenden, 1976), and *People* (1978) printed articles with lurid titles such as "How Sun Myung Moon Lures America's Children"; "Why I Quit the Moon Cult"; "The

Incredible Story of Ann Gordon and Reverend Sun Myung Moon"; and "A California Teenager Goes Underground to Investigate Life Among the Moonies." Each sought to outdo the others in finding a sensational story line, and taken together such articles created the impression that "cults" were growing rapidly in size and that innocent children (not adults) were being plucked from the streets and from college campuses at an alarming rate. Further, numerous radio and television talk-shows featured apostates, and major television network documentaries (*e.g.*, on ABC and NBC) drew heavily upon apostates for eye-witness confirmation of the true nature of "cults." Finally, in addition to the extensive media coverage accorded to these individuals, there were numerous books in which apostates presented their own accounts of their experiences while members of the new religions. Some of the more notable (and best-selling) books of this genre included *Peoples Temple; Peoples Tomb* (Kerns, 1979); *Escape* (Martin, 1979); *Walled In: The True Story of a Cult* (Conner, 1979); *Six Years with God* (Mills, 1979); *Moonstruck* (Wood and Vitek, 1979); *Crazy for God* (Edwards, 1979); and *Hostage to Heaven* (Underwood and Underwood, 1979). These tracts were paralleled historically by titles with much the same flavor and which had much the same impact on earlier new religions. Examples of these earlier apostates included the following: *Watchtower Chaos* (Tomsett, 1974), *I Was Raised a Jehovah's Witness* (Hewitt, 1979), *Awful Disclosures of the Hotel Dieu Nunnery* (Monk, 1836), *Six Months in a Convent* (Reed, 1835) and *Wife No. 19: or, The Story of a Life in Bondage, Being a Complete Expose of Mormonism* (Young, 1835).

The result of these apostate accounts was not only that the media regularly aired apostate-inspired atrocity stories but also that the new religions were accorded relatively little positive or balancing media coverage. It was not surprising, therefore, that, in a national poll of teenagers, 41% said they had heard of Reverend Sun Myung Moon and the Unification movement, and 32% reported holding an unfavorable opinion of the movement.[29] Representatives of various institutions with whom members of the new religions came into contact were similarly influenced. Thus, when the institutional leaders deliberated over setting policies that might affect the new religions, whether in local town councils or congressional committees, one major source of data upon which they drew was the large volume of almost exclusively negative media reports.

There were numerous illustrations of apostates playing an important role in swaying public opinion, and of discrediting the new religions to groups seeking to investigate them or to legislate against them. For example, in mid-1979, Christopher Edwards, author of *Crazy for God* (1979), made public charges that child abuse was rampant in both East and West Coast branches of the UM. He alleged that children were separated from their parents, not given proper medical attention, kept in overcrowded living quarters, and not allowed to attend school. Howard Lasher, a Brooklyn Assemblyman and lawyer chairing the New York State Assembly Committee on Child Care, instituted hearings based on these charges. The hearings began by probing the treatment of children in the Unification movement, but the committee was soon distracted by the sensational (larger) questions concerning the movement's operation and resources. While these hearings did not produce any substantive governmental actions (indeed, under examination Edwards' charges were revealed to be grossly exaggerated), a parade of anti-cult witnesses used the occasion—at least tacitly supported by the government—to discredit the new religions in general and the Unification movement in particular.

There were other instances. As we have shown, former UM members testified at the "Fraser Committee" inquiry into "Koreagate" during 1976-78, and following the Jonestown, Guyana, tragedy in 1978, a small number of UM apostates suddenly claimed to recall having received suicide instructions from UM leaders on the West Coast (Carroll and Bauer, 1979). Suffice it to say that in the many cases where apostates could not claim to have inspired a totally new investigation (in the fashion of Edwards) they could at least take credit for having added more fuel to an ongoing fire.

Summary and Conclusions

In this paper, we have considered apostates and atrocity stories as one outcome of the process which anti-cultists have termed deprogramming. It is our contention that apostates and the atrocity stories which they recount* have played a major role in discrediting social movements throughout history. Because most new religions—movements that we have termed world transforming movements—rely upon persuasive rather than coercive tactics to bring about the change they envision, the struggle for credibility and legitimacy is vital to their interests. It is this critical resource which apostates have been relatively successful in denying them, and the lack of legitimacy has significantly altered the new religions' strategies, tactics, and success. Thus, it would be difficult to assess the course of social movements from a sociological perspective without an understanding of this powerful mechanism of social control.

From our perspective, apostasy has its roots in basic conflicts of interest and in the exertion of power. It was the violation of fundamental familial interests which precipitated strain and conflict between parents and their offspring who had joined new religions. When satisfactory resolution of this strain was not forthcoming, and when sensible open discussion on differences of interest could not develop, parents began to entertain extreme explanations for their offspring's aberrant behavior. What emerged was the brainwashing and programming ideology which led, in turn, to the concept and procedure of deprogramming. In fact, deprogramming constituted an exertion of power although parents and deprogrammers both had a strong interest in depicting it in therapeutic terms. We have contended that a number of results were possible in any instance of deprogramming, and that apostasy constituted a special case of exit from the new religions, in which former members accepted a reinterpretation of their experiences in terms

*Editor's Note: The authors recount these atrocity stories as examples of what has been said. They are not necessarily evidence of what happened, nor—as is apparent from the analysis which follows—do the authors accord them credence. They are, however, evidence of what some people allege happened, and what the media and some official bodies have been prepared to consider as reports of things that have occurred. This evidence is reproduced here without attempt at refutation by the publishers, who, nevertheless, believe that there is another perspective from which the cases presented in this section should be regarded.

consistent with the anti-cult ideology. Because apostates claimed retrospectively and publicly to verify the claims of the anti-cultists, both achieved considerable visibility and legitimacy. It was their availability to the media which influenced both public opinion in general and institutional decision-makers in particular. Thus, although apostates were relatively few in number, their influence on the development of the new religions has been immense.

FOOTNOTES

1. See David G. Bromley and Anson D. Shupe, Jr., *"Moonies" in America: Cult, Church and Crusade,* Beverly Hills, Calif.: Sage 1979.
2. See for example, William Gamson, *The Strategy of Social Protest,* New York: The Dorsey Press, 1975.
3. For example, H. Richard Niebuhr, *The Social Sources of Denominationalism,* New York: Holt, 1929.
4. See, for example, John McCarthy and Mayer M. Zald, *The Trend of Social Movements in America: Professionalization and Resource Mobilization,* Morristown, N.J.: General Learning Press, 1973; *idem,* "Resource mobilization in social movements: a partial theory," *American Journal of Sociology,* 82, 1977, pp. 1212-39; Mayer N. Zald and Roberta Ash, "Social movement organizations: growth, decay, and change" in R.R. Evans (ed.), *Social Movements: A Reader and Source Book,* Chicago: Rand McNally, 1973, pp. 80-101; Mayer N. Zald and M.A. Berger, "Social movements in organizations: coup d'etat, insurgency, and mass movements." *American Journal of Sociology,* 83, 1978, pp. 823-861.
5. See Bromley and Shupe, *"Moonies" in America...op. cit.*
6. We have referred to specific publications wherever we draw upon particular data or methodologies. For a complete set of references and discussion of methods, see Bromley and Shupe, *op. cit.; idem,* "Evolving foci in participant observation: research as an emerging process," in V. Shaffir, R. Stebbins, and A. Turowetz (eds.), *The Social Experience of Field Work,* New York: St. Martin's Press, 1980, pp. 191-203; Anson D. Shupe, Jr., and David G. Bromley, *The New Vigilantes: Deprogrammers, Anti-Cultists, and the New Religions,* Beverly Hills, Calif.: Sage, 1980; *idem,* "Walking a Tightrope: dilemmas of participant observation of groups in conflict," *Qualitative Sociology,* 2, January, 1980, pp. 3-21.
7. See Bromley and Shupe, *"Moonies" in America...op. cit.*
8. See Bromley and Shupe, " 'Just a few years seem like a lifetime:' a role theory approach to participation in religious movements" in Louis Kriesberg (ed.),

Research in Social Movements, Conflict and Change, Greenwich Conn.: JAI Press, 1979.

9. We have described these in A.D. Shupe, Jr., and D.G. Bromley, *The New Vigilantes, op. cit.,* p. 331.

10. See Erving Goffman, *Asylums,* Garden City, N.Y.: Doubleday, 1961, pp. 306-7.

11. Evidence for this assertion is to be found in our research on the motives and predispositions of recruits to the UM, and its sources of attraction for them: see Bromley and Shupe, *"Moonies"...op. cit.; "Just a few years..." op. cit.*

12. See Shupe and Bromley, *The New Vigilantes, op. cit.; idem.,* "The Moonies and the Anti-Cultists: Movement and Countermovement in Conflict," *Sociological Analysis,* 40, Winter, 1979, pp. 325-66.

13. David G. Bromley, Anson D. Shupe, Jr., and Joseph C. Ventimiglia, "The role of anecdotal atrocities in the social construction of evil" in James T. Richardson (ed.), *The Deprogramming Controversy: Sociological, Psychological, Legal, and Historical Perspectives,* New Brunswick, N.J.: Transaction Books, forthcoming.

14. See Eileen Barker, "With enemies like that... some functions of deprogramming as an aid to sectarian membership" in James Richardson (ed.), *op. cit.,* forthcoming, for a discussion of the functions for movement solidarity served by such anecdotes in the British Unification movement.

15. See Jim Siegleman and Flo Conway, "Playboy Interview: Ted Patrick." *Playboy,* March, 1979.

16. *Ibid.,* pp. 70-1.

17. Barbara Underwood and Betty Underwood, *Hostage to Heaven,* New York: Clarkson N. Potter, Inc., 1979.

18. Allan Tate Wood and J. Vitek, *Moonstruck,* New York: William Morrow, 1979.

19. See Bromley, Shupe, and Ventimiglia, *op. cit.*

20. Christopher Edwards, *Crazy for God,* Englewood Cliffs, N.J.: Prentice-Hall, 1979, pp. 157-71.

21. See Underwood and Underwood, *op. cit.,* pp. 79-95.

22. See CEFM (National Ad Hoc Committee Engaged in Freeing Minds) *A Special Report. The Unification Church: Its Activities and Practices.* Vols. I and II, Arlington, Texas: National Ad Hoc Committee, A Day of Affirmation and Protest, 1976.

23. *Ibid.,* p. 24.

24. U.S. Government, 1976, "Activities of the Korean Central Intelligence Agency in the United States" (Hearings before the Subcommittee on International Organizations of the Committee on International Relations, U.S. House of Representatives, Part II) Washington D.C.: U.S. Government Printing Office, 1976, pp. 20-42; and U.S. Government, Investigation of Korean-American Relations (Report of the Subcommittee on International Organizations of the

Committee on International Relations, U.S. House of Representatives) Washington, D.C.: U.S. Government Printing Office, 1978, pp. 338-48.
25. *Ibid.*, 1976, p. 24.
26. *Ibid.*, 1976, p. 51.
27. *Ibid.*, 1976, p. 53.
28. For a broader view of these effects, see Bromley and Shupe, *"Moonies..."* *op. cit.*, and Shupe and Bromley, *The New Vigilantes, op: cit.*
29. *Religion in America 1979-80,* Princeton, N.J.: Princeton Religious Research Center, 1979.

TIME, GENERATIONS, AND SECTARIANISM

Bryan Wilson

The Visibility of the New Religious Movements

It is perhaps a reflection of the increasing relativism of modern society and with it of the associated demise of cohesive social values, that what at one time were easily designated as "sects" or "cults", both by the public at large and by sociologists, have now become "new religious movements".[1] The old terms had, for many, pejorative connotations, and perhaps that reflected certain widely-held social values which, in a pluralist society, are somehow no longer tenable or respectable. The newly-developed usage reflects something more than this, however. It indicates, first, that we are aware that many of the new movements do not quite fit the assumptions that were commonly made of sects—which were often thought of as break-away groups from a central tradition, often with the implication that a process of schism had occurred at their origins (an assumption which was not, of course, by any means always true). And second, it suggests that during the past two or three decades, we have become very much more aware of the emergence of new religions than we were at any earlier time, even though it might be very difficult to show that there were now in fact a larger number of new religions than at previous periods of history. We learn of groups that operate in regions remote from our own society, but we also know that news about them may itself be the first step towards their dissemination to our own locale. Thus, many members of the public heard about Scientology, the Ananda

217

Community, the Moonies, and Krishna Consciousness, *before* these groups had actually spread to their own areas, and this is a qualitatively different circumstance from any that prevailed for most sectarian groups in the past. Whereas, fifty years or more ago, sects were known because they were locally observed—because people at least knew someone who knew people who belonged—today, quite a lot is recounted by the media about religious movements before people have any other sort of acquaintance with them. The movements are more newsworthy (partly *because* they are not local schisms, but are of exotic origin); the media are more effective; the movements themselves know how to exploit the opportunities for publicity, and devote themselves to this as a means of disseminating their ideas; and, perhaps most important of all, they now generally recruit a different and more conspicious section of the population—the young.

It is largely the shift in generational appeal that keeps modern sectarianism in the eye of the media. New sects in the past tended to recruit from among sections of the population that were—as social strata—less the focus of attention. Of course, their appeal in the initial stages (with which alone we are concerned) varied from case to case: the relatively poor, working class, urban and industrial clientele of the Pentecostalists; the middle-aged, middle-class, genteel, largely female following, by relatively isolated individuals, of Christian Science and Vedanta; the lower middle-class, self-employed votaries of the Plymouth Brethren; the down-and-outs to whom the Salvation Army took its message; and the small town, rurally-minded (if not always rurally-bred) converts to Seventh-day Adventism. Of course, all of these groups, even in their early days, received some press publicity. Sects always make attractive copy for the press, even if journalists rarely take the time to really understand what a sect stands for and what it does. But, in these cases, press publicity was mainly localized. Occasionally, some celebrated issue, such as the death of the patient of a Christian Science practitioner, or the disappointed adventual hopes of the Seventh-day Adventists, attained wider newspaper coverage, but the sustained interest of the press, such as was manifested, from the late 1960s until the present time, in groups such as the Unification Church, the Scientologists, and Krishna Consciousness, is a relatively new phenomenon. And we may attribute that persisting fascination at least in part to the fact that contemporary new religious movements draw into their ranks a disproportionate number of the relatively young. And the young, as a class, are themselves something of an obsession with the media.

That that should be so should cause no surprise. In a rapidly changing society, youth is at a premium and age at a discount. In a society which pins its faith to technology, education (of the young) is a paramount concern. Experience is most probably a handicap (at least in the technical matters which are, today, socially evaluated as of far more importance than are moral matters) and hence age is a disadvantage. The redistribution of income in Western societies reflects the enhancement of the young, who constitute a class of consuming non-producers. A consuming class in a consumer society becomes a principal target for advertising, and the advertisers, seeking to sell, espouse luxury and hedonism as their values, and these are the most widely canvassed values of modern society, and they are directed vigorously at the young.[2] The news media are themselves powerfully influenced (not necessarily in a sinister way) by advertising, and it is not surprising that advertising values percolate the media themselves, become the "common sense" of modernity. In a world of increased and increasingly diverse leisure possibilities, youth stands more to profit from, and to become more involved in, new leisure activities, from hang-gliding to punk rock, from surfing to marijuana. When, occasionally, older people take up such pursuits they do so, often, to persuade themselves that they are young, since it is among the young that life is still being lived. The media men themselves, following their instinct for whatever is new, recognize in the young their obvious source of copy, and hence provide the means for a change in the society's generational centre of gravity (given the nature of its values one might call it a generational centre of frivolity). In the light of these changes, we may say that the things in religion that concern the media are likely to be those things that involve the young.

That the new religious movements today should have a dispro-portionate appeal to the young in part appears to be a conse-quence of the diversification of life-chances that now exist for young people, and the bewildering uncertainty of life-styles and values. One need not argue that there is a vacuum in the value system of modern society, so much as that there is a plethora of life-styles with no centre. The constellation of values that, at least in traditional societies, were part of what it meant to be a Frenchman, a Bavarian, a Piedmontese, or a Briton, and (at least in parts of the United States) an American, has undergone considerable erosion. Patriotism is now neither itself an automatic value nor the core of other virtues which, in the past, men were accustomed to identify as their peculiar national heritage. The virtue has largely gone out of nations, and even more dramatically has gone out of those states—such as America—which never settled down long enough really to be "nations". Many of the new movements represent exotic values that stem from other—apparently unsullied, cultures which retain some element of continuity and tradition, and the aura of the mystery of which—is seen as still "authentic", because it is mystery untrammelled by the impediments and accretions that have grown up around the central Western religious traditions. The young know so much less of the corruptions and the levels of mendacity and duplicity of other cultures than they know of their own. Exotic cults appear to come from a noble and more integrated tradition. Alternatively, science, or meta-science, with the offer of new "beyond the establishment" techniques of therapy or emotional enlargement may also be attractive. It is not, however, my purpose to speculate on the appeal of new movements, nor their special attraction for the young, so much as to suggest that it is because of the appeal to this particular clientele that the new movements have obtained their impact on Western societies, and that this is partly so because, in the course of the past three decades, we have seen, especially with respect to consumption and leisure, a marked shift towards preoccupation with the young.

The Sectarian Sense of Time

New movements arising in Western cultures have, at their outset, generally presented themselves as the purveyors of urgently needed religious truth and practice, in a way which is not true either for the traditional churches or for sects that have achieved the status of being long established. What new movements claim—and this is also true of sects of the past at the moment when *they* were new—is that they have new truth to be communicated *now*. They present themselves, therefore as arising *now*, at this specific present, with the implication that all history has been but a prelude leading to this moment—the moment of the sect's emergence. Theirs is always a Whig view of history: what has unfolded hitherto has all been in the course of ushering in the opportunity for the sect to arise on the world scene. The sect appropriates to itself a central place in the scheme of historical time. The very totalism of sectarianism makes this claim clear. All else in history, no matter how long a course one surveys, recedes into insignificance beside the momentous significance of the emergence of the new movement. Time comes to take on a different perspective, and history a new meaning.

Christian sects in particular, of course, have a repertoire of reasons for urgency, and clearly, urgency has a close connection with the effectiveness of a proselytizing religion. Paramount among these causes of expedition is the millennial tradition. Most millennial sects have embraced the pre-millennialist position in which an early second advent of the messiah is awaited: indeed, we generally deny the term "millennialist", or "millenarian" to groups that espouse a post-adventual conception of the millennium (which is the characteristic orthodox position of both Roman and Protestant Christianity). Second adventist sects arise in the expectation of an early advent: they do not arise to proclaim the advent centuries hence. Their truth is urgent, and the advent is to be sudden and soon. This was so for the early Christians, if New Testament and patristic evidence is to be relied upon. It was true for the radical sects of the Reformation in Europe. James Nayler did not enter Bristol in imitation of Christ merely as a symbolic gesture, and

George Fox would not have proclaimed "Woe unto the wicked city of Lichfield" without the expectation that something was soon to befall that quiet country town. I need not catalogue the anticipations of Shakers, Southcottians, Millerites and Christadelphians, nor in our own day of Jehovah's Witnesses and the Children of God to justify my assertions concerning the millennial tradition. All have been new movements which, in their newness, have seen themselves as operating in the last moments of time.[3]

A similar sense of destiny is to be found even in those Christian movements in which the advent and the millennium is not the primary focus of concern (and I say "not primary" since what literalist sect could deny these elements?). Among even the post-millennialists, the pressing need to convert as many people as possible to usher in the millennium on earth, lent a spirit of eagerness to their activities. The revivalist tradition, whether pre- or post-millennial (or doctrinally vague on the issue) applied the same sense of pressure to the masses who exposed themselves to the ministrations of the preachers. The typical appeal of the revivalist, whether in the spontaneous revival of the kind evident in Wales in 1905, or in the organized campaign that developed following, on both sides of the Atlantic, the activities of C.G. Finney, made the greatest use of the idea that men were currently living in the last moments of time—of their own time, if not of the world's. The demand that people should "give" themselves before it was too late, was a commonplace. The idea that a man's life might at any time be required of him, justified the importunity with which he was urged to embrace the faith. The preachers, and the sects that developed in the revivalistic style— sometimes arising as a direct consequence of free-lance, interdenominational revivalist preaching—knew that the idea that "the time is at hand", no matter in what sense the words were uttered or received, was a vital element to the success of their work. And so it was that revivalistic sects shared with more exclusive millenarian movements, a self-interpretation which made the sect itself the vital turning point of post-biblical history.

Given the frequency of this claim, it would be surprising if movements manifestly in neither the millennialist nor revivalist tradition did not in some measure also adopt this powerful reinforcement of their own claims to importance. Even therapeutic and manipulationist groups like Christian Science and Scientology present themselves as ushering in a transformed world of opportunities which better be grasped as soon as possible. Sometimes there are dark hints about the shortage of time to accomplish all that must be done—in the case of Scientology, by way of enhancing human intelligence in the face of the threat of disaster. It cannot be said that Christian Science or any of the New Thought movements made quite the same case for urgent action as millennial or revivalist sects, but even here the claims of these movements had to be validated by the implication that the present was a special time, the time ripe for the discovery of new truth, in the optimistic expectation that once that truth was understood its appropriateness for the times would be unquestioned.

New religious movements share a radically elliptical perspective of history. Often they move from the New Testament, or the early church, to their own foundation and teaching: little that happened in between can be of much consequence. What was started at the beginning, lapsed throughout subsequent history, and is being worked out now. The intervening centuries, and the life of faith of the generations between, have played little if any part in the divine purpose or the movement's own programme. In proclaiming themselves to have restored, recovered, or revivified the truth, the sects in Western culture also implicitly claim that they are the movement of the times, and that "now is the accepted time".

The sectarian sense of time differs radically from that of traditional church religion. The Church is engaged in offering an opportune truth, not an importunate truth. It is concerned to make the offer recurrently and repetitively to successive generations. Even if, as must be the case, the idea of an ultimate millennium persists, it does so only as a remote, shall we say a very ultimate, concern, and not as an early prospect requiring present canvass. The Church's religious functions throughout history were adjusted to the need to socialize each new generation in a repertoire of value orientations that are themselves socially entrenched and supportive of stable social order. This is particularly manifest in the Church's commitment to maintain relative natural law as long as man remains in a fallen state and the world forgoes God's perfect law. Thus, the Church counsels the rich and powerful to exercise mercy, and urges the poor and suffering to adopt attitudes of subservience and contentment with their lot. In all of this, the significance of the Church as an agency for social order and control is clear, supporting established authority, (providing always that those authorities do not depart too radically or too abruptly from the canons of religious truth).

The balance of Church/State power is not our concern, but clearly it is a balance which, over the course of history, has increasingly—if, albeit, not invariably and uniformly—favoured the state. Over the long run, the Church is increasingly integrated into secular culture, and although, initially, it may have done much to shape that culture, gradually it compromises its own early sense of urgent mission, accommodates diversity and apathy, and eventually ceases to condemn, or even to identify, heresy. It continues to offer its ministrations and to perform its rituals recurrently and repetitively for successive generations, and it continues to state, albeit *sotto voce,* its ideological commitments, but it abandons any hope it had of sudden or early prospect of change. If the Church travels in hope, it has ceased to speculate about what it might be like to arrive. In the preservation of traditional rituals, may be seen the extent to which the Church has committed itself to the long view of itself, its mission, and the purpose of religion. Its own role-structure has reassured its professionals of continuity. Its rites of passage have been undramatic servicing of a population: social change for the Church, as for Talcott Parsons, was for generational change not the radical transformation of society. Its scholars built up a sophisticated sense of historical time into which original revelation is rather curiously accommodated. So it is that the Church's entire operation has come to convey a sense of time wholly different from that according to which new movements have always operated.

Whereas the Church has offered timeless truth, the sect has always canvassed timely truth.[4] The Church, acting now, seeks to act as it assumes that it has always acted. The sect tends to urge the finality of opportunity, offering *now* what has not been offered before, and what, in high probability, will not be offered ever again. It is this lack of historical perspective that permits so many new movements to appear as especially destined for the hour. Such a movement appeals to the strong sense of personal destiny that inheres in every man: to his feeling that something must happen, and mixed with that his feeling that it ought to be happening now, whilst he himself is alive to perceive it. Of course, there is, in all religion, churchly or sect-like, a strong egocentric element. Men are concerned with their own destiny—in any case. But the time-sense of sectarianism and tradition diverge radically, and it is always possible in the churchly context, or, more accurately, the traditional context, to see the present as merely another moment in a long, perhaps unending, series. There is nothing special about it, only something special in that it is *I*, who see it: *it* is special for *us*, we are not special to *it*. This relativism is alien to sectarian assumptions: in the new movement "I" and "it" converge to make this a vital, perhaps a final, moment in time.

It is precisely because the Church has this sense of its own continuity, and because it has a traditional commitment, that it shares a sense of time with the more cultivated and educated classes of the society in which it operates. The masses, however, do not share this historical sense, although it can be brought to their awareness through agencies such as the Church and—under the types of education that were fashionable in at least European countries until three decades or so ago—the school. The abandonment of education in history, in classics, and in human culture, exposes a larger population to an ahistorical sense of time, and it allows them to exult in their sense of the contemporary. In some respects, the detachment from historic culture creates a predisposition towards the espousal of the radical sense of timely truth which is offered by sectarianism. When men do not test religious claims against the data of history; when they do not enquire into the history of prophetic ideas; when they fail to compare particular accounts of the discovery (or recovery) of religious truth against all the other similar accounts—then they are more likely to be impressed by whatever religion is now canvassed. When they do not know what has happened before, how many messiahs there have been, how many false dawns, and how many ineffective therapies, they are more likely to accept the latest new ideas. They are more likely, given this escape from the weight of the past, to believe in their own importance and the global, cosmic, or epochal significance of the specific time in which they live. They are not here by chance, they are here to reap destiny.

The Sense of the Modern

All of this is in itself neither to endorse nor to condemn the teaching of the humanitarian liberal perspective. It is only to suggest that the neglect of such an education is one factor which promotes the sectarian consciousness. The effect of this neglect is that even educated contemporary man has a different time consciousness from that of his educated predecessors, and that this alone makes the present age appear to more people as more significant, more special, and more unprecedented than perhaps any period was regarded in the past. And all of this contributes to the attractiveness of the new, including new religious movements. Of course, this argument, if it is sustained, does not specifically explain any particular new religious movement, nor does it by any means exhaust the evidence from which causal imputations might be made: it offers one limited precondition which appears to favour the acceptance of new religious ideas in contemporary Western society. (It says nothing, for example, about the proclivity to schism within religious organizations, which is another source of diversity in sectarianism.) Today the scale of man's vision, and particularly that of the young, is foreshortened, not because they lack education but because of the impress of the modern world itself, because, that is, present time and the contemporary scene are so powerfully represented to us all. Whilst we may have little direct personal communion with our fellow men, we have instantaneous, multifarious, urgent communication about them and a stronger sense by far than ever before of the importance of "now".

The sense of the modern is a familiar theme of contemporary literary criticism employed in explaining the changing pattern of literary consciousness, and in an age of widespread literacy, its extension to a wider public. There has been a radical shift in man's consciousness from a time when the present was largely a time for the celebration of the past, in societies which devoted perhaps their best energies to memorializing past events and former leaders, to a type of consciousness in which men live only for the present and in eager anticipation of the near future. It needs little documentation, except to add that not only are we committed to planning techniques for the ordering of our resources, including our future time, but that we also perceive the rapid erosion of structures that in the past could readily, albeit often mistakenly, be taken as timeless and enduring. It is this erosion, and the sense of a supposed possibility that we might make all things new, which feeds the modernist impulse. Yet, despite the optimism born of planning and technology, it is clear that some of the forces that re-order our sense of time and value are not amenable to any sort of control. The everyday phenomena that promote radical change include not only the new planning procedures and technical facilities, but forces which are manifestly at work beyond the programming apparatus and the arena of political decision-making. In the face of such forces, even the planners are rendered hopeless and defenceless. Inflation, for example, is the monetary expression of the erosion of values, and a potent source of uncalculated and perhaps uncontrollable change. Democracy, espoused as the political logic of the times, and itself a contributor to the optimistic modernist consciousness, entails a concomitant status-uncertainty which leads, paradoxically to processes of status inflation, and so to the enfeeblement of the agencies of legitimation in social life. Migrations, which we often acknowledge as necessary for humanitarian reasons, create structural disruption of social systems and promote the confusion of values and problems of socialization.

Politicians and planners, media men, and all the other makers of the modern consciousness, usually acknowledge only the most visible effects of these disruptions. Because the socialization process is very slow, political men, who seek quick solutions—solutions that will bring them credit whilst still in office—fail to comprehend the cause of some aspects of social breakdown. They tend to treat only symptoms, and then often only for the cosmetic effect. Yet the breakdown of value-consensus and the failure of socialization have consequences which fatally flaw the optimism of modern consciousness.

In the new religions of our own time we may readily perceive how fully the time-sense of modernism has been espoused. The new world order is soon to come, and there is a need self-consciously to recreate society, and to defend men from the consequences of modern planning and technology and all that this implies. At the same time, it is characteristic for these movements also to point to the deficiencies that are manifestly evident in modern social systems.

It is in their claim to have the solutions to the problems of modernity that the new religions are most decisively up-to-date. The very circumstances that have created the decay of integrated social values, stable class structures, clear patterns of authority and adequate agencies of social control, and which are virtually those that are the preconditions necessary for the success of new movements, are also the circumstances to which the new movements address much of their attention. Pick up a copy of religious literature circulated by the new movements and contemporary sects, and you will discover nostrums to resolve the world's problems, society's contemporary distress, and the people's discontents. Not infrequently, the leaders of the new movements comment on the disintegration of modern society, at times with sophisticated comprehension of the sociological causes of contemporary problems.

For these commentators, their own faith is an urgent response to the needs of the times—a final offer of salvation for mankind. For traditional religionists, the new religions are, of course themselves a contributory element to the disruption of values and the cohesion of society. For the sociologist, the new religious movement is to be located in the social context in which it emerges and grows, as an expression of modernity, of radical contemporaneity, as well as a participatory reaction to it.

The new religious movement may be equated with the sect in its earliest stages. Such movements, at least within the Christian tradition, and perhaps this is generally true of the movements arising in advanced Western societies, tend to lack a historical sense of time, and to be unaware of their own longer term significance in relation both to the past and the future. Their perspectives of such a movement are transient, locked into the modern and contemporary idea not only of the style and purpose of worship, but also of the way in which to cope with the passing problems of that section of society that it seeks to recruit. At times it adopts a message couched in the most radical neoteric mode:—"Stay high all the Time with Hare Krishna", or, as in the case of "flirty-fishing" by the Children of God, the latest indulgence of the passing moral mood. New movements of course have always seized on contemporary fads or fantasies, hence the food reformism incidentally embraced by SDA; the pyramidology by Pastor Russell's International Bible Students; freemasonic worship in Mormonism, and the influence of anti-Mason ideas of the late 1820s; lost tribism in the British Israel movement, in one of the schisms of Christian Science, and even in the pentecostal Elim Foursquare Gospel Church. The new movement meets its potential clientele on their own terms, even if those terms reflect the casual or even deviant temper of transitory cultural and sub-cultural styles.

That new movements should address contemporary issues is, of course, expectable, but that they should so readily adopt strategies that imitate secular modern methods of operation indicates the measure to which they are hostages to the cultures in which they work. Getting high; easy sex; giant promotions and extravaganzas (of the kind that have been promoted by the Divine Light Mission); intelligence testing, in the manner of the Scientologists; or even academic conferences sponsored by the Unification

Church—are all borrowed *modi operandi* from secular society. When transcendent Truth comes to earth and is made flesh—it is dressed in the style of the times. The exigencies of the hour do more than merely colour the message, they appear to occasion the message, and if not to dictate its substance at least to determine its mode of expression. And all of this occurs with little, if any, awareness of how often such things have happened before, and of the inevitable compromise that a message must sustain if it is to stand the test of time and to be transmitted from generation to generation. The longer-time perspective; the need to acknowledge the slow unwinding of history, and the even slower growth in grace; recognition of tensions that can never be eliminated but may at best be contained; acceptance of the process of maturation and the expansion of learning; and of the necessarily slow transfusion of higher values to a wider public—are not elements encompassed normally in the understanding of new movements or their prospects and possibilities. Even those movements which do not embrace a millennialist conclusion to history, which canvass therapy or spirituality, such, for example, as Transcendental Meditation, tend to expect early, profound and relatively dramatic change in human society. It is the emphasis on the sudden that must raise other questions, for the expectation of sudden change of the kind that new movements expect has, hitherto, always been disappointed.

A new movement which anticipates sudden change prompted by divine agencies, or which expects that very rapid growth will permit the movement to dictate social change, is faced with compromise when it comes to terms with the need to make provision for its own continuance. If the advent is expected very soon, long-term planning might itself be seen as a contradiction of faith. If millions being "born again" is expected to bring in a new era, in which society will be made new, then even schemes of social amelioration, let alone proposals for structural change in society, suggest that conversion is, after all, not enough. Even those aspects of bureaucratic organization that are almost taken for granted in any modern concern, may be challenged within the context of a new religion—as they have often been in cases as divergent as those of Christian Science and Pentecostal movements—as indicating some insufficient faith about the adequacy of pure dependence on the spiritual.[5]

Persistence and Generational Transmission

Yet, hitherto, all movements that were to survive have required the evolution of agencies and techniques to cope with the diverse problems of self-maintenance, from the acquisition and management of property to processes for the induction of the second generation and subsequent generations. One facet of the problem is well recognized in all religious movements, as they lose their newness. It is recognized as an ambivalent and controversial process, described—in the case of Christianity itself—by Rudolf Sohm as the process of change from love to law. Max Weber discussed it, in the specific case of charisma, as routinization. And Thomas O'Dea specified some of its sub-divisions in his work on the dilemmas of institutionalization. Yet, more is involved than merely the creation within the new movement of agencies that—in their legalism, their mundane preoccupations, and their necessary accommodation to the structures, systems, and values prevalent in the secular world outside—exist as a type of Trojan Horse, impugning from within the adequacy of the spiritual. There must also be a change in the movement's self-interpretation, in its understanding of itself in history, and there must be a re-orientation of its expectations concerning its own effect on society. It must eventually abandon its belief that as a movement it in itself (or the truths which it espouses) will transform the world, and it must come to concern itself rather with its own survival within the world.

Obviously, the specific nature of such a shift must vary according to the specific teachings and expectations of each new movement. The longer time perspective may become necessary as suddenly as the expected advent, when adventual prophecy fails, even though the reappraisal and readjustment may in themselves take longer. Or the change may be a slow, almost imperceptible process, when it is gradually realized that the new therapy is not always successful as the world judges success. Or it may be an irregular and persisting struggle as the expected tide of revival appears first to rise only to ebb again, as the born-again lapse into old ways and as spiritual momentum diminishes. Clearly, a variety of strategies exist for the reappraisal and redeployment of a movement's ideological resources, even though one cannot represent these as being consciously perceived or rationally evaluated. What a movement does when, say, adventual hope fails, must depend on a variety of idiosyncratic, and perhaps even purely adventitious factors, and I do not think that it would be useful to engage in abstract sociological speculation about the specific possibilities. If one were to examine known cases, one would see that movements have had recourse to various stratagems: the revision of prophetic calculations; the invocation of alternative sources of legitimacy; the spiritualization of erstwhile materialistic expectations; the gradual accretion of other concerns; the shift in the locus of religious aspirations from the objective world to the subjective community—to name some.[6] Obviously, the case of the millennial movement is the most dramatic and arresting, but other new movements have also been obliged to find ways of coping with the diminishing sense of urgency as events have failed to meet expectations. Revivalist groups, even while retaining a strong belief in the value of the spontaneous operation of the spirit, increasingly routinize their revivalist activities; and therapeutical movements steadily offer metaphysical re-interpretations of the benefits of therapy, pointing to mind and morals, and even to social welfare, more than solely to physical well-being and recovery. If secular movements sometimes inflate their compensatory offers by launching them at more abstract, metaphysical levels, so religious movements, too much extended by promises of terminal events or the final solutions to all historical problems, sometimes lower their sights.[7]

For all new movements, however, it is the arrival and socialization of the second generation of believers, the children of converts, which most signally indicates the shift in time-orientations, and in the mood and meaning of ideological commitment. Of course, by

no means all the second generation is retained, but most movements increasingly perceive the children of members as some
kind of natural inheritance, and most of them take some steps to
bring them into the truth—by Sunday schools, youth groups,
uniformed brigades, special programmes of one type or another,
and always by supporting their shared association, but most
important of all, by the intimate and subtle processes of socialization in the home. The shift of perspective, from converting outsiders to socializing children, was long ago recognized by both H.
Richard Niebuhr and Liston Pope, both of whom, however, saw in it
the mark of a transformation of the sect into the denomination.[8] But
this change of orientation is to be interpreted by no means so
narrowly: it occurs in all new movements, whether they are movements that successfully retain their sectarian posture or even in
religions which emerge without the explicitly exclusivistic orientations that is one of the criteria of sectarianism. For all of them, the
question of persistence beyond the first generation is crucial. The
process is likely to bring a movement to terms with a variety of
social imperatives, chief of which is the necessarily slow cultivation
of the sense of particular values in the young. Those values in
themselves, over time, come to reflect longer-term perspectives
than those embraced by the urgent new movement. Moral worth,
dedication, enduring commitment, consistency, high standards of
personal comportment, the acquisition and maintenance of respectability in the world beyond, are all likely to grow in importance for
any persisting religious movement. Whatever may be the tempo-
rary strategies for recruitment, the likelihood of taking on more
abiding values as time passes seems to me to be considerable. As
urgency diminishes, intensity of moral commitment, the cultivation
of the self in the context of the movement is likely to increase.
Preparation for the new order soon to come may give way to
preparation of the individual to take his sectarian place in the wider
world. The search for the philosopher's stone becomes its own
reward, no matter if the stone is not found, nor even if it never
actually existed. The impact of a new movement on the world may
be, at times, considerable: but the impact on any new movement,

of the need to survive in the world must, in the long run, be somewhat greater.

FOOTNOTES

1. For a discussion which clarifies the concept of the cult, and which sets forth the bases for conceptual differentiation, see Roy Wallis, "The Cult and its Transformation" in Roy Wallis (ed.), *Sectarianism,* London: Peter Owen, 1975, pp. 35-52.
2. Some of these ideas are enlarged in B.R. Wilson, *The Youth Culture and the Universities,* London: Faber, 1970.
3. There is, of course, an extensive literature available, but see for discussions of adventism in recent Western history, Ernest Sandeen, *The Roots of Fundamentalism,* Chicago: The University of Chicago Press, 1970, and J.F.C. Harrison, *The Second Coming: Popular Millenarianism 1780-1850,* London: Routledge, 1979.
4. Of course, it must be acknowledged that modernity has not left the churches unaffected either: indeed, it has profoundly unnerved them. In consequence, we see the abandonment of timeless truths for the sake of the momentary allure of styles that appear, in the modern argot "to be with it"—hence the demolition of the entire liturgical apparatus of those churches most exposed in contemporary societies, the Roman, Anglican, and Episcopalian, and with it of their linguistic, musical, cultural, doctrinal, and ethical traditions. In spite of this process, the image of the church remains—and may yet remain for some time—as that of a stable structure with long historical roots.
5. The Stetson schism in Christian Science challenged the need of material organization for a spiritual movement: see A.K. Swihart, *Since Mrs. Eddy,* New York, 1931. The charismatic leader of the Elim Foursquare Gospel Church in Britain left the movement he had founded after a disenchanting experience when he deputized for the ailing secretary-general of the movement: see B.R. Wilson, *Sects and Society,* Westport, Conn.: Greenwood Press, 1978 rept.
6. The allusions are respectively to Jehovah's Witnesses; Seventh-day Adventists; orthodox Christianity, and particularly to the Augustinian reappraisal of adventist expectations; again to Seventh-day Adventism; and to the Christadelphians and Quakers.
7. See Rodney Stark, above, pp. 159-177.
8. H. Richard Niebuhr, *The Social Sources of Denominationalism,* New York: Holt Rinehart, 1929; Liston Pope, *Millhands and Preachers,* New Haven: Yale University Press, 1942.

PARTICIPANTS IN THE SOCIAL IMPACT OF NEW RELIGIOUS
MOVEMENTS CONFERENCE, BERKELEY, CALIFORNIA,
JUNE 19-22, 1980

Dagfinn Aslid, graduate of UTS and student, Claremont Graduate
School, Claremont, California

Eileen Barker, Professor of Sociology, The London School of
Economics and Political Science, University of London, London,
England

David G. Bromley, Chairman, Department of Sociology, University
of Hartford, Hartford, Connecticut

David Carlson, graduate of UTS and student, Pacific School of
Religion, Berkeley, California

Donald W. Dayton, Librarian and Assistant Professor of Historical
Theology, Northern Baptist Theological Seminary, Lombard,
Illinois

Joseph. H. Fichter, Professor of Sociology, Loyola University, New
Orleans, Louisiana

Anthony Guerra, graduate of UTS and student, Harvard Divinity
School, Cambridge, Massachusetts

Tyler Hendricks, graduate of UTS and student, Vanderbilt University, Nashville, Tennessee

James D. Hunter, student, Rutgers University, New Brunswick,
New Jersey

J. Stillson Judah, Librarian and Professor Emeritus of History of
Religions, Graduate Theological Union, Berkeley, California.

David S.C. Kim, President, Unification Theological Seminary,
Barrytown, New York

John Maniatis, Conference Coordinator, Unification Theological
Seminary, Barrytown, New York

David Martin, Professor of Sociology, The London School of Economics and Political Science, University of London, London,
England

Michael Mickler, graduate of UTS and student, Graduate Theological Union, Berkeley, California

Stephen Post, graduate of UTS and student, The Divinity School, University of Chicago, Chicago, Illinois

Richard Quebedeaux, freelance writer, Berkeley, California

Lewis Rambo, Professor of Psychology of Religion, San Francisco Theological Seminary, San Anselmo, California

James T. Richardson, Professor of Sociology, University of Nevada, Reno, Nevada

Rodney Sawatsky, Director of Academic Affairs, Conrad Grebel College, University of Waterloo, Waterloo, Ontario, Canada

Anson D. Shupe, Jr., Professor of Sociology, University of Texas, Arlington, Texas

Rodney Stark, Professor of Sociology, University of Washington, Seattle, Washington

Roy Wallis, Head, Department of Social Studies, The Queen's University of Belfast, Belfast, Ireland

Bryan R. Wilson, Professor of Sociology, All Souls' College, Oxford, England

Patricia Zulkosky, graduate of UTS and student, School of Theology at Claremont, Claremont, California